MIXED-BLOODS AND TRIBAL DISSOLUTION

MIXED-BLOODS AND TRIBAL DISSOLUTION
Charles Curtis and the Quest for Indian Identity

William E. Unrau

 University Press of Kansas

For Andrew

© 1989 by the University Press of Kansas
All rights reserved

Published by the University Press of Kansas (Lawrence, Kansas 66045), which
was organized by the Kansas Board of Regents and is operated and funded by
Emporia State University, Fort Hays State University, Kansas State University,
Pittsburg State University, the University of Kansas, and Wichita State University

Library of Congress Cataloging-in-Publication Data

Unrau, William E, 1929–
          Mixed-bloods and tribal dissolution: Charles Curtis and the quest
for Indian identity/William E. Unrau.
          p.   cm.
          Bibliography: p.
          Includes index.
          ISBN 0-7006-0395-6 (alk. paper)
          1. Curtis, Charles Brent, 1860–1936.   2. Kansa Indians—Biography.
3. Kansa Indians—Mixed bloods.   4. Kansa Indians—Cultural
assimilation.   5. Indians of North America—Kansas—Biography.
6. Indians of North America—Kansas—Mixed bloods.   7. Indians of
North America—Kansas—Cultural assimilation.   8. Legislators—
United States—Biography.   I. Title.
E99.K2C878   1989
973'.0497502—dc20
          [B]   89-31799
                                                                                                        CIP

British Library Cataloguing in Publication Data is available.

Printed in the United States of America
10 9 8 7 6 5 4 3 2 1

The paper used in this publication meets the minimum requirements of the
American National Standard for Permanence of Paper for Printed Library
Materials Z39.48-1984.

Contents

Illustrations

Whispering Hope

Soft as the voice of an Angel
Breathing a lesson unheard,
Hope, with a gentle persuasion,
Whispers her comforting word.
Wait till the darkness is over,
Wait till the tempest is done,
Hope for the sunshine tomorrow,
After the shower is gone.
Oh, how welcome Thy voice,
Oh, how welcome,
Making my heart in its sorrow,
Rejoice, rejoice!

—Septimus Winner (1868)
An inspirational song that was popular
during the lifetime of Charles Curtis.

Preface

Mixed-bloods played a pervasive role in the diminution of the Indian land base in the United States. A critical examination of certain articles that were inserted in land-cession treaties from the Jeffersonian era until the termination of the treaty mechanism in 1871, granting allotments or special concessions to mixed-bloods, suggests that without the cooperation of the mixed-bloods, tribal dispossession by the federal government would have been more difficult to accomplish.

Building on antecedents dating back to pre-Revolutionary America, exclusive benefits for mixed-bloods were regarded as rewards for assisting Indian Office personnel and for services on reservations or at the treaty table and, more often than not, were justified on grounds of the "civilizing" impact they would have on the tribes as a whole. Exemplary conduct on the part of the mixed-bloods, it was assumed, would generate envy among the full-bloods, lessen the shock of acculturation, and provide much-needed time for Indian traditionalists to alter their way of life and take up the agrarian enterprise that was so central to the culture of the invader.

In the nineteenth century, however, the dramatic numerical decline of American Indians gave rise to the belief that the total demise of the continent's first inhabitants was virtually irreversible. But this belief was not accompanied by good evidence that the mixed-blood was an endangered species as well. In fact, even the most pessimistic and critical observers reported quite the contrary. The consequence was a dilemma of significant proportions, which prompted arguments about the essence of Indian identity and debates among scientists and pseudo-scientists of various persuasions regarding human hybridity and the virtues of monogenism versus multiple creation as a means of dealing with the reality of the mixed-blood increment. Likewise, until the closing years of the nineteenth century, when problems over guardianship, heirship, individual native competency, and the final determination of the allotment rolls could no longer be evaded, there was a paucity of discussion in Congress as to how the mixed-blood might require a modification of basic Indian policy.

An important exception to this reticence was Charles Curtis, a mixed-blood Kansa-Kaw attorney and congressman from Kansas, who eventually was elected to the second-highest office in the land and who, with great personal confidence, insisted on the positive role that mixed-bloods should play in post–Civil War assimilationist policy. Although it was overshadowed by his later political career in the Senate and his frustration as vice-president during the Hoover administration, his earlier involvement in the mixed-blood issue was more important than is generally recognized. The intent here, then, is to assess that contribution within the context of what made him the kind of aggressive mixed-blood that he was and how he emerged as one of the most influential Indian policy brokers of his time. The intent also is to demonstrate that the government's design to use the mixed-blood as an instrument of "progressive" Indian policy was real, but that it was, certainly in the eyes of Curtis, largely deficient in accomplishment.

For one who was in public life for nearly half a century and who held some of the highest political stations in America, the paucity of Curtis manuscripts, correspondence, speeches, and reminiscences seems baffling. But excluding the possibility that some of this material has been either lost or disposed of by Curtis's family, this was no mere accident. Curits preferred to keep his public pronouncements to a minimum, while in the meantime engaging in much personal, informal discourse—both in Washington and Indian country. Those individuals and groups toward whom the discourse was directed, in conjunction with the available Curtis manuscripts, newspaper accounts, genealogical records, travel accounts, government documents, and a wealth of legal material, constitute the major sources for this study.

"Whispering," as his verbal technique came to be called by some of his admirers and most of his critics, was truly Curtis's forte. While it prompted either snide inferences regarding his intelligence and even his good common sense or, worse, racist beliefs that his silence and long-suffering were expected responses to his personal insecurity and the Indian blood that flowed through his veins, the fact is that on matters relating to Indian policy, tribal and intertribal politics, and the allotment revolution that unfolded after 1887, Curtis was as informed as any national leader of his time. Certainly, he took great pride in his so-called partial Indianness.

I am aware that the use of "mixed-blood" as an adjective or a descriptive noun runs counter to the preferences of some contemporary scholars, who define it in pejorative terms. James Axtell, for example, in a recent issue of the American Historical Association's *Perspectives* (vol. 2, no. 2 [Feb. 1987], 10–13), places mixed-blood in the "forked tongue" category and approvingly notes others who have relegated the phrase to the level of a "damning folk biology." They prefer "métis," although they concede that its application is more appropriate to the nineteenth-century descendants of Indian and French parents in Canada and the northern regions of the United States.

Through both his paternal and maternal lines, Curtis was very remotely a part of this culture, if at all, but he was a mixed-blood, and he used the phrase freely in dealing with his own identity and his efforts to have other mixed-bloods share in the bounty that was supposedly accruing to all Indians under government trusteeship before World War I. Congressional and other documents that were contemporary with Curtis, his associates, and his relatives through several generations used the phrase as well, as does George Woodcock in his 1986 English translation of Marcel Giraud's monumental *La Métis Canadian* (1945). I have used "métis" sparingly, principally in relation to the syncretic culture that in the 1830s and 1840s existed near the confluence of the Missouri and Kansas rivers.

A number of persons warrant recognition for their part in this study, and I wish to thank them for their assistance: Robert M. Kvasnicka, Robert Fowler, and Renée M. Jaussaud of the National Archives; Kent Carter of the Fort Worth branch of the National Archives; Reed Whitaker of the Kansas City branch of the National Archives; Jack Haly of the University of Oklahoma; Frances J. Majors, Phillip D. Thomas, and Thoburn Taggert, Jr., of Wichita State University; David Austin of the University of Illinois, Chicago Circle; L. G. Moses of Northern Arizona University; William H. Seiler of Emporia State University; Patricia A. Michaelis, Larry Jochims, and Robert J. Keckeisen of the Kansas State Historical Society; Andrea I. Paul of the Nebraska Historical Society; James A. Cavanaugh of the State Historical Society of Wisconsin; Tom Dennison of Ponca City, Oklahoma; Sam Witham of Cushing, Oklahoma; Constance K. McCullom of Woodstock, Vermont; William T. Hagan of the State University of New York, Fredonia; Tannis C. Thorne of the University of California at Los Angeles; and Dianne Rahm of Pennsylvania State University, whose research on the Curtis Act at an early stage in this project provided me with valuable insights into the complex character of Charles Curtis.

I would also like to thank the Office of Research and Sponsored Programs at Wichita State University for financial support.

William E. Unrau
Wichita, Kansas

1

"What Is an Indian?"

On 24 February 1896, during debate on the annual Indian appropriation bill, Congressman Charles Curtis of Kansas proposed that mixed-blood children of white men and Indian women should have "the same right and privileges to the property and annuities of the tribe to which the mother belongs, by blood, as any other member of the tribe." Interior Secretary Hoke Smith had only recently denied those rights, based on his interpretation of an 1888 federal statute barring non-Indian husbands from acquiring a legal right to the property of their Indian wives. It was wrong and short-sighted to penalize the children, complained Curtis, for the mixed-blood was a powerful instrument in the government's assimilation program. "We may talk all we please; missionaries may say what they please," said Curtis; "but the only way to solve the Indian question is by education and by intermarriage of Indians and whites."[1]

It was a personal defeat for Curtis when the House voted down his proposal. As a prominent attorney, successful land developer in his home state, dedicated member of the House Committee on Indian Affairs, and a mixed-blood member of the Kaw tribe, Curtis was sensitive to the problem of mixed-blood identity, particularly as it related to property and inheritance rights. Certainly, his defeat on the House floor affirmed his longstanding belief that the mixed-blood was being served up as a sacrificial lamb in the movement to assimilate Indians.

Curtis's principal opponent in the 1896 congressional debate was Samuel M. McCall of Massachusetts, who viewed the 1888 law as a means of preserving Indian lands for Indians, not for mixed-bloods. When an Indian woman married a white man, she surrendered her tribal rights as far as her children were concerned, said McCall, who summarized his objections to Curtis's proposal with what amounted to

1

a personal rebuke of his mixed-blood colleague from Kansas, "Our people are willing to support Indians but draw a line as to who are to be considered Indians."[2]

Curtis and McCall were not alone in the debate regarding Indian identity in the 1890s. In his 1892 annual report to Congress, Indian Commissioner Thomas Jefferson Morgan submitted an analysis of the problem which dated back to the Columbian invasion of 1492. Noting that the federal government had passed numerous laws "without discriminating as to those over whom it has a right to exercise such control," Morgan was sympathetic to the position taken by Curtis. To suggest that mixed-bloods were not Indians in terms of their right to claim the property of the tribe, wrote Morgan, "would unsettle and endanger the titles to much of the lands that have been relinquished by Indian tribes and patented to citizens of the United States." On numerous occasions in the past, mixed-bloods had been counted in treaties requiring a three-fourths tribal majority for the validation of land cessions; they had also been counted in censuses required by federal law when "recognized by the Indians themselves as members of their tribe." Under the General Allotment Act, mixed-bloods had been allotted alongside full-bloods "without distinction," and if mixed-bloods were not Indians, then it was a serious question as to whether "real Indians" might not have an equitable claim against the government for the misappropriation of their annuities.[3]

The genealogical galaxy that underlay Charles Curtis's one-eighth Indian blood quantum dated back to the early years of the nineteenth century, a time when certain prominent public figures were advocating Indian-White miscegenation as a means of drawing the savage "within the pale of civilization." In 1816, only a few years before the birth of Curtis's Indian grandmother, Secretary of War William H. Crawford interceded on the side of the mixed-blood. After efforts to introduce the Indians to the importance of private property had failed, said Crawford, "let intermarriage between them and the white be encouraged by the government. This cannot fail to preserve the race, with the modifications necessary to the enjoyment of civil liberty and social happiness." Crawford's proposal, however, prompted a storm of protest, including that of Judge Thomas Cooper of the University of Pennsylvania, who wrote to President James Madison a series of angry letters that were printed in the *Democratic Review*. Asserting that it was no more possible to convert an Indian barbarian to civilization than to change a black man to white, Cooper warned that Crawford would "find his filthy proposal treated with the execrations they deserve, by those whom he marks out as the victims of his flagrant want of sense, and his unnatural want of taste."[4]

Certainly, racist fears regarding the inevitability of a mongrel progeny were not uncommon in the half century preceding Charles Curtis's birth on the Kansas frontier in 1860. While monogamists, polygamists, comparative zoologists, craniologists, and devotees of the American School of ethnology refused to accept the virtues of human hybridity, the literary community articulated similar fears and thereby added to the confusion regarding Indian identity. Washington Irving predicted that the amalgamation of Indians and whites would produce a monstrous hybrid similar to the Asian Tartars; in *The Oregon Trail* (1849), Francis Parkman characterized the mixed-bloods as "half Indian, half white man, and half devil." And in *The Confidence Man* (1857), Herman Melville's fictional James Hall was the very embodiment of the civilized-savage dichotomy's besetting mankind in general.[5]

Nonetheless, careful students of mid-nineteenth-century Indian demography were obliged to conclude that while the full-blood population was declining dramatically, the opposite was true of the mixed-bloods. Many had accepted the white man's dress and eating habits and had responded reasonably well to instruction in the mission and governmental schools. Merchandising and agricultural pursuits did not seem to be beyond their grasp, and some—including Curtis's half-blood grandmother—had displayed considerable talent in land speculation. In fact, most mixed-bloods seemed eager to share in the material bounty of the trans-Mississippi West; and as Charles Curtis reminded his fellow legislators in 1896, it was the mixed-bloods who had cooperated to the fullest extent in the negotiation of land-cession treaties that had opened the Indian country to yeoman farmers from the East.[6]

Curtis was an attorney who knew well that the framers of the Constitution had provided no legal definition of the term "Indian." Nor had the War Department or the Interior Department, the cabinet offices that had successively been responsible for the administration of Indian affairs in the United States. As a result, William T. Hagan has noted, the matter was left to the courts. In the decade and a half preceding Curtis's birth, the most fashionable considerations were that the individual must have some Indian blood or be accepted by the tribe with whom the individual wished to affiliate. By the time Curtis had taken his seat in Congress in 1892, the most widely accepted principle of identity was that the tribes were the authority in the determination of their membership.[7]

Curtis also realized that Congress could make or unmake an Indian, regardless of genealogy, ethnological data, treaty commitments, or tribal preference. So could an employee of the Indian Office, acting under his interpretation of federal law or the directive of an administrative superior, as Curtis knew well from personal experience. Even though his great-great-grandfather had been the principal chief of the Kansa (later, Kaw) tribe during the 1820s[8] and though as a young boy, Curtis himself had resided on the Kaw reservation, he was dropped from the tribal roll in 1878 by a field officer of the Indian Office for not having taken up residence on the reservation established for the Kaws in 1872 in Indian Territory.[9]

The dramatic growth of a mixed-blood population in the trans-Mississippi West was especially perplexing to outside observers. "Our Indian Question seems to take on new intricacies and perplexities as the decades go by," lamented the Reverend William Barrows in 1889. "Among these is the complex and diffuse fact of intermarriage and half-breeds." A resident of Reading, Massachusetts, Barrows was well traveled, and he reported favorably on the mixed-blood family who served as his host on a journey from Canada to the Green River country of Wyoming and south into the very heart of Indian country. All beyond the Mississippi, he found himself among "the bleached and the browned, till races are obscured, and one brings himself unconsciously to taking his fellow-travellers on quality, and not shades of color or facial structures." From Montreal and Winnipeg to the streets of St. Louis and Muskogee, Barrows found it difficult to tell which blood "had the mastery and which brings the honor."[10]

With guarded approval, the New England clergyman noted that the mixed-blood was instrumental in the forming of "a new people or race, as distinct as were the Aryans, or Romans, or Scandinavians." They were especially evident in Indian Territory, where no white man could reside unless he had an Indian wife and thereby had secured "the noble title of 'squaw man.'" Here, it seemed, the mixed-blood was "taking over."[11]

To his contemporaries, "squaw man" implied one of the more nefarious characters in Indian country. His disdain for authority, his often manipulative role in tribal politics, and especially his quest for tribal annuities and real property through marriage to an Indian woman prompted complaints from reservation full-bloods and governmental agents alike. In his 1896 proposal, however, Curtis was concerned with the children of Indian-white marriages. Prior to the 1888 statute, common law that applied to Indians held that descent was patrilineal, so that the children of an American citizen and an Indian woman were American citizens. But in the majority of tribes, including the one from which Curtis was expelled in 1878, descent was matrilineal. Why exclude the children from the traditional rights enjoyed by their mothers? "You may go to the Indian Territory, you may go to any Indian reservation that you please," said Curtis, "and you will find that the children who are advanced in education and intelligence are the children of white men and Indian women or the children of white women and Indian men.'' And in response to those who argued that his proposal was ''taking a step backward,'' Curtis asked: ''If indeed it is taking a step backward then why has not Congress the courage to take the proper step and say that hereafter no Indian man shall marry a white woman and no Indian woman marry a white man?'' His query did not alter the negative vote on the proposal, but it did affirm his belief in miscegenation and, by implication, his views on Indian identity.[12]

Being an Indian, for Charles Curtis, was less a matter of blood than the fusion of Indian and white into a cultural composite that was committed to private property as the most effective means of fulfilling the assimilationist dream. As a conservative Republican during the closing years of the nineteenth century, Curtis was anything but a disciple of Thomas Jefferson. Yet toward the end of his presidency, the Sage of Monticello had addressed a delegation of visiting Indian dignitaries in a manner acceptable to Curtis: ''Let me entreat you, therefore, on the land now given you to begin to give every man a farm . . . and when he dies, let it belong to his wife and children after him. . . . When once you have property, you will want laws and magistrates to protect your property and persons. . . . [You] will unite yourselves with us . . . form one people with us, and we shall all be Americans.''[13]

In his 1816 memorandum to Congress, Secretary Crawford agreed; and two decades later the Baptist Isaac McCoy, an advocate of removal, reported, on the basis of personal observation in the Indian country west of Missouri and Arkansas, that the majority of the nearly seventy-five thousand removal Indians—many of them mixed-bloods—were doing much better ''in the field or the shop . . . than are found among the whites in the frontier settlements.'' Heads of the Indian Office during the three decades preceding the Civil War agreed. Indian Commissioners T. Hartley Crawford, William Medill, Orlando Brown, Luke Lea, and George W. Manypenny, while they admitted that there were important differences between whites and Indians, even that the latter possessed certain savage and barbaric traits, nevertheless attributed such characteristics to environment and conditioning, not to innate racial differences that were immutable by modification and improvement.[14]

Expansion into Texas and the Southwest during the 1840s, however, prompted new concerns regarding the mixed-bloods in the United States. One popular emigrant guide described ''the indolent, mixed race of California as scarcely a visible grade, in the scale of intelligence, above the barbarous tribes by whom they are surrounded,'' and in 1847, Secretary of State James Buchanan worried about the governing of ''the mongrel race" that was inhabiting the vast area soon to be obtained from Mexico. Even Alexander Ross, who had married an Indian woman, was the father of mixed-blood children, and was a long-time resident of the fur trader's frontier, reported in 1856 that "amalgamation" was detrimental to both Indians and whites and that it would be best to separate the two races by a buffer zone at least fifty miles wide. And as late as 1874, Francis A. Walker, a former Indian commissioner, insisted that extermination was preferable to intermarriage as a solution to the Indian problem.[15]

By the early 1880s, when Charles Curtis was coming to his maturity and the government was moving toward the passage of a general allotment law requiring greater precision in identifying Indians who might qualify for individual land ownership, attitudes towards mixed-bloods were moderating. The research of Lewis Henry Morgan, which suggested that amalgamation was beneficial to both races, was filtering down to the nonscholarly community. In 1879, the *Atlantic Monthly* reported that the best plan for alleviating discord among the Five Civilized Tribes was "a harmonious blending of the races"; and a decade later, Thomas A. May, in *Popular Science Monthly*, insisted that "natural unions" between Indians and whites had accomplished more toward a resolution of the Indian problem than had the actions of all statesmen past and present.[16]

Philip C. Garrett, of the Board of Indian Commissioners, reported to the Lake Mohonk Conference in 1886: "Some prejudice, it is true, appears against intermarriage and entire loss of race identity, but it is impossible to prevent the mingling of blood on the same soil, even if desireable. . . . Nor am I sure that the fusion of the whole Indian population in that of the United States would be to the detriment of the latter." Less than a year later, on 8 February 1887, the General Allotment (or Dawes) Act became law, precipitating what one recent study has termed a "flurry of activity generated by non-Indians trying to cash in on severalty program allotments." One result was the more restrictive 1888 statute, also sponsored by Senator Henry L. Dawes of Massachusetts, which was followed by Curtis's abortive attempt in 1896 to protect the property of mixed-blood children.[17]

As Curtis predicted, confusion abounded regarding Indian identity at the turn of the century. Legislative relief at the individual and tribal levels, expensive legal action, or intense maneuvering and lobbying within the tribal political structures emerged as the most practical means of determining the identity and the economic well-being of most mixed-bloods. While there is no evidence that Curtis (who by then was a member of the United States Senate) made any effort to intervene during the land-allotment crisis among the White Earth Chippewas during the decade after 1906, he surely was distressed when prominent anthropologists were called upon "to measure, to scratch the skin, pull the hair, and otherwise physically examine the Chippewa people" in order to differentiate between mixed-bloods and full-bloods.[18]

In his public pronouncements and in his private correspondence, Charles Curtis seldom alluded to his Indianness. In part, it was the consequence of his disdain for public speaking and his preference for pursuing his goals behind the scenes. Many of his critics and even some of his admirers erroneously attributed this reticence to the stereotypical silence and long-suffering that was allegedly characteristic of Indians of his time in general. Yet, Curtis was anything but long-suffering, and he certainly spoke out when the honor and the character of mixed-bloods were called into question.

Still, there were reasons for his taciturnity beyond a shyness of character, reasons that stemmed from the cultural duality of his childhood and from an awareness during his adolescent and early adult years that for mixed-bloods, action spoke better than words. As he came to a better understanding of the assimilationist role that the government had assigned to his Indian grandmother and a handful of her mixed-blood relatives during the mid 1820s, Curtis committed himself to vindicating his Indian ancestry by study, work, and performance, not verbiage. "Rely on yourself, use common sense, and believe in God's plan for human progress," he said to a graduating class in Philadelphia at the height of his political career. That he had succeeded seemed apparent to a writer for the *Nation* in 1928. On the occasion of Curtis's candidacy for the vice-presidency of the United States, Eric Kiel wrote: "The Indian has been betrayed, conquered, pauperized, and is now facing extinction. Out of the wreck of his old culture but one thing has been saved; there is no social stigma on his race, a fact for which the romantic episode of Pochahontas and Captain John Smith may have more than a little to do. The Star of the Red Man [i.e., Curtis] now seems to have almost touched its azimuth."[19] Frank P. MacLennan, the publisher of the *Topeka State Journal*, agreed: "I have strongly admired his integrity, ability, loyalty and conscientious devotion to duty and to his friends. He gets things done and may be called the Great Accomplisher."[20]

In Oklahoma, Curtis's Indian relatives also agreed. To celebrate their brother's remarkable achievement, eight Kaw full-bloods led a long procession to the tribe's dancing grove a mile and a half from Kaw City. After "five old chieftans" called a halt to the crooning and dancing, Curtis's sister apologized for her brother's absence and stated, "I want you to know that I—that we—are all very proud of Charles." Grunts from all, it was reported, marked the approval of her words. Then followed a feast of chicken and waubushe (fried bread), the prized delicacy of the Indians. Curtis's campaign biographer reported that when it was all over, the Kaws had gone back to their cabins, ''after such a day as the Kaws had not enjoyed since the long-bearded stranger was initiated in the tribe sixty years before and sang to them the song of the Muscolgee!''[21]

2
Kinship Beginnings

In a short biographical sketch written nearly three decades ago, the late James C. Malin noted the absence of reliable data regarding the Curtis genealogy when he said that "peculiar gaps exist in [the] family history." In a subsequent monograph dealing mainly with the national political career of Curtis, Marvin Ewy agreed: "The childhood of Charles Curtis is shrouded in mystery and romance, a curious mixture of fact and legend, a story containing many conflicting opinions and omissions, a story in many instances based upon the word of Curtis after he had attained an advanced age."[1]

Curtis and his half sister, Dolly Gann Curtis, did not agree on some of the most essential details of their ancestry. The rapid and uncritical composition of campaign profiles, particularly in the late 1920s, complemented by an almost endless drivel regarding the social activities of Curtis and his family in the nation's capital during the congressional and vice-presidential years, contributed little to an understanding of Curtis's Indian background. Some reminiscences did, however, confirm the important role that women played in the private and public careers of the mixed-blood from Kansas. "Curtis was conspicuously a man's man," conceded Malin, but no one could deny "the important, if not critical, role of the women of his family in influencing his career: his grandmothers, his wife, and in later years, his half-sister, Dolly."[2]

It was from the maternal line that Curtis received his share of Indian blood. His mother, Ellen (sometimes listed as Helen or Helene), was the quarter-blood daughter of Louis Pappan,[3] a Frenchman from the St. Louis or St. Charles area of Missouri, and Julie Gonville, a half-blood member of the Kansa (later Kaw) tribe, whose villages in the early years of the nineteenth century were located in the lower Kansas River valley between modern Manhattan and Topeka, Kansas. Julie's father was

Louis Gonville, a French- or Scots-Canadian from the Michilimackinac area, according to most accounts. Her mother was Wyhesee (sometimes listed as Waisjasi), a full-blood Kansa-Osage daughter of Chief White Plume (variously listed as Nompawarah, Nampawarah, Wompawara, or Mannschenscaw, meaning "He Who Scares All Men" or simply "Fury"). He was born near the end of the Seven Years War in the Osage country southeast of modern Kansas City, and he married a daughter of the renowned Osage leader Pawhuska (or Papuisea, meaning "White Hair"). From this distant union, Curtis could claim an Osage heritage as well.[4]

There is no doubt that Curtis took pride in his modest Indian blood quantum. To Curtis, White Plume provided the primordial foundation for "progressive" Indianness: that is, acquiescence to the whites' invasion of Indian country west of Missouri, hard bargaining over Indian land for the benefit of all parties concerned—whether Indian or white—and especially the acceptance of a pragmatic strategy of accommodation that would inevitably contribute to the assimilation of Indians in the United States. Recalling White Plume's assistance to the Lewis and Clark expedition in 1804, his ability to speak at least some English, his "urbane" character, and "his liberal and hospitable hand," Curtis proudly described his great-great-great-grandfather as "one of the ablest and most progressive Indians of his day."[5]

The untimely death of Curtis's mother in 1863, when he was only three years old, prompted his father to place young Charley in the care of his grandmothers. From the age of six to nine, he resided on the Kaw reservation near Council Grove, Kansas, in the care of Julie Gonville Pappan. Because it was she who, in 1873, advised Curtis to abandon the tribe and "make something of himself" at a time when the Kaws were being forced out of Kansas into Indian Territory, it is important to understand the kind of mixed-blood society in which Julie came to her maturity.[6]

An important factor was the fur trade that developed between the Kansas and the invading Europeans toward the end of the seventeenth century. Trade in horses was also important, for on 10 July 1700, Father Gabriel Marest of the French mission at Kaskaskia in the Illinois country wrote that the Kansas were carrying on a valuable and diplomatically disturbing commerce in horses with the Spaniards to the southwest. French colonial officials responded with a recommendation to Paris that both Spain and England be expelled from upper Louisiana and that a post to encourage the fur trade be established west of the Mississippi. The Indians should be armed with French weapons, and more freedom should be given to the independent traders who might serve as valuable allies in the effort to win the Kansas and the other tribes to the French banner in the lower Missouri valley.[7]

Kansa Chief White Plume, or Nomparawarah (1765?–1838), great-great-grandfather of Charles Curtis. Portrait by Charles Bird King (early 1820s), reproduced from Thomas L. McKenney and James Hall, The Indian Tribes of North America, *vol. III. Courtesy of the Kansas State Historical Society.*

From then on, until the end of the American Revolution, the tribe of Julie Gonville was periodically embroiled in the struggle between France, Spain, and England over peltry, horses, and profits in the trans-Missouri West. By generally refusing to make a lasting commitment to any of these foreign powers, the Kansas provided a testament to their tenacity, diplomatic flexibility, and cooperation with neighboring tribes. Despite schemes for trade monopolies, the increased use of alcohol provided by the invaders, and epidemic disease, which during the 1750s cut their ranks in half, the Kansas were able to sustain a firm hold on their strategic position at the confluence of the Missouri and Kansas rivers.[8]

In the decade preceding America's acquisition of Louisiana, a number of individuals and groups competed for the Kansa trade, which William Clark estimated to be worth at least $8,000 a year. Among the competitors were independents such as Gregorio Sarpy and J. P. Cabanné; more powerful companies were Jacques Clamorgan's Discoverers and Explorers of the Missouri, Manuel Lisa and his associates, and the affluent and politically well-connected Laclède-Chouteau group, headed by the half brothers Auguste and Pierre Chouteau of St. Louis. With their close ties to governmental officials in Washington, D.C., and St. Louis and their commercial associations with the powerful Osages, the Chouteaus extended their influence among the Kansas through the cooperation of White Plume and several other tribal leaders under his sway. Certainly, by the early years of the nineteenth century the Chouteaus constituted an important factor in the increasing power of the mixed-bloods in Kansa society.[9]

"Fundamental to the growth of a fur-trade society," Sylvia Van Kirk has written, "was widespread intermarriage between traders and Indian women." The majority of these marriages were neither casual nor promiscuous. Biological unions were not simply private affairs, characterized by sexual exploitation and peripheral to the traders' commercial ventures. Rather, the bonds thus established were purposeful, ones in which the Indian spouse served "in the role of cultural liaison between traders and her kin." Indian women played important social and economic roles and were central to the emergence of a close-knit mixed-blood community that flourished and placed a premium on family life. Van Kirk's focus was on the métis in the Canadian West, but the advent of an influential mixed-blood faction among the Kansas after 1800 suggests that her conclusions can be applied elsewhere. Certainly, the commercial society of Charles Curtis's maternal grandmother bears this out.[10]

Under Spanish rule, the Chouteaus cultivated and eventually secured a preferential position in the Osage trade. In 1794, for example, in return for promises to construct Fort Carondelet to police the Osages' predatory activities south and west of St. Louis, the Chouteaus were granted exclusive control over the Osage trade. President Thomas Jefferson abrogated the monopoly in 1804; but the appointment of Pierre Chouteau as the first United States Indian agent in Louisiana that same year, coupled with Louisiana Governor James Wilkinson's practice of withholding rival licenses regardless of Jefferson's orders, ensured that the Chouteaus' commercial domination of the Osages would remain intact. Support from within the tribe strengthened this domination.[11]

Both Auguste and Pierre Chouteau secured membership in prominent Osage clans and, without legally abandoning their French wives
and families in St. Louis, took Osage wives in Pawhuska's village on the
Osage River, some two hundred miles to the west. Their native spouses
were in a position to promote and temper, if need be, the generally
demanding mercantile tactics that were a hallmark of the Chouteau
enterprises in Indian country, for in traditional Osage society the
division of labor was such that women were expected to play a
prominent role in the tribe's commercial operations. And as a vital
liaison between cultures, they were able to enhance dramatically the
power of subsequent mixed-blood generations.[12]

The experience of Paul Loise (or Louise), the mixed-blood son of
Pierre Chouteau and his Osage spouse, bears this out. Through his
father's influence, Paul received the valuable federal appointment as
official Osage interpreter, and through the maternal line, he was
designated the headman of one of the Little Osage villages. In 1806,
when Pawhuska headed a delegation of Indian leaders to Washington
for an audience with President Jefferson, Loise went with him, and in
the important Kansa land-cession treaty of 1825, a treaty that bore
directly on the future of Charles Curtis, Loise served as one of the
interpreters.[13]

The incidence of closer connections between the Kansa and the
Osage people at the turn of the century also had a significant impact on
the developing Curtis genealogy. During the eighteenth century, the
linguistically related tribes of the parent Dhegiha-Siouan stock had gone
their separate ways, but common interest, occasioned by the advance of
the St. Louis merchants, tempered the intertribal animosity. The marriage of White Plume to a daughter of Pawhuska was of symbolic
importance to both groups and certainly was taken by the Chouteaus as
an important incentive to penetrate the Kansa trade.[14]

Growth of a mixed-blood community at the mouth of the Kansas
River was thereby greatly encouraged. In 1811, Fort Osage's factor,
George C. Sibley, noted that marital connections between the Osages
and the Kansas were so extensive that he doubted "that any serious
difference will ever occur between the two tribes." Included in these
connections were both French-Osage and French-Kansa unions. Eight
years later, Thomas Say reported such widespread intermarriages that
the features of the Kansas "more and more approach those of the
Osages." Certainly, the long-range consequences were profound, as the
former Osage agent Laban J. Miles reported during the Osage allotment-
enrollment hearings before a congressional committee a century later:
"The mixed-bloods [of the two tribes] are nearly all related, and the
probabilities are if we could get their history . . . , we would find that

the Kaw is only a band of the Osage who went in another direction when they left St. Louis."[15]

A French traveler among the Kansas in 1802 learned that sexual unions involving outsiders who had been welcomed into the tribe were open and public, not "private, libidinous affairs," and that marital unions with Kansa women were an essential aspect of the tribe's mercantile economy. "They feasted me in turn," reported Perrin Du Lac, "and, according to their customs, offered me their daughters. I accepted those of the great chief, whom I was afraid of displeasing by a refusal." With no regrets, the Frenchman went on to explain that "to accept the daughter of head man" was absolutely a prerequisite to negotiating for Kansa furs. Such accommodation was in sharp contrast to a Catholic missionary, Joseph Anthony Lutz, whose failure to establish a permanent mission among the Kansas in 1828 obviously contributed to his negative response about the French traders among the Kansas and Osages: "They are slothful bellies, and not much different from the Cretans, addicted to drink and much idle talking. . . . Some of them live with Indian concubines, refusing the grace offered to them by my ministry. Only two could I prevail upon to dismiss their concubines and contract in legitimate marriages."[16]

One such marriage may have been that of Curtis's great-grand-parents Wyhesee and Louis Gonville. Michilimackinac baptismal records indicate that on 3 July 1752 a Jesuit missionary baptized the thirteen- or fourteen-year-old son of "a Mr. La Plante and of a Savage of Cammanettigouia [or Potawatomi nation]." The godmother was recorded as "a M. Bourassa" and the godfather as "a Mr. de Gonneville." The boy was named Louis, and he took the surname of Gonville. In view of a known migration of Gonvilles from Canada to the St. Louis area not long thereafter, this individual may have been the father of the Louis Gonville whose marriage to a daughter of White Plume was legitimated by Father Lutz in 1828.[17]

In the syncretic society that developed in the lower Kansas valley and east toward St. Louis, such unions were anything but unique. Indeed, the area was a veritable melting pot of cultures and creeds. Washington Irving emphasized this when he commented, albeit with considerable trepidation, on St. Louis society of the time,

> The old French houses engaged in the Indian trade had gathered round them a train of dependents, mongrel Indians, and mongrel Frenchmen, who had intermarried with Indians. These they employed in their various expeditions by land and water. . . . All these circumstances combined to produce a population at St. Louis even more motley than at Mackinaw. Here were to be seen,

about the river banks, the hectoring, extravagant, bragging boatmen of the Mississippi, with the gay, grimacing, singing, good-humored Canadian voyageurs. Vagrant Indians, of various tribes, loitered about the streets . . . and now and then the scraping of a fiddle, a strain of an ancient French song, or the sound of billiard balls, showed that the happy Gallic turn for gayety and amusement still lingered about the place.[18]

What economic activity Louis Gonville was engaged in prior to 1807 is not known, although he probably worked at odd jobs associated with the fur industry. More certain is that on 12 September of that year, with the help of Pierre Chouteau's son Francis, he was granted a one-year's federal license to "hunt on the Kansas river." Years later, Pierre's brother Frederick recalled the circumstances: "Louis Gonville was a trapping Before I came to Kansas he got his outfit from my Brother Francis Such as trap Rifle powder & lead he would Start in the fall and Return in the Spring he would make successful hunt he followed that for several years. . . . I imploy Louis as a laboring hand he remain with me until his death in 1852 he was a very good man that you could depend upon."[19]

Like others who lacked land, social standing, and the economic resources to compete with the rapid influx of the Americans into Missouri after 1803, Gonville found it difficult to survive in the changing St. Louis economy. The independent trade that had thrived in Illinois and Canada under Spanish control was gone, and the lone trader had fallen victim to more stringent controls, dictated by the Indian Office in distant Washington. A temporary respite was furnished by the employment that Francis Chouteau provided in 1807, but the disruption that was occasioned by the War of 1812 undermined the profitability of even this. On 20 May 1815, Louis Gonville was incarcerated in the St. Charles prison as an insolvent debtor.[20]

But the government's postwar policy of negotiating friendship treaties with the western Indians presented new opportunities for men like Gonville. While he languished in prison, Auguste Chouteau received the appointment as a federal commissioner to assist the Indian Office in winning tribal allegiance to the United States. An arrangement on this model was concluded in St. Louis with the Kansa tribe on 28 October 1815, and among the nineteen headmen who affixed their "Xs" to the document was Gonville's future father-in-law, White Plume. As a son-in-law of Pawhuska and as an increasingly prominent leader among the Kansas, White Plume could attribute his ascendency to his marital ties with the Osages and the federal government through the Chouteaus. A decade later, after he had consolidated his power among the

Kansa mixed-bloods and had committed them to the cause of the government, White Plume proudly informed the Indian superintendent William Clark: "This is my wife, the same woman you took by the hand some time ago [as an Osage]. . . . My father, I consider myself an American and my wife an American woman—I want to take her home with me and have everything like white people."[21]

After being released from the St. Charles prison, probably in 1816, Louis Gonville moved west to the Kansa country near the confluence of the Kansas and Big Blue rivers, to begin life anew in a setting where opportunities for getting ahead were much more attractive. He first married Hunt Jimmy, the eldest daughter of White Plume, and then, in late 1817 or early 1818, Hunt Jimmy's younger sister, Wyhesee. The termination of marriages under Kansa custom generally were uncomplicated affairs: if there was a mutual agreement—as there apparently was in the case of Gonville and Hunt Jimmy—no outside counsel or interference was required. In fact, having married two of White Plume's daughters, Louis Gonville's status as a respected family man was enhanced, while in the meantime his connections with the Chouteaus became correspondingly more secure.[22]

The westward movement of the next generation of Chouteaus provided still other opportunities for Gonville. On 16 August 1816, Gabriel (the twenty-two-year-old son of Auguste) and Francis (the nineteen-year-old son of Pierre) were awarded licenses to trade with the Kansas, Osages, and Pawnees. Shortly thereafter, the two young men constructed the Four Houses trading post on the Kansas River, twenty miles above its confluence with the Missouri; and by October 1819 it was reported that their capitalization for the Kansas and the Osages alone had reached $4,000. Gonville, their employee, was a family man and a dependable hunter; and through his father-in-law, Gonville was a valuable tribal contact.[23]

The world into which Curtis's maternal grandmother was born, probably in late 1818, was the main Kansa village at the confluence of the Blue (or Blue Earth) and Kansas rivers, near present-day Manhattan. In the late eighteenth century, the Kansas had their villages on the Missouri just above future Fort Leavenworth, but pressure from the Iowas and Sacs, in addition to the fear of smallpox, prompted the shift. A movement west to the mouth of the Blue also placed the Kansas closer to the buffalo plains. Fort Osage's factor, George C. Sibley, who visited the main village in 1811, counted 128 lodges arranged in "a rather neat and cleanly" appearance. Nearby were about a hundred acres of corn, beans, and pumpkins, only recently planted by the village women; and on a beautiful prairie, hundreds of children were herding a large number or horses and mules. All was "bustle busy hum and merriment'' in preparation for the summer buffalo hunt, which Sibley described as ''the greatest enjoyment of their life.'' He was pleased to see American flags flying in various parts of the village, and especially the large one that ''gracefully waved over the lodge of the great chief.'' Writing to William Clark in St. Louis, Sibley reported that at one time the Kansas had been ''the terror of the lower Missouri,'' but now they were becoming ''one of the best tribes in your agency.''[24]

How long Gonville and Wyhesee stayed at the Blue Earth village is not certain, although it was not later than the spring of 1822. In August 1819, Louis served as a guide for Thomas Say's return from Blue Earth to rejoin Major Stephen H. Long's expedition to Yellowstone, then on to the Missouri below the mouth of the Platte. That may have been the time when the Gonvilles moved to the mouth of the Kansas River. Here, at a strategic point for the fur trade, a small but growing community of French and mixed-blood families was in the process of being established, and it was here that White Plume moved his family in 1821. That same year, Superintendent Clark selected White Plume to join a delegation of other Indian leaders to journey to Washington to confer with President James Monroe about peace and allegiance to the United States. The seeds for a government, or what later would be called the ''half-breed'' faction of the Kansa tribe, were thus planted.[25]

In Washington, the first meeting with President Monroe took place in early December 1821; this was followed by a three-week tour of New York, Baltimore, and Philadelphia. A New Year's reception was held at the White House, where White Plume and leaders of the Otoes, Pawnees, Omahas, and Missouris met with Secretary of War John C. Calhoun, Secretary of State John Quincy Adams, the British and French ministers, Chief Justice John Marshall, and diplomats from Russia and Sweden; and members of Congress were there as well. The French minister Baron Hyde de Neuville was so impressed with the visitors from the West that he invited them to his private residence to demonstrate their native dances. Several days later, they performed ''their war dances and other feats of agility'' on the White House lawn. At a meeting in the White House on 4 February 1822, President Monroe listened to each of the Indian emissaries and then addressed them in regard to the enormous population and military power of the United States. The United States was at peace with all nations, said Monroe, but if war were to break out, its citizens would quickly mobilize and become brave warriors. The Indians were urged to maintain peace and to listen to no other voice than that of their Great Father. The president concluded with a description of the many gifts they would receive and with a promise that they would be safely escorted home to their wives and families.[26]

Back at the mouth of the Kansas River, White Plume reported that his trip to Washington had been personally satisfying and diplomatically instructive. Mexican independence, he had been told, would lead to more regular commerce between the United States and the vast region formerly controlled by Spain. Missouri's statehood would inevitably lead to rapid white expansion up the Missouri River, and perhaps even onto the Kansa domain itself. Tribal movement to the west and north was blocked by the Pawnee and Dakota people, while on the plains the supply of buffalo and other game was diminishing. And in Washington there was talk about moving vast numbers of eastern Indians into the area west of Missouri. Hard bargaining would be necessary to save the Kansa tribe from becoming extinct.

With the government's blessing, the help of the French traders, and the support of the mixed-bloods at Kawsmouth (as the settlement at the mouth of the Kansas River was called), White Plume viewed himself as the one to assume the mantle of leadership during these difficult times. White travelers noted that the several bands of Kansas joined only rarely, mainly on important hunting expeditions ''or when the greatest danger requires it.'' White Plume understood this; governmental officials understood this; and in terms of mounting pressure for a massive land cession to accommodate eastern Indians, the officials saw in White Plume a valuable ally and a potentially unifying leader. Fortunately, there was precedent for tampering with the Kansa leadership, because in 1805, Wakanzare, whom the St. Louis traders called ''le chef Americain,'' had accepted an invitation to meet with President Jefferson in Washington. Wakanzare had gratefuly taken the ''appointment'' as ''Chief of the Kansa tribe'' and had promised to open trade relations ''with the Europeans.'' But no significant concessions were made—only a promise of peace and understanding. Eighteen years later, when visited by Paul Wilhelm (duke of Württemberg), Wakanzare admitted that Anglo-American culture had certain advantages, but he insisted that these were ''unsuited to the Indian nations which are so close to the state of nature.'' In 1823, his village was located at least sixty miles west of Kawsmouth and the French traders, and his deference to White Plume at that time was minimal at best. ''He knows,'' reported Wilhelm, ''that a too early acceptance of such laws [i.e., treaties] would bring harm to the aborigines.''[27]

White Plume was obviously more conciliatory. During the meeting with President Monroe, a much clearer distinction regarding tribal leadership and rank was made than in Jefferson's time. ''Full Chiefs'' were awarded two silver epaulettes to adorn their costumes, whereas ''Half Chiefs'' were given but one. This was manipulation at its finest, and the higher rank that was given to White Plume created a lasting impression on him, the father-in-law of Louis Gonville. With European ministers and representatives of Congress looking on approvingly, his Great Father had endowed him with special authority, authority that would transcend the troublesome disputes among the less fortunate pretenders to a unified Kansa leadership in the Indian country.[28]

The task, of course, was difficult. By the early 1820s, at least three village leaders were attempting to assert the very authority that White Plume coveted. To Superintendent Clark, White Plume admitted that to maintain his own authority, he was obliged to crop the ears and strip the backs of too many unimportant chiefs who were vying for control of the tribe. "My people are bad and need to be corrected," he told Clark in 1827, but "with the authority of good council he had received in Washington," buttressed by the support of the Chouteaus at Kaws-mouth, his confidence had not faltered. "I am determined to come and live near the whites," said White Plume, "and in doing so I have come with the feeling of a white man."[29]

White Plume's resolve was fortified by the increasingly mixed-blood community at Kawsmouth, not the least of which were the grandchildren born to Louis Gonville and White Plume's two daughters. In order of birth, they were Josette (or Josephine) and Pelagia, the daughters of Hunt Jimmy; and Julie, Victoria (or Margaret), Louis, America, Rosalia, and Baptiste, the children of Wyhesee. Louis and America died as infants, Baptiste died before reaching maturity, Rosalia eventually married a mixed-blood Shawnee-Delaware, and the remaining (including Julie, Curtis's grandmother-to-be) married Frenchmen. Louis Gonville's brother Baptiste also married a Kansa woman, and similar unions constituted the nucleus of a settlement that one day would be metro-politan Kansas City. In addition to Francis and Bernice Chouteau, who served as Josette Gonville's foster parents, the other residents at Kaws-mouth by the late 1820s were Calice Montary, Francis Tremble, Pierre Revalette, Louis Roy, and James McGee. In the immediate vicinity also were Joseph and Gabriel Philibert, Clement Lessert (who also took a Kansa wife), Andrew Woods, and "Grand Louis" Bertholet. Like the Gonvilles, these men had moved west from St. Louis for greater economic opportunity and the social security that circumstances at the mouth of the Kansas could provide. Joining the Gonville men and Lessert as fathers of half-blood Kansa children by 1825 were Francis Laventure, Pierre Brisca, Baptiste Ducherute, Cecile Compare, Joseph James (Little Chief, or Kyhegashinga), James Joncas, and three males whose surnames were Butler, Rodgers, and Cote.[30]

Whether the German aristocrat Paul Wilhelm actually met the family of Louis Gonville in the summer of 1823 is not known. But Wilhelm was in the immediate vicinity where they resided, and his

Julie Gonville Pappan (born 1818?), Charles Curtis's maternal grandmother, the recipient of Half-Blood Tract Number 4 under the Kansa Treaty of 1825. Standing beside her is her quarter-blood granddaughter Isabelle Pappan (born 1881), Charles Curtis's cousin. The photograph was probably taken at Julie's home on the Kaw Reservation in Indian Territory in the early 1890s. Courtesy of Kansas State Historical Society.

observations—biased by his racist preferences—afford some details of the society in which Charles Curtis's grandmother spent her childhood. A dinner prepared for him by "a good natured woman" at the cabin of Andrew Woods was "as good as the circumstances afforded." Wilhelm noted that the settlers had domestic animals and fowl but still preferred to maintain themselves primarily by the hunt. He met "Grand Louis" Bertholet, "an unspoiled son of the wilderness . . . whose inclination to drink and immorality often exceeds the bounds of human dignity" but who, when sober, "was not insensible to better feelings." On a hunting trip with Bertholet, Wilhelm noted:

> In the afternoon several creole hunters and halfbreeds together with a number of Indian women and children camped on the right bank of the [Missouri] river, opposite the dwelling of Grand Louis. These hunters soon came to pay my host a visit. They repeated this visit the next day. On both occasions they were drunk. In spite of a natural goodheartedness they were repulsive in this condition. The Indian women in their company deported themselves in the manner customary to their people. They were scantily dressed in red and blue shawls. Their decoration consisted of glass beads, coral and porcelain sticks. Their faces were stained with red, blue and green paints, which disfigured their otherwise rather pretty faces. They were all concubines or squaws of these hunters.[31]

Important here to the kinship of Charles Curtis were the circumstances of the Kansa women at Kawsmouth. With a mixed-blood progeny that could not be reversed, they were trapped in the crucible of cultural change beyond their individual capacities to alter this condition. Isolated from their full-blood relatives to the west and positioned at one of the most important commercial crossroads west of St. Louis, these women took on the primary responsibility for sustaining the fabric of mixed-blood family society. Alcohol flowed freely, husbands and fathers were regularly absent on hunting excursions or visits to St. Louis, while in the meantime the government's closing of the nearby trade factory at Fort Osage placed them more firmly under the domination of the private traders, led by the Chouteaus. White Plume had determined to follow the white man's path and, with the encouragement of the government, to use the mixed-blood children under his domination as instruments of tribal "progress."

3

The Estate

There is a persistent notion that Charles Curtis, in his rise from the lowly circumstance of an orphaned mixed-blood on the Kansas frontier to a position of national political prominence, accomplished his goals by tenacity and hard work on the pattern of Horatio Alger himself. Newspapers and magazines extolled these alleged virtues, particularly after Curtis was elevated to the United States Senate in January 1907. "The Government had not begun giving out the prize packages to its wards when he was a boy," offered the *Saturday Evening Post,* "and Curtis had a tough time of it." The *New York Times* explained that Curtis had to work hard as a child because his grandmothers simply "had no money to spare."[1]

Other periodicals of the time joined in complimenting Curtis on his remarkable achievements, but the strongest testimony came from the Indian commissioner Charles H. Burke in 1925. Curtis had only recently been designated Senate majority leader by the Coolidge Republicans, and Burke made the most of it. A personal friend and admirer of Curtis's efforts to expand the allotment revolution that had been inaugurated by the General Allotment Act of 1887, Burke and the Indian Office issued a pamphlet, for distribution in agency and governmental boarding schools, entitled "To the Indian Youth Everywhere." Here, it seemed, was the archetypical, self-made man:

> It should be of lasting value to every young man who will keep steadfastly in mind as a guiding force the elements of success in this distinguished career, prominent among which . . . were self-reliance, hard work, persistence of honest purpose, careful attention to details, thorough mastery of the job in hand, respect for the views of others, a desire to harmonize contention into results, and loyalty to enacted laws.[2]

In the same pamphlet, under the official letterhead of the United States Department of the Interior, Senator Curtis confirmed the laudatory appraisal of Commissioner Burke: "There was little in my early days that offered me particular advantage in reaching this goal. Since the journey has been possible for me who started so obscurely and who had so many early handicaps, is there any reason any boy anywhere should not consider that to him all things are possible?"[3]

In the twentieth century, Curtis could recall his humble beginnings and childhood adversity. He could talk about the value of property rights for mixed-blood Indians and even about the "progressive" qualities of White Plume. But in none of his public pronouncements was there so much as a hint that a substantial material inheritance through his maternal grandmother had given him an edge in his rise to power and fame. Indeed, even after he had bridged the gulf between traditional Kansa culture and the non-Indian power base that propelled him to national political prominence, Curtis was reticent regarding the material estate that had been established for him through his maternal grandmother in the Kansa treaty of 1825.[4]

The treaty of 1825 dated back to 9 January 1817, when the Senate Committee on Public Lands suggested the "expediency" of appropriating money for treaties that would allow Indians in the East to exchange their lands for new estates in the West and thus place them in a more isolated, hospitable setting for the government's emerging "Civilization" program.[5] On 16 March 1818, the approximate birthdate of Julie Gonville, the Missouri territorial delegate John Scott presented a statehood petition to Congress that bore directly on the future of the Kansa domain, especially the strategically located Kawsmouth area. With its fertile bottom lands, its ample hardwood timber, and its water connections with St. Louis, the area was coveted no less by white settlers and merchants than were the soon-to-be-ceded Indian lands in the East. It was, in short, a situation that required careful and firm negotiations with the resident tribal leadership.[6]

In St. Louis, the Indian superintendent William Clark instructed Fort Osage's factor, George C. Sibley, to hold preliminary talks with the Kansas. His task was not easy, for in addition to the fluidity of tribal leadership, there was the problem of the mixed-blood community at Kawsmouth. On 20 September, at Fort Osage, some forty miles below the mouth of the Kansas River, Sibley and Clark met with eight Kansa warriors and three of their chiefs: Shonganega (or Shonejenegaice), a prominent chief; his son Fool Chief (or Kahegawataninga or Cahegawatpiege); and a lesser leader, Wawhuachero. Sibley insisted that they were recognized leaders of the Kansa nation who "had consulted with nearly all the principal persons of their nation and without the least persuasion or compulsion'' were ready to treat with the United States. The preliminary arrangement provided for the cession of all Kansa lands in the future state of Missouri south of the Missouri River, and, in the future state of Kansas, for a massive cession bordered by Kawsmouth and the site of the future city of St. Joseph on the east, then southwest to the mouth of the Delaware River where it joins the Kansas River, then due south to present-day Iola, and finally back to the Missouri by way of the southeastern corner of present-day Miami County, Kansas. For this first land cession ever for the Kansas, the tribe was to receive $1,000 in merchandise simply for signing, plus $2,000 every September thereafter, in either merchandise or cash. A blacksmith was also promised, and the United States promised to provide ''a convention of protection'' against any nation that might threaten the security of the tribe.[7]

A number of factors precluded the adoption of the agreement. For one thing, an annuity in perpetuity was unacceptable to Congress, and with the statehood movement in Missouri gaining force, it was desirable to eliminate Indian title to land north of the Missouri River as well. Chief Shonganega was then in the process of relinquishing his authority over the main village at Blue Earth to his son Fool Chief, who had yet to prove himself among the rank-and-file Kansa warriors. Wakanzare, who, it will be remembered, had visited Washington in 1805, was not party to the talks; nor was White Plume, a rising star in the increasingly complex galaxy of Kansa leadership. No provisions were made to pay the debts owed the Chouteaus, and most important of all, the mixed-bloods were ignored. As their leader, then, White Plume was in the position of being a possible power broker in the reduction of the Kansa domain, especially when Clark and Sibley learned that White Plume and his followers were receptive to individual land ownership. Such preferences, after all, were a vital part of the government's civilization program.[8]

A month after the War Department had turned down the agreement of 1818, Sibley wrote to Clark: ''I am certain that I can point out a tract of 20 miles square, in the Territory offered for sale . . . which will in two years . . . be equal to ten years the annual payment to be made to the Kansas.'' This was no mere speculation, for by 1819, land in the Franklin district on the eastern border of the Kansa lands in Missouri was selling at an average of four dollars an acre, nearly twice the price then being received at the St. Louis office. By the time White Plume arrived in Washington in the fall of 1821, pressure from the settlers for an extensive Kansa cession had increased dramatically. The Missouri statehood bill had been passed on 10 August; William Becknell had embarked on a commercial journey to the Southwest that would open up the lucrative Santa Fe trade with Mexico and thus establish Kawsmouth as an important site for urban development, and squatters were beginning to occupy adjacent lands. Clearly, a permanent settlement with the Kansas was mandatory.[9]

In the field, Sibley worked hard. On 10 January 1824, he informed Missouri's Senator David Barton in Washington that the Kansas were willing to sell their lands ''for a mere trifle as compared with the immense value of the land'' and that it was useless to restrain white men who coveted the fertile land surrounding Kawsmouth. In fact, insisted Sibley, a higher law demanded a change in ownership.

> Besides the uncommon excellence of the soils and beautiful aspects of the country, it possesses other great natural advantages that would render it a garden indeed if once settled and owned by our enterprising citizens. This fine tract of country now lies an unproductive wilderness, utterly useless to the savages who claim it; and interdicted to our people, thousands of whom are anxiously waiting for our govt. to purchase it, and reap from it those great advantages which it is presumable the God of Nature designed for the use of civilised man.[10]

Sibley's plea represented little more than an amalgamation of assumed native deficiency and the belief that agriculture, the very foundation of New World civilization, was the true source of wealth. In this scheme, which enjoyed widespread public approval because of the pronouncements of Benjamin Franklin, Thomas Jefferson, and the transplanted Frenchman Michel Guillaume Jean de Crèvecoeur (pseudonym, J. Hector St. John), man had a natural right to land and ultimately a fee-simple title to that plot if he engaged in productive cultivation. The proper role of government, certainly for the Jeffersonians, was to encourage such activity and to extend the benefits of such policy to the Native Americans as well. It was a foregone conclusion, then, that Sibley's plea would receive a positive response among his superiors.[11]

At the more practical level, the government's removal policy demanded a quick and sweeping land cession from the Kansas. In the East, the bellicose posture of Georgia against numerous Indians prompted the Monroe administration to push hard for tribal removal to the West. In a series of urgent messages to Congress in 1824 and early 1825, Monroe recommended a voluntary removal bill that would prevent white intrusion, provide a governmental structure for the emigrant Indians, and promote the high ideals of white ''civilization.'' Senator Thomas Hart Benton of Missouri was elated, and on 1 February 1825 he introduced a bill that incorporated the president's recommendations, including funds to purchase large tracts of land from tribes such as the Kansas. Eleven days later, at Indian Springs in the Creek Nation, certain Creek leaders signed a treaty—which was later judged to be fraudulent—providing for the selection of a vast reservation on the Red, Canadian, Arkansas, or Missouri rivers, with the stipulation that "if the territory so to be selected shall be in the occupancy of other tribes, then the United States will extinguish the title of such occupants for the benefit of said [Creek] emigrants."[12]

A cursory examination of the Kansa treaty that Clark engineered in June 1825 reveals no overt evidence of chicanery on the part of the government. Indeed, by comparison to many other agreements, it appears reasonably generous. For a narrow strip on the western Missouri border and a good part of future Kansas bordering on the eastern edge of "The Great American Desert," the tribe was granted $70,000 in annuities to be distributed over a twenty-year period. For agricultural development, a distribution of five hundred domestic fowl, three hundred cattle, three hundred hogs, three yokes of oxen, two carts, and sundry hand tools was authorized. Agricultural instructors were to be provided, and for emergency assistance the Kansas were to receive an immediate issue of provisions valued at $2,000. To educate the children, thirty-six sections of prime bottom land in the Big Blue valley in western Missouri near Kawsmouth were to be sold from the ceded lands; and from the total cession, which amounted to more than twenty million acres, the tribe was to retain a reservation thirty miles wide, beginning sixty miles west of Missouri and extending west to a point in the Smoky Hill watershed that would be determined by the government in the future.[13]

The treaty was signed on 3 June, one day after the Osages had concluded a similar agreement. Superintendent Clark was delighted, and in a letter to Secretary of War James Barbour one week later, Clark reported: "In the negotiation of these treaties the two nations were fully represented; the Chiefs with a party of warriors from every village being present and fully authorized before they left home according to their discretions." A careful examination of the Kansa leadership at the time, however, presents a different picture. In fact, the St. Louis parley was a classic example of manipulation and the use of mixed-bloods as a device for the government to make chiefs and to dispossess the entire tribe of its material wealth.[14]

The four chiefs who signed the 1825 treaty were White Plume (Nompawarah), Fool Chief (Kahegawataninga), Hard Chief, (Kyhegawachehe), and Little Chief (Kyhegashinga). Eight warriors also affixed their Xs to the document, which was signed by Clark for the United States and was witnessed by fifteen non-Indians, including the United

States commissioner George C. Sibley. Notably absent from the document were the signatures of Wakanzare, who, after his visit to Washington in 1805, had signed a peace-and-friendship agreement in St. Louis ten years later, and Shonganega, who was clearly the most distinguished Kansa leader until White Plume became the choice of Clark and Sibley.[15]

As in mid-nineteenth-century Kansas, when chief making by the government reached its zenith, the federal agents were required to identify a flexible tribal leader who enjoyed enough followers so that the government's dispossessory objectives might not seem so blatantly pernicious. Such had been Sibley's strategy in 1818. By signing this treaty, Shonganega replaced Cayezettanzaw as the most powerful leader at Blue Earth, and the former tried to retain this position until White Plume's visit to Washington and the consequent 1825 treaty undermined his power. Indeed, it was precisely the negotiations in 1818 and 1825 that prompted the Kansas to abandon Blue Earth, break up into contending factions, and establish segregated villages. Thus by 1830, in modern Shawnee County, some sixty miles east of Blue Earth, were the village of Wakanzare, the village of Shonganega and his ambitious son Fool Chief, and the village of the Hard Chief (Kyhegawachehe). Still farther east, near the newly established Kansa Agency headquarters and the future site of Topeka, resided White Plume and his mixed-blood entourage that had moved west from Kawsmouth after the treaty of 1825.[16]

Shonganega, who commanded the largest following, was ill informed or unaware of the agreement that White Plume, Fool Chief, and Hard Chief had reached with Clark and Sibley in St. Louis. On 3 March, three months before the St. Louis treaty, a bill was passed authorizing the government to mark the Santa Fe road from "the Western frontier of Missouri to the confines of New Mexico." Included in the legislation was the stipulation that the commissioners who would be assigned were to "obtain the consent of the intervening tribes of Indians, by treaty, to the marking of said road and to the unmolested use thereof to the citizens of the United States and the Mexican Republic." Appointed as commissioners were Benjamin Reeves, Thomas Mather, and the ever-present Sibley, who on 16 August (more than two months *after* the St. Louis treaty) met with a group of tribal leaders at Sora Kansas Creek in present-day McPherson County, eighty miles southwest of Blue Earth. Here, for an immediate payment of three hundred dollars in merchandise and the promise of an additional five hundred dollars in merchandise or cash, "the Chiefs and Head Men of the Kansa tribe of Indians" agreed to the government's offers.[17]

Heading the list of signatories was Shonganega, who, as in the preliminary agreement of 1818, was identified as "the great chief of the Kanzas Nation." Other "chiefs" who signed were Moneerata and Neeakershall, who was identified as "a chief, brother of the great chief." Among the thirteen warriors who also signed were Keheabashee, "eldest son of the great chief," and Haheeseeshe, who was identified as "White Plume's deputy." In Kansa–United States relations, there was no precedent for such a delegation of power.[18]

None of these individuals had signed the St. Louis treaty, and it is doubtful if they were even aware of the massive cession of land that Clark and White Plume worked out. Had Shonganega agreed to the cession, he certainly would have realized that the Santa Fe road was to go through the area that only recently had been ceded in St. Louis. But he apparently did not realize this, and in good faith, he had signed the Sora Kansas Creek treaty, collected the payment typically required for such services, and continued on with the summer hunt. Sibley, who served as the government's tribal contact for nearly a decade, had the advantage of attending both parleys. While the St. Louis treaty was concluded on 3 June, it was not until the following 20 December that it was entered into the statute books.[19]

In 1818, Shonganega had agreed to a cession that included only a small strip of land west of Missouri, whereas White Plume in 1825 relinquished nearly half the future state of Kansas, including most of the buffalo country drained by the Smoky Hill and Republican rivers. At stake was not only a large amount of land but also the horticulture/hunting economy that had sustained the traditional Kansa way of life before the arrival of the white man. Pressure from the Republican Pawnees to the northwest over the shrinking supply of buffalo was now aggravated by White Plume's concessions to Clark. The miserly bribe that was given to Shonganega at Sora Kansas Creek was less an easy bargain to provide security for the Santa Fe traders than it was an attempt to placate the aging Kansa leader as the government proceeded to restructure the tribal leadership to suit its own needs.

Certainly, Sibley was not uninformed regarding the diversity of the Kansa economy and the importance of hunting to their survival. He had visited the village of Blue Earth as early as the spring of 1811 and had observed nearly a hundred acres of flourishing corn, beans, and pumpkins, recently planted by the women. On a nearly prairie were hundreds of Kansa children herding a large number of fine-quality horses and mules, and the tribe as a whole was happily planning the summer buffalo hunt, which Sibley described as "the greatest enjoyment of their life."[20]

At Blue Earth also, Sibley had observed the political system whereby the tribe was governed by a head chief and council of the oldest and most distinguished warriors. He noted some jealousy arising from the ambitions of certain "minor chiefs," but he remained confident that the head chief, Cayezettanzaw, "a man of sense and firmness, as well as a great warrior," would soon reestablish his authority. Seven years later, however, it was the more flexible Shonganega with whom Sibley negotiated for Kansa land, thus establishing the policy of chief making that culminated in White Plume's rise to power.[21]

Mixed-blood factionalism and Indian removal were not major issues when, later that spring, Sibley distributed peace medals and American flags among the Kansas and the Pawnees. More important then were intertribal relations and the promise of allegiance to the United States in the impending war with Britain. But by 1818, Indian removal and the future of the Kansa domain were mounting in importance, and by 1825, they could no longer be deferred. Close cooperation between the Kawsmouth mixed-bloods and the French traders, coupled with the end of the factory system, which was so despised by the traders, dictated that a new Kansa leader was needed in order to implement the government's Indian policy in the trans-Missouri West. White Plume was the logical choice.[22]

George Sibley's boast that the Kansas were ready to sell "for a mere trifle" in 1825 was cause for optimism, but in no way did it provide for the mixed-bloods. Here, then, was the challenge to Clark. The Kawsmouth faction would have to be rewarded in a manner commensurate with their apparent commitment to the government's removal and civilization program. So, with the guidance of the Chouteaus, an offer was made on 3 June to White Plume: it provided individual plots of 640 acres for each of the twenty-three half-blood Kansa children, on the pattern of a similar offer accepted by the Osage half-bloods on the preceding day.[23]

The arrangement was more than acceptable to Superintendent Clark, who told the secretary of war that the ceded area would easily accommodate the Creeks, as well as other removal Indians who surely would benefit from the wonderfully productive terrain that the Kansas had relinquished. The Chouteaus were also pleased, since the treaty provided for the payment of the money owed to the French traders. White Plume and the mixed-bloods came out even better, for the all-important article 6 granted "reservations, of one mile square, for each of the half breeds of the Kanzas nation . . . to be located on the North side of the Kanzas . . . commencing at the [eastern] line of the [new] Kanzas reservation, and extending down the Kanzas river for quantity." Included in the twenty-three half-bloods enumerated in article 6 were the four daughters of Louis Gonville: Josette, Pelagie, Julie, and Victoria. Julie's section was subsequently designated "Kaw Half Blood Mile

Four." It was located directly across the Kansas River from the future town site of Topeka, and it constituted the 640-acre estate that would one day belong in part to Charles Curtis.[24]

In his letter that accompanied the treaty of 1825 to Washington, Clark insisted that the tribe had been well represented at the treaty table in St. Louis. In fact, this was not the case. For one thing, there was only one village in 1825, and the permanent division into three villages with recognized leaders did not take place until 1829—even then, it was primarily the result of dissension over the treaty itself. Shonganega, it will be recalled, did not sign the treaty; nor did his brother or his eldest son. Wakanzare's signature was absent, as were those of Hurasogee and Moneerata, both of whom were to certify the Sora Kansas Creek agreement later that year. Clark's letter to the contrary, the Kansa nation was rent with factionalism, and Indian Office agents in the field were exploiting the situation almost at will.[25]

Heading the list of those who did sign, of course, was White Plume. From a group of no fewer than nine and possibly as many as twelve so-called chiefs, only three were certified in the document as official chiefs: Fool Chief, Hard Chief, and Little Chief. Eight lesser individuals also signed, including Little White Bear (Mechuchinga), an individual who was to be of some prominence in the future. Superintendent Clark was the principal contracting officer for the government, while Sibley added his name as an official commissioner. Among the official interpreters was Baptiste Ducherute, whose daughter Elizabeth was a recipient of one of the half-blood tracts.[26]

Little Chief, the fourth to sign, provides important insights into the inner workings of the mixed-blood faction. In fact, Little Chief, White Plume's son-in-law, was better known to Clark and Sibley as Joseph James, or "Jo Jim." After Wyhesee had replaced Hunt Jimmy as Louis Gonville's second wife, Hunt Jimmy married James, who thus became White Plume's second son-in-law. To the Hunt Jimmy–Joseph James union was born Joseph James, Jr. ("Jo Jim, Jr."), who, not surprisingly, was also awarded one of the prized mile-square tracts along the Kansas River. Why the senior James, rather than Louis Gonville, was selected by White Plume and William Clark to serve as a treaty chief tells much about the growing power of the mixed-blood faction during the 1820s.[27]

On the surface, Louis Gonville had equal or even superior credentials. He had provided White Plume with four grandchildren, had been living among the tribe longer than James had, and was a faithful employee of the Chouteaus. An important difference, however, was that, as a half-blood Osage, James had better connections with White Plume's extended genealogy, and perhaps even more important, he was

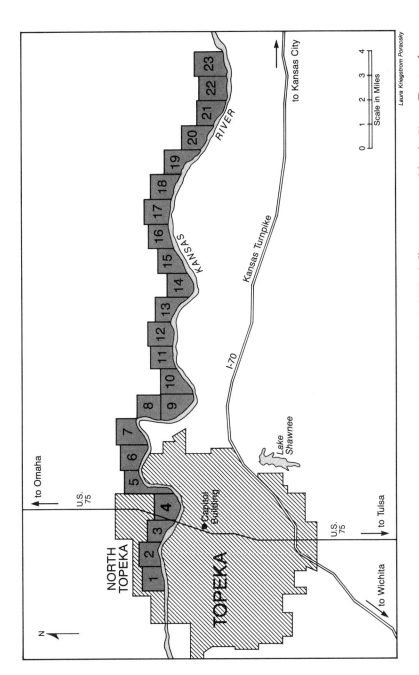

A map of present-day Topeka and vicinity, showing the twenty-three half-blood allotments granted by the Kansa Treaty of 1825. Number 4 was awarded to Julie Gonville (Pappan), the maternal grandmother of Charles Curtis.

Laura Kriegstrom Poracsky

fluent in English to the degree that in the future he would qualify for the position as official interpreter for the Kansas.[28]

Additional factors favored James over Gonville. Hunt Jimmy bore James four children, two of whom survived infancy, including Jo Jim, Jr. In addition to Wyhesee and Hunt Jimmy, White Plume had at least three more children, all of them males. According to Kansa custom, one of these could expect to be elected to chieftain status upon the death of White Plume. But by the mid 1820s, it was uncertain if any of these offspring would be able to carry out this function. The eldest, Chinga-cahega, was sickly and was not expected to reach maturity. Another was a bastard whose name is not known, and the third, Wasabase, was only nine years old at the time of the treaty of 1825. Given White Plume's advanced age, it was doubtful if Wasabase would achieve maturity before White Plume would die. Certainly, White Plume was concerned about the succession of power, for in 1827 he told Clark that he had already decided to purchase two black slaves to take care of him in his aged and sickly condition. Thus, the male offspring of Hunt Jimmy and Joseph James, Sr., were the only logical individuals who might be expected to assume the mantle of mixed-blood leadership once White Plume was gone.[29]

There is no question that Indian superintendent Clark was pleased with the deal struck with the mixed-bloods. To Secretary Barbour he wrote: "Reserves of this kind have been heretofore made in behalf of such persons, and in my opinion have a good effect in promoting civilization, as their attachment is created for a fixed residence and an idea of separate property is imparted without which it is vain to think of improving the minds and morals of the Indian or making any progress in the work of civilization."[30] But having extolled the virtues of land ownership by mixed-bloods, Clark was less optimistic regarding contacts between the Kansa traditionalists and the white settlers of western Missouri: "Experience having convinced me of the necessity of preventing a White and Indian population from remaining in immediate contact with each other and the Indians themselves being fully sensible of the inconvenience of such neighborhoods . . . it has been stipulated that the Kansa reservation be about fifty miles west of Missouri, *to prevent the stocks of the two parties* from intermixing" (emphasis added).[31]

The thinking, then, was that the Kansa full-bloods would be far enough removed from the white settlements to prevent them from adopting the more pernicious qualities of white culture, while, in the meantime, the mixed-bloods would demonstrate, by exemplary agrarian living, the means whereby their less fortunate relatives might one day enjoy the civilizing lessons of land ownership by individuals. Miscegenation—Curtis's solution to the problem years later—was to be discouraged; hence the buffer zone between the main Kansa villages and the white farmers of Missouri.

Central to such thinking were several assumptions, none of which was wholly fulfilled in the years following the 1825 treaty. For one thing, White Plume's influence over the mixed-bloods was greatly exaggerated in the minds of Clark and Sibley, and Jo Jim's contrived status as a Kansa chief was never recognized by the tribe as a whole. White Plume's health was faltering—indeed, his brief involvement with the Catholic missionary effort in 1828 was more the consequence of a near-death experience than it was a commitment to the theological overtures of the missionary Joseph Anthony Lutz. In the end, the disillusioned Kansa leader moved west to the main tribal villages, most likely to be on hand at the time of the semiannual annuity distributions authorized in 1825. When White Plume died in 1838, probably the result of excessive drinking while on an autumn hunt, the Reverend Henry Gregory reported that the chief had "returned to the old Indian habits."[32]

Another misguided assumption was that the half-bloods would take up the agrarian life. This was unrealistic. All of the twenty-three allottees were minors in 1825, and none took possession of his or her tract before 1840. It was not until 1827 that A. L. Langham surveyed the tracts, and shortly thereafter the boundaries that he located became embroiled in survey problems resulting from the Delaware removal treaty of 1829. The ensuing conflict ultimately focused attention on the value that the mixed-blood tracts had for speculation, not for cultivation by the Indians.[33]

By what may have been an oversight, or at least the result of poor communication between governmental surveyors, the treaty of 24 September 1829 awarded the half-bloods' reserves to the Delawares. Assisted by a Delaware interpreter and Jo Jim for the Kansas, Isaac McCoy and his two sons were authorized to survey the reservation in 1830. It was truly an unprofessional job, for there is no evidence that the survey party even ventured onto the half-bloods' lands. Not until 1837, when the Delaware chief Captain Swannach visited Washington, was any question raised as to what right Jo Jim, the Gonville sisters, and the other half-bloods had to the reserve that the Delawares assumed was theirs.[34]

For the next several years, the government pursued a policy of vacillation which was characterized by occasional efforts to convince the half-bloods to sell to the Delawares at a maximum price of $1.25 per acre. McCoy advised that it would be "an advantage to the half-breeds to sell," while St. Louis's superintendent, Joshua Pilcher, Clark's successor, was certain that it would be possible to extinguish the titles at "the Government price or less." In Washington, however, the Indian commissioner T. Hartley Crawford engaged in delaying tactics, especially after he had learned that certain traders among the half-bloods were urging them to hold out for a higher price. By late 1841, the government backed off from any plan to force the sale to the Delawares.[35]

While the tracts remained vacant, the majority of the half-bloods and their families moved to St. Louis, where they hounded Pilcher for permission to sell to speculators. By the spring of 1842, Crawford was informed that the half-bloods were "so destitute of the necessities of life" that a sale at any price was preferable to starvation. Congress, however, refused to issue the fee-simple titles needed for such transactions. The intent had been for the half-bloods to farm their lands, not to speculate, as the white frontiersmen across the border in Missouri were doing. A further complication was traffic over the Oregon Trail in Kansas, which crossed the Kansas River in the vicinity of Julie Gonville's reserve number 4. Clearly, hers and the adjacent reserves were appreciating in value dramatically, and what was needed, of course, was someone to exploit the commercial potential of the location.[36]

Timothy Flint wrote in 1826: "I have already hinted at the facility with which the French and Indians intermix. There seems to be as natural an affinity of the former people for them, as there is repulsion between the Anglo-American and them. . . . The French settle among them, learn their language, intermarry, and soon get smoked to the same copper complexion [and] a race of half-breeds spring up in their cabins." A decade later, a certain Baptiste, Victor Tixier's companion on his journey to the Osage prairies, was greatly impressed with the beauty of the Kansa females whom he met in the vicinity of Kawsmouth. They boldly bathed near Tixier's party, were "prettier" than the Osages, "and their glances were ever encouraging." It was Baptiste's studied conclusion that their morals "were not very strict" and that cohabitation with Frenchmen was their main objective. "Lasciva puella et fugit ad salices, et se cupit ante videril" (Virgil, in *Aeneid*, "The wayward girl runs behind the willow and hopes I see her first before she hides!") was his lusty observation.[37]

Four years later, Matthew Field had the pleasure of meeting the Gonville sisters on half-blood tract number 3. While he certainly agreed with Baptiste's alluring description of Kansa femininity, his perception of the situation dealt more with the economic realities of mixing the races:

5 sisters—really beautiful—educated at the Mission near Westport—talk French, English, Kaw, and Iowa—4 married to Frenchmen—one to an intelligent half-breed Delaware—a sixth now growing to make some shrewd fellow happy—for these men get a certain quantity of land in right of the Kaw women.[38]

Land was the consideration—land made all the more attractive because of
its increasing value and because it was owned by beautiful young Indian
women who obviously had experienced a significant degree of acculturation by the time Field visited them in 1843. By then, the half-bloods
named in the 1825 treaty had divided into two factions: one, the larger
group, who gravitated to St. Louis and were anxious to sell to speculators; and the other, the smaller group, dominated by White Plume's
grandchildren, including the future grandmother of Charles Curtis.[39]

White Plume's flirtation with Catholicism was an important factor
in the acculturation of Jo Jim and the Gonville sisters. In his 1827
meeting with Superintendent Clark, White Plume had voiced his
disapproval of the Protestants, which dated back to the abortive
Methodist Episcopal Mission established near Kawsmouth by William
Johnson in the spring of 1825. "The American [i.e., Methodist] ministers
among us are all married men," complained White Plume. "I don't like
that—I want Catholic priests, to teach our children." A year later, at the
Kansas subagency, he said to the Catholic missionary Anthony Lutz:
"Oh my Father, you are welcome. At last you are here whom I have so
long desired. . . . It is my intention to assist you in all things that you
wish to do among the Kansas."[40]

White Plume was not alone in his religious preferences. The
Chouteaus played a no-less-important role in the acculturation of White
Plume's progeny. Josette, the eldest of the Gonville sisters, was raised in
the home of Francis and Bernice Chouteau at Kawsmouth, and at the
age of eighteen she was baptized a Catholic by Father Benedict Roux in a
rude chapel erected by the Chouteaus. Also baptized in 1834 were the
two half-blood children of Clement Lessert (the Kansas' interpreter) and
Mehatonga and the two children of the former Kansa agriculturist
Daniel Morgan Boone. A year later, the Chouteaus erected a more
permanent church, which was known as the Church of St. Francis Regis
after 1839.[41]

On 1 November 1840 the Reverend Nicholas Point, S.J., arrived to
take charge of the parish at the mouth of the Kansas River. "The district
. . . was peopled by an assemblage of 23 families, each family comprising
a Frenchman and his Indian wife and half-blood children." Included in
the small parish were half-blood allottees Clement and Adel Lessert, and
Pierre Carboneau. Absent by then, however, were Josette and Julie.[42]

Like her sister Josette, Julie Gonville had resided at the parish since
its founding. Sometime before 1829, apparently in her early adolescent
years, Julie had lived with Louis Roy. The union had not lasted, and on
13 June 1829, in a civil ceremony conducted by Justice of the Peace
Andrew P. Patterson, she had married Clement Lessert, who by then
had left Mehatonga. Clement and Julie's daughters, Mary and Martha,

were baptized by Father Roux at Kawsmouth on 24 February 1834, and two years later, on 18 July 1836, the civil vows of Julie and Clement were renewed in a Catholic ceremony conducted by Father C. F. Quickenborne. Not long thereafter, both Josette and Julie contemplated building permanent residences on the 640-acre tracts that had been awarded to them in 1825. The death of White Plume in 1838 may have been a consideration, but the arrival of still other French fur traders appears to have been equally, if not more, important.[43]

In an important study of marriage and settlement patterns among the trappers and traders of the Rocky Mountains, William R. Swagerty has emphasized that by the late 1830s, certainly after the last rendezvous in 1840, "residential settlement communities provided a viable alternative to going 'white' or 'native' for those trappers and traders who had Indian wives and mixed-blood children."[44] Certainly, the Gonville history supports Swagerty's view, albeit in a different setting. On 5 October 1837, Josette married Joseph Pappan in the home of the widowed Bernice Chouteau; two years later, Julie left Lessert and married Joseph's brother Louis.[45]

Little is known about the Pappan brothers before they married Josette and Julie. Based on his acquaintance with the Pappans during their later years, the Shawnee County historian William W. Cone recalled: "These French gentlemen were born in St. Louis, Missouri, their father, Louis Pappan, Sr., having moved there from Montreal, Canada, in the latter part of the last century." While available evidence for Louis's activities prior to his marriage to Julie is minimal, it is known that his brother Joseph was a former employee of the American Fur Company and that he may have been the "J. Papin" who reportedly had saved the Oregon missionary William Gray from a hostile Sioux party in the summer of 1837.[46]

In the spring of 1840, Joseph and Louis Pappan constructed a cabin on Josette's allotment number 3, across the river from what would become north Topeka. Directly east were tracts 4, 5, and 6—the reserves of Julie, Pelagia, and Victoria, respectively. In that same year, Ellen Pappan was born to Louis and Julie, in the cabin that had only recently been completed. More children were soon born to the two unions, including Ellen's brothers, Henry and Louis. By the mid 1840s, "Kansa Half Blood Survey No. 3" formed the nucleus of a growing mixed-blood settlement west of Kawsmouth.[47]

We are again indebted to Matthew Field, reported for the *Picayune* (New Orleans), for a perceptive description of the Pappans' home in mid October 1843:

> Two bed steads and a crib—a dozen loose planks laid over the rough cross-beams formed the second story . . . and 5 tender juvenillians,

of as many colors, romped over and under and around everything to the infinite merriment and heart's delight of their tender, copper colored mamas. Around the walls hung, on wooden pegs and old nails, a little red framed look glass, with a picture of a red brick house, that seemed to be of fire, painted on an upper panel of the glass. There as something by the side of the house resembling Vesuvius in eruption, though the painter may have meant it for a tree, prefering red to the common color of green. Under this hung a common glass liquor flask, with some sort of dirty oil in it, and next to the flask a vial, containing something altogether unguessable. Then there was a white coon skin, a woman's sunbonnet, a string of praying beads, with a little brass crucifix, several soiled engravings, of the Archangel's slaying of the serpent, the Holy Ghost descending &C.&C., pinned to a towel and the towel nailed to the wall.[48]

Field described the generous if not altogether tasty repast that was presented as the supper meal before he spent the night on the cabin floor with his two companions:

When about to get us our supper, the lady of the house pulled up a couple of planks from the floor, and jumped down, threw a pile of potatoes out, which were forthwith peeled and washed and put on the fire. Boiled pumpkin, cold & insipid, wild turkey, warmed in hot water, potatoes, *nearly* cooked, strong coffee, without sugar and unsettled, and flour biscuits, homemade, heavy and cold, were laid before us; and we fancied it was something like home, inasmuch as we sat on raised seats at a four legged platform.[49]

Field's description provides a powerful contrast to another description, penned by Charles Curtis some thirty-five years later for the *North Topeka Times*. Referring to the same location described by Field, Curtis wrote:

The only human inhabitants of the land on which our beautiful city [of North Topeka] now stands were the noble red men of the West. Here in the sands of the Kaw [River] his footprints could be seen; here the noble warrior wooed his first dusky squaw, and chased the wild deer and buffalo, and no white man disturbed their quiet hours but an occasional trader.[50]

On the eve of the great Oregon and California migrations and the soon-to-be-joined legal struggles accompanying the land speculators' assault on the half-blood reserves, this description would have been unrecognizable to the Pappans who were residing on half-blood tract number 3.

4
Born in a Log House

In his study of white renegades on the American frontier, Colin G. Calloway observed that mixed-blood children of Indian-white parentage were "at best marginal people of minor significance, and at worst, 'mongrel half-breeds' who combined the worst characteristics of each parent." While a majority became snared "in a rapidly diminishing 'no-man's-land,' a few readjusted to life in the white man's world but remained objects of curiosity." Jacqueline Peterson, on the other hand, basing her observations on the métis population living south and west of Lakes Superior and Huron to about 1815, emphasized their considerable power in the numerous small trade towns and challenged the view of the métis as being mainly "transient vagabonds." But, Peterson has cautioned, "because fur trade society was not an agricultural society, its members did not develop [the] keen sense of individual property rights" that was essential to preventing them from losing their improved land to more "sanguine Americans" for much less than its actual value.[1]

During the 1840s, in the strategic Kansas valley, which commanded access to the Santa Fe, Oregon, and California trails, there unfolded an intermediate state of commercial venture that temporarily insulated the Gonville-Pappan estates from land jobbers who were determined to fill the economic vacuum created by the collapse of the fur trade. In the larger setting of tribal dispossession, it was an important episode of mixed-blood tutelage and, at a more limited level, a development that established the foundation for the estate that one day would be the inheritance of Charles Curtis.

According to Francis P. Prucha, "Treaties became instruments of American paternalism." In the early years of the republic, they may have resulted from deliberations between sovereign nations, particularly if the United States were confronted by Indian nations of considerable power, but by mid century they were little more than "civilizing instruments intended by the federal government to move the Indians from their aboriginal cultural patterns to the agricultural existence that was deemed necessary for the Indians." Fraud, Prucha admits, did occasionally occur, but a more important characteristic that shone through at mid century was a truly "benevolent paternalism."[2]

Included in the paternalistic plan were (1) the reduction of the Indian land base and the establishment of more limited reserves; (2) annuities for education and "civilization"; (3) grants for farms, mills, and shops; and (4) allotments to individual Indian families. Family allotments were viewed as important models for other, less acculturated Indians to follow.

A quarter of a century earlier, however, the Indian superintendent William Clark displayed less interest in the welfare of Indian families than in individual mixed-bloods when he authorized grants to the Osage and Kansa mixed-bloods on grounds that "reserves of this kind have been heretofore made in behalf of such persons, and in my opinion have a good effect in promoting civilization." The large cession obtained from the Kansas, which totaled nearly 20 million acres, provided room for emigrant Indians from the Old Northwest, and other articles in the 1825 treaty provided much of what Prucha views as the main features of treaty making. But previous individual grants to individual Chippewas in 1819, to Ottawas, Chippewas, and Potawatomis in 1821, to the Florida tribes in 1823, to the Quapaws in 1824, and to selected Osage mixed-blood individuals prior to the Kansa agreement of 1825, indicated that the government was more than casually interested in the mixed-blood individual landowner as an instrument of white civilization.[3]

Because the Kansa grants were made in the name of civilization, there is little evidence that the government provided the direction and the practical assistance essential to make them viable, demonstrative enterprises. In fact, quite the opposite was the case. Surveys were tardy and poorly executed, and little account was kept of the activities of these new landowners. While interlopers soon invaded the lands, litigation over land titles became commonplace, and tribal factionalism—in large measure the result of awarding the individual reserves in the first place—was exploited as a device for further dispossession of the tribes. In the meantime, it was left to the Pappan brothers and their families to provide some credibility to the "civilizing" components of the treaty of 1825.

In the transition from employment with the Chouteaus to commercial agriculture, the Oregon migration of the early 1840s provided the Pappan brothers with an opportunity to sustain themselves on their spouses' reserves. Whereas the majority of the twenty-three reserves that were named in the treaty either remained at Kawsmouth or nearby Westport or moved to St. Louis, Joseph and Louis Pappan located on reserve number 3 and took advantage of some of the very basic needs of the Oregon emigrants. Inexperienced travelers were fortunate to have the Pappans' services, especially advice as to where best to ford the major streams, which usually were swollen at the beginning of the travel season in early spring.[4]

On 12 May 1841, at the Sapling Grove rendezvous some eight miles west of Westport, Missouri, the John Bidwell–John Bartleson party of approximately sixty persons embarked for Oregon. Preceding this party, generally recognized as the first organized emigrant train to the Pacific, was the small party of Father Pierre Jean De Smet, whose guide, Thomas Fitzpatrick, was to pilot the two companies to Oregon. After crossing Wakarusa Creek, just south of present-day Lawrence, and Shunganunga Creek, within the limits of present-day Topeka, the De Smet party reached the "Kansas crossing" on the sixteenth; the Bidwell-Bartleson party arrived on the following day. As nearly as can be determined, the location was directly across from Josette Pappan's reserve. On hand to transport the baggage, wagons, and emigrants across the river in a "hollowed tree trunk" (which reminded De Smet of a Venetian gondola) and in rawhide boats made of buffalo skins were two "Kansas Indians." Although not identified by name, they almost certainly were Louis and Joseph Pappan.[5]

A year later, on 15 June 1842, Lt. John C. Frémont, on his first journey to the Rocky Mountains, purchased twenty pounds of coffee and exchanged a yoke of oxen for "a fine cow and calf" from a "Louis Pepin" near the point where De Smet and the Bidwell-Bartleson party had crossed the Kansas River. Six of Frémont's carts were taken across the river by the Pappans in what was described as an "Indian rubber-boat." The husbands of Josette and Julie Gonville were beginning to exploit a profitable alternative to the agricultural endeavors that the government had envisaged in the treaty of 1825, although at the time they had no way of knowing about the enormous increase in western travel that would develop following the discovery of gold in California six years later.[6]

Josette Pappan's reserve number 3 was the first location of the Pappan ferry. A writer in 1856 noted that when crossing from the south side of the river, one could see "Papan's house on the right, peeping cosily out from its environment of trees."[7] Indications are that the enterprise was profitable from the start, although by no means as lucrative as similar operations farther west, were ferrymen who had no competition could take in as much as $50,000 in one season. Prior to the great flood of 1844, which temporarily disrupted the Pappan ferry, the

P. 1. *Lane's command crossing at*
PAPPAN'S FERRY. K.T.
Friday morning, Sept. 12ᵗʰ 1856.

A sketch of the Kansas River ferry operated by Louis Pappan, Charles Curtis's maternal grandfather. The view here is looking south across the river from North Topeka. Courtesy of the Kansas State Historical Society.

Indian agent Richard W. Cummins reported that he had paid two dollars and fifty cents to have his horses and baggage ferried across the Kansas River. Five years later, the Pappans were charging two dollars for each wagon, twenty-five cents for a mule or horse, and ten cents for each man. Later that month, a competing ferry at Uniontown, some fifteen miles above the Pappan location, forced the price down to one dollar per wagon, although, as a result of the "forty-niner" traffic, the volume was up dramatically, as each ferry took care of between sixty-five and seventy wagons a day. Other competition soon developed, including the operation of Charles Fish, a Delaware who had married Julie Pappan's sister Rosalie and whose business was located on the Kansas River just below the Pappans'.[8]

Nevertheless, the Pappans enjoyed advantages that were not available to Fish, Uniontown, or the Weld ferry nearby. Until the opening of Kansas Territory in 1854, they could, on the basis of being married to the Gonville sisters, claim title to the north bank of the river and, from a legal position, try to fend off would-be competitors. Although not always successful, the situation was one of advantage and relative security. Commenting on the "remarkable" Pappan enterprise, which by the early fifties had been expanded to include a toll bridge over

Shunganunga Creek and a mercantile house for the emigrants, an army officer who was headed for Santa Fe in May 1852 reported: "I was surprised to find at the Kansas river Ferry a young Canadian Frenchman, apparently proprietor of the ferry, who, with note-book in hand, was all day long busily occupied in taking down the number of wagons, horses, mules, sheep, &c., crossed over in his boats. Between the emigrant trains and those belonging to our command you may be sure he had a task to attend to."[9]

By contrast, life at the villages belonging to Fool Chief, Hard Chief, and American Chief was anything but secure. The failure of missionary activity was matched by chronic disease, periodic starvation, and very little progress in the agricultural arts, which presumably were to be encouraged by the treaty of 1825. A smallpox epidemic hit during the winter of 1831/32, and a severe outbreak of "high fever" struck during the fall of 1839. Many lives were lost. Because of the more powerful Cheyenne and Dakota tribes, hunting on the buffalo plains became more and more dangerous, and a deadly confrontation with the Republican Pawnees in the fall of 1840 threw the Kansa full-bloods into a frenzy of dancing, feasting, and consequent agricultural inactivity. No less discomforting was the flood of 1844, which destroyed the few acres of beans and corn that had been planted at Mission Creek, while in the meantime, governmental annuities under the treaty of 1825 were woefully inadequate. As for missionary efforts, the Reverend C. W. Love admitted in November 1843 that preaching Methodism to the Kansa "heathen" was like "water spilling upon the ground."[10]

More and more, the full-bloods resorted to raiding the overland trains, begging at Fort Leavenworth, and preparing themselves for yet-another land-cession treaty. This came in 1846, when the Kansa leadership relinquished an additional two million acres (at just over ten cents an acre) in exchange for a concentrated reservation on the upper Neosho River near Council Grove. By the time the tribe had made the move to the new reservation two years later, the mixed-blood group that had been singled out for special considerations in the treaty of 1825 were living as a separate band at the sites that were to become Topeka and Kansas City to the east.[11]

After the Mexican War and the Compromise of 1850, the Kansas-Nebraska Act was signed into law on 30 May 1854. Kansas Territory soon became a testing ground for the ideal of popular sovereignty, but underlying this momentous experiment was one of the most intense episodes of land speculation in the history of the Republic. Writing from west of St. Louis in July 1854, "Philos" reported: "They come by boats, stages, carriages, wagons, on horse-back and mule-back . . . making their way into the forests of [eastern] Kansas and Nebraska, to hew out a home. The emigration to these territories is unprecedented except in the history of California. . . . The ferry-boats here are busy transporting them from daylight until dark."[12]

But as Paul Wallace Gates noted more than three decades ago, a cardinal feature of this mass migration was that when the territory was officially organized in the spring of 1854, not one acre of land was available for legal sale. Plunder, privilege, and patronage fueled the speculative mania in farmsteads, railroads, and town sites, and reservations were overrun, without any regard for the rights of the Indians. On assignment in Kansas for a New York paper, William Phillips wrote in 1856: "I do not know whether the originators of the Kansas-Nebraska Bill contemplated an amalgamation of whites and Indians, to vindicate the faith of treaties and the progress of American civilization westward. If so, it was a blunder. Some few of the more intelligent and industrious Indians may be absorbed in the population of Kansas, but the great mass can neither use nor be used by civilization."[13]

The Kansa treaty of 1846 was a mere stopgap leading to the eventual removal of the entire tribe to Indian Territory in 1873, but for "more industrious" mixed-bloods such as Julie Pappan, other alternatives were available. Real-estate transactions with land speculators emerged as a more profitable enterprise than ferrying, particularly when Julie and her husband learned about the enormous interest in the so-called Wyandot floats then coming up for sale west of Missouri. By the Wyandot removal treaty of 1842, certain mixed-bloods of that tribe were assigned sections of land "out of any lands west of the Missouri River set apart for Indian use, not already claimed or occupied by any person or tribe." These floats, thirty-five in number, were made assignable to non-Indians and soon thereafter became the object of intense speculation. Simply put, they were the most attractive means for town promoters to secure legal title to 640 acres of land before preemptors or cash buyers could obtain Kansas real estate. The first transfer of a Wyandot float—to the Baptist missionary Johnston Lykins for $800—was registered the day after the 1855 treaty went into effect. On 24 March 1855 the Robertaile float—the future town site of Lawrence—brought $1,000; and a year later the Topeka Association voted to buy the Walker float of 621.8 acres for $1,200, at a rate well above the government's minimum price. Directly across the river from the Topeka Association's purchase were the allotments of Josette and Julie Pappan, and almost overnight the value of these lands increased dramatically.[14]

In fact, interest in the half-bloods' tracts dated back to the opening of Kansas Territory. In late 1854, an unidentified company offered to purchase the entire block of twenty-three reserves for five dollars an acre; another firm offered six dollars, or a total of $88,320. That same

year, Kansas' territorial governor, Andrew H. Reeder, District Attorney
Andrew J. Isacks, and Judges Rush Elmore and Sanders W. Johnston
agreed to pay up to three dollars an acre for the reserves of Adele Lessert
Bellmard, Julie Gonville Pappan, Pelagie Gonville Aubry, and Joseph
James.[15]

Under article 11 of the 1825 treaty, however, these transactions
required the permission of the United States.[16] Indian Commissioner
George W. Manypenny was appalled at the developing frenzy of land
grabbing. He flatly refused to certify the deals that Reeder and his
associates had allegedly arranged "in good faith" with the half-bloods.[17]
Personally furious and determined to retain his public office in the face of
mounting public criticism, Governor Reeder struck back at Manypenny:

> I assert that these vendors whom you have probably led the public
> to regard as wild, untutored savages, are, in fact, as competent to
> manage their own affairs as you and I. Louis Papin [Pappan] is a
> white man—a shrewd and intelligent Frenchman, who speaks the
> French and English well, is quite at home in all ordinary transac-
> tions of life, and so far from being an Indian that he has not the
> slightest admixture of Indian blood, and cannot speak the language.
> Aubrey is precisely the same, their wives are the daughters of Louis
> Gondil [sic], a French trader, and his Indian wife—quite as intel-
> ligent, as their parentage and station would indicate, and with
> whom the French is their daily and domestic language. . . . Indeed,
> if I were allowed to venture an opinion, I should say that they are
> quite as competent to superintend your bargins [sic] as you or your
> agent are to superintend theirs.[18]

While Reeder's abortive attempt to obtain these valuable tracts
eventually contributed to his dismissal, the publicity surrounding the
event did nothing to quell the speculators' interest in the half-blood
lands, at least not in the reserve of Louis and Julie Pappan. Indeed, the
Pappan's dealing with Reeder and his associates suggested that their
modest log cabin on the banks of the Kansas opposite Topeka was
situated on realty that was not much less valuable than a mining claim in
California and that the influx of squatters into the region was as
potentially profitable to them as it would be disastrous to their full-blood
relatives at Council Grove. Although the 640-acre Gonville-Pappan tract
was not included in government estimates at the time, the Kansa agent
John Montgomery estimated that it was worth between twenty-five and
forty dollars per acre at the time Reeder made his bid.[19]

Ellen Gonville Pappan was fourteen years old when the Kansas-
Nebraska Act opened the floodgates of white intrusion west of Missouri.

While she doubtless made occasional trips with her mother to the tribal reservation at Council Grove, most of her childhood and adolescent years were divided between playing on the riverbank at the foot of the ferry, helping her mother in the small garden plots nearby, and securing an education at a Catholic convent in St. Louis and at the Catholic Potawatomi Mission of St. Mary's, some twenty-five miles to the west.[20] Across the river was Topeka, which by 1859 had six hundred residents, most of whom were white Protestants from the Old Northwest, although a few were from New England, and most of whom were champions of the Free State faction of the Kansas Republican party. Two miles to the northwest, in a secluded bend of Soldier Creek, was the proslave but much less politically agitated community of Indianola, which was, conceded the Right Reverend John B. Miege of St. Mary's, a "solid Catholic town," but by no means a model, Christian community: "It is composed of half-breeds, nearly all of them Canadians, rangers of the mountains and plains, who have ended by marrying one or more Indian women. With the exception of one or two families who lead a good life, the rest are a perfect *canaille* in the matter of immorality, drunkenness, bad faith, stupid ignorance, [and] indifference to all instruction."[21] Soon to be designated as the capital of Kansas and often heralded as the very bastion of abolitionist morality in the fight against the Missouri border ruffians, Topeka also had its share of secular indulgences. Lamenting the absence of religious fervor among the men of Topeka, a Leavenworth reporter, on a visit to Topeka in 1861, wrote: "Suggest to a friend the propriety of attending church; he stares at you for a moment with a look of ineffable surprise, then indulges in a boisterous guffaw, subsiding, at length, into low gutturals, amidst which such syllables as 'pshaw,' 'damn,' and the like are plainly discernable."[22] In short, the area where Charles Curtis's father met Ellen Pappan in 1856 was largely deficient in social and institutional restraints, and contradictions in the treatment of racial minorities were the norm there. Partisans with conflicting views regarding the "peculiar institution" in Kansas could display intractability and engage in violence over the question of slavery, while simultaneously consorting with their opponents over wresting Indian land from its legal owners in defiance of federal law. Indeed, the consensus that it was morally proper to seize tribal land for farmsteads, timber, railroads, and town sites by illegal or quasi-legal means was nothing short of amazing.

In the early summer of 1855, a group of squatters took possession of several Kansa-half-blood tracts east of the Pappan reserves. Other squatters illegally harvested timber for houses and commercial establishments in Lecompton, Tecumseh, and Topeka. Emboldened by Governor Reeder's venture into land speculation, they voiced only contempt for the Indian Office's efforts to have them expelled. The Kansa agent John Montgomery finally was able to obtain token military support for his efforts to remove the squatters, but when he burned their cabins to discourage their return, he was charged with arson by local law-enforcement officials and ultimately was forced to flee to the more protective cover of the Kansa reservation at Council Grove. In late December 1856, Commissioner Manypenny learned that nearly a hundred squatters, "totally ignorant of land matters," were comfortably situated on the half-bloods' lands. A few months later, in a book that was widely distributed in the East, Governor John W. Geary's private secretary reported: "The [half-bloods'] reserves, like every other in the territory, are now covered with squatters who are making fortunes by cutting the fine timber for the neighboring saw-mills, and are unmolested by the Indian agents." For the venturesome, Kansas Territory had truly become the land of promise.[23]

That Orren Arms Curtis was a venturesome individual seems indisputable. He was born on 1 June 1829 in Eugene, Vermillion County, Indiana, the first of William and Permelia Hubbard Curtis's fourteen children, and at the age of fifty-nine, Orren boasted that he had traveled through twenty-nine states and nine territories. While less nomadic, his parents nevertheless participated in the western migrations during the early national period. William Curtis, of "solid English stock," was born near Albany, New York, on 22 December 1800. From there, he moved to Eugene, where he operated a flatboat on the Wabash River and on down to New Orleans. In 1860, ostensibly to help free the west from slavery, he went to Kansas Territory, where he squatted on Delaware land and established a stagecoach station at Mount Florence, in Jefferson County, within walking distance of the Kansa half-bloods' reserves. Permelia Hubbard claimed ancestry dating back to early-seventeenth-century New England and a great-grandfather who had established the first Presbyterian church in Sheffield, Massachusetts, where Permelia was born on 14 May 1807. Soon thereafter, her parents moved to Michigan Territory, converted to Methodism, and then journeyed to Indiana, where Permelia married William Curtis in August 1828. She was a strong-willed person and an ardent Christian, but her strong influence over her grandson Charles was countered by her obvious failure to exert a similar influence over Orren.[24]

River trips with his father to New Orleans stimulated young Orren's interest in travel and his seemingly insatiable quest for new experiences. On 31 January 1849, Orren married Isabel Jane Quick of Vermillion County, who bore him three children, two of whom survived infancy. In 1851, the young family moved to Platte County, Illinois, where Orren worked for a circus company. The move to the Indiana

Permelia Hubbard Curtis, Charles Curtis's paternal grandmother. This photograph was taken shortly before her death in 1903 at the age of ninety-six. From Dolly Gann, Dolly Gann's Book *(Garden City, N.Y.: Doubleday, Doran & Co., Inc., 1933), following p. 4.*

farm that he and his wife had located with the help of his father proved unsatisfactory, and Orren decided that his destiny lay elsewhere. He deserted his wife and children and headed for the more exciting frontier of the trans-Missouri West. After arriving in Kansas City in early April 1856, Orren moved to the Free State stronghold of Lawrence, where for a short time he worked for the mercantile firm of Gaius and Jenkins. From there, he traveled to Kickapoo and then to Leavenworth, where slavery partisans threatened him and forced him to retire to St. Joseph, Missouri, and then to Winterset, Iowa. There he joined the Free State "Grizzlies," commanded by Preston B. Plumb, who were then engaged in shipping arms and ammunition to the forces of freedom west of Missouri.[25]

In company with the Grizzlies, Curtis arrived at Indianola on 25 September. With his experience in flatboating on the Mississippi, it was not difficult for him to obtain employment as a ferryman for Joseph and Louis Pappan; nor was it difficult to become attracted to Louis's sixteen-year-old black-eyed and black-haired daughter, Ellen. After a brief return to Indiana in 1858, at which time he learned that Isabel had divorced him and had sold their farm, Orren returned to Indianola, where in February 1859, in a Catholic ceremony conducted by Father Ignatius Maes, he was married to Ellen Pappan. Less than a year later, on 25 January 1860, "in a log house located near the landing of the Pappan ferry," Charles Curtis was born.[26]

An important aspect of the mythology regarding Curtis's dramatic rise to national prominence has its origin in the allegedly humble circumstances of his birth. Curtis himself contributed to the distortion. In his reminiscences, written in the twentieth century, he recalled his father's circumstance in the late 1850s as that of a lowly employee and son-in-law of a struggling French merchant and his half-blood Indian wife on the Kansas frontier. In a letter to the Kansas State Historical Society in 1933, however, Curtis remembered well the vitality of the ferry business and how his grandfather Louis Pappan had sold the ferry charter and business to his father and other investors. Years earlier, Curtis recalled other events that documented the material advantage that had resulted from the marriage of his father to the daughter of Louis and Julie Pappan.[27]

In 1858, for example, Orren and his father-in-law erected several houses and a saloon on Julie's tract number 4. That the saloon was illegal under the Trade and Intercourse Act of 1834 did not concern them, since it was their view that the enterprise was on a private Indian reserve and thus beyond the jurisdiction of the 1834 prohibition. In fact, it blatantly disregarded the 1825 treaty, which described the half-bloods' tracts as "reservations," granted to Indian individuals who retained legal membership in the Kansa tribe. Profit, of course, was the objective, particularly in the spring of 1859, when hordes of gold seekers, headed for the Cherry Creek mines in western Kansas Territory, pushed ferry income to as high as three hundred dollars a day.[28]

On 14 January 1860, less than two weeks before the birth of Charles, Orren Curtis assumed sole ownership of the ferry and ran this ad in a Topeka newspaper:

> TOPEKA FERRY! This first class ferry across the Kansas river, is again in the hands of the subscriber, who is making quick trips with the greatest of safety. My boats are good and my hands experienced. This is certainly the best and most reliable ferry on the river.[29]

Later that month, Orren Curtis formed a new partnership, this time with Joseph Middaugh, who was a member of the Topeka Association that had purchased the Walker float. The two men secured a charter from the territorial legislature, which granted them a five-year monopoly for ferry service within two miles of the Topeka town limits. To complement this, Curtis invested in several municipal bridge companies in Topeka, one of which eventually spanned the river with a pontoon structure in 1865.[30]

William Clark's prediction, made a generation earlier, that the half-bloods' reserves would have a civilizing influence on the Kansa tribe had by now been forgotten, as squatters, town promoters, lawyers, and railroad corporations joined in the struggle to control the valuable river valley between Kansas City and Topeka. Based on personal observation, indeed having examined the very land that in part would one day belong to Charles Curtis, Horace Greeley observed in 1859: "As to the infernal spirit of Land Speculation and Monopoly, I think no State ever suffered from it more than this." Two decades later, after the government had presided over the dissolution of the Council Grove reservation and had determined that the only solution to survival for the Kansas was forced removal to Indian Territory, a report confirmed the more nefarious implications of Greeley's statement: "It seems as though the D——l had changed his residence, & gone to Kansas, for certainly no such atrocities could be committed without his leadership." The eve of the Civil War was indeed a difficult and exciting time for young Charles Curtis to learn about bushwhackers, jayhawkers, and land speculators and especially about how lawyers and the Great Father dealt with Indians on the Kansas border.[31]

5

The Estate Endangered

On 29 January 1861, four days after Orren and Ellen Curtis had celebrated their son's first birthday, Kansas was admitted as a free state under the Wyandotte Constitution. The objective of one New England emigrant was consequently fulfilled, as he recalled years later: "We came to Kansas to better our conditions, incidentally expecting to make it a free state." While many joined in the crusade against slavery, the majority of the thousands who came to Kansas during the seven years after the formal opening of Kansas Territory were attracted by land and little else. In fact, the typical squatter, whether from Indiana or the South, viewed chattel slavery as a troublesome obstacle to the small farmers, whose principal goal was to improve their economic status. Most of them considered the inability to secure a good title to Indian land as the ultimate barrier to progress in the area west of Missouri.[1]

The unrestrained celebration over statehood, which had prompted a mighty rush to the saloon, soon gave way to more somber conduct. Less than four months after Kansas Day, Fort Sumter was shelled by South Carolina, and the consequent "War of the Rebellion" abruptly rendered futile any efforts to compromise the slave issue in the trans-Missouri West. Fort Sumter surrendered on 13 April, and on the fifteenth, President Abraham Lincoln issued a call for seventy-five thousand volunteers. Nearly two-thirds of all Kansas males eventually served with the Union forces (including three Indian regiments), and among those who responded immediately was Orren Curtis—that is, if we can believe the recollection of his son, Charles.[2]

No other records corroborate this account; therefore a more credible version is that Orren continued to operate his ferry in Topeka until April 1863, when his wife suddenly died of "black fever," perhaps cholera. Ellen Curtis had given birth to a second child, Elizabeth, in September

Captain Orren ("Jack") Curtis, Charles Curtis's father. Courtesy of the Kansas State Historical Society.

1861, and until Ellen's untimely death less than two years later, there is reason to believe that Orren was content with his family circumstance. Very probably, then, his personal loss prompted him to seek escape by organizing a militia at Indianola for service against the border ruffians. The following August, at Fort Leavenworth, he obtained a commission as captain of Company F, Kansas Fifteenth Cavalry, and in October the unit was mustered into the service for guard and scouting duties on the Missouri border. Included in "Jack"—as he now was called on the streets of Indianola and Topeka—Curtis's recruits were Henry and Louis Pappan, Jr., brothers of his recently deceased wife.[3]

Under traditional Kansa tribal custom, young Charles and Elizabeth would have been sent to live with their maternal grandparents, Julie and Louis Pappan. But alternatives prevailed that had a dramatic effect on the formative years in Charles's life. He and his sister were placed under the care of their paternal grandparents, William and Permelia Curtis, at their farm and stage station in Mount Florence, some ten miles northeast of Topeka, on the Delaware lands. At the insistence of his parents, apparently, Orren was persuaded that his children would be safer at Mount Florence from the Missouri bushwhackers than in the home of the Pappans across from Topeka. Other considerations were involved, including the scores of Kansa relatives who, after the distribution of annuities, often came from Council Grove to camp on the half-bloods' tracts. Indeed, the saloon on tract number 4 and another saloon operated by Orren at Indianola were major attractions, as well as a source of bickering and occasional violence. J. S. Dowdell, among others, soon entered into the nefarious business; his Antietam Saloon on tract 4 (the future sight of North Topeka) posted an income of $2,500 in just five days in 1866, with most of the patrons being "camped-out Indians." Dancing and celebrations of many kinds, as well as begging from the overland emigrants at the ferry, were popular activities which in some instances lasted from early summer to late fall. The daughter of one white squatter "greatly feared the hundreds of wild Kaws." She and her playmates "never could be convinced by their elders that those Indians were not casting covetous eyes upon our scalps." In short, the Mount Florence home of William and Permelia Curtis seemed a more desirable place to raise young Charles and Elizabeth.[4]

It was an exciting place for young Charles to be. In his autobiography, he recalled: "I can remember the old stage coaches, and the reckless and fearless drivers, the curriers [sic] on horse back, the long line of freight wagons drawn by oxen, mules and horses, the old prairie schooners and the wild many soldiers and the dances that were given in their honor in the large dining room."[5] But in addition to the excitement, there was an agrarian order more characteristic of the Indiana frontier—a frontier that emphasized independence, hard work, enterprise, and especially, land ownership as the cornerstone of ultimate worth. Thus, Curtis also recalled

> the great corn crib full of corn; the cattle; the horses; the chickens and guinea hens; the hog killing in the fall; the great piles of apples; potatoes, turnips and cabbage that were covered with straw and dirt to keep for winter use; the render'ng of lard, the making of soap and candles, the boiling of hominy, the making of rag carpets and the quilting bees, the knitting of all kinds of comforts for the folks at home and the soldiers in the field; the taking of the wheat and corn from the fertile field to the mill and bringing back our own flour and corn meal. The nearest mill was several miles away at Ozawkie. We drove over in the morning and back in the late afternoon. The Grasshopper river near the dam was a great place to fish and the channel cats were plentiful, so some times we would stay all night and do a little fishing. Youngster as I was, I can still remember the trips and the great joy it brought me when I was allowed to go along.[6]

Whether William was attracted to Kansas Territory because of rumors that the lands of the Kansa half-bloods would soon be on the market or whether he was attracted by the Delaware treaty of 1860, which authorized the Leavenworth, Pawnee and Western Railroad (LP&WRR) to receive 223,966 acres of land for sale to non-Indians after tribal members had selected their individual allotments, is difficult to determine. What is certain is that William Curtis came, not to render lard or to boil hominy, but to speculate in Indian land—Delaware, Kansa, or otherwise. Certainly, the situations of the Kansas and the Delawares were interconnected with the exciting prospect of constructing a transcontinental railroad through eastern Kansas, and surely the fact that his son had married a daughter of one of the half-blood reserves was not unrelated to William's plans for the future.[7]

Even before Governor Reeder's attempt to secure title to four of the half-bloods' tracts—including tract number 4—several of the half-bloods had attempted to sell, based on the erroneous inclusion of the tracts in the Delaware reservation, established in 1829. While on an official visit to Washington in 1837, the Delaware chief Captain Swannach learned about the error, and soon thereafter the issue of conflicting ownership was plaguing Indian Office officials in Washington and St. Louis. At the suggestion of Isaac McCoy, efforts were made to have the government purchase the tracts from the half-bloods for a maximum of a dollar and twenty-five cents an acre, with the intent of granting the tracts outright to the Delawares once the sales had been completed. The Delawares, however, were not taken in by this promise; they feared that the purchase would be funded out of their own treasury. The effect was to publicize the issue, and in St. Louis, the Indian superintendent Joshua Pilcher was besieged by absentee half-bloods who were determined to sell what they believed was their increasingly valuable realty. It was not until the Delaware cession treaty of 1854 had extinguished all Delaware claims that more serious speculators such as Andrew Reeder moved onto the scene. Meanwhile, the resident half-bloods, such as the Pappans, the Clements, and Joseph James, petitioned Congress either to expel all interlopers or to authorize sales at much-higher prices, including damages for timber that had been taken to build the towns of Lawrence, Topeka, Tecumseh, and Lecompton. The half-bloods' progress in acculturation was evident in their recognition of the appreciating value of their lands. Like the speculators who were attempting to displace them, the half-bloods were determined to profit from the benevolence that the treaty of 1825 extended to them.[8]

A legal problem that the half-bloods faced was whether they enjoyed the fee-simple titles that were essential if they were to sell their land without the permission of the government or whether they were in fact legal members of the Kansa tribe and thus were under the authority of section 11 of the Trade and Intercourse Act of 1834, which prohibited any non-Indian intrusion in Indian country unless it was specifically authorized by the president of the United States. Article 6 of the 1825 treaty specifically referred to ''the half-breeds of the Kansa nation,'' which suggested that unilateral action on the part of the half-bloods was questionable in the extreme.[9]

Certainly, the full-bloods at Council Grove took the position that their relatives at Topeka were bona-fide members of the tribe. In early April 1857, it was reported ''that the whole Nation Is at This Time in a state of Confusion and Excitement'' over the outcome of the issue, and two months later, five full-bloods journeyed to Washington to complain that ''interlopers, farmers, and timber cutters'' were invading the Topeka tracts, which they believed were as much the property of the tribe as were the tracts of the half-bloods singled out in 1825. Moreover, article 9 of the 1859 Kansa treaty stipulated that forty acres of the Council Grove reservation were to be assigned to each of Julia and Josette Pappan's children, in addition to the other children of the 1825 half-bloods, as a means of ''manifesting their good-will toward their half-breed relatives now residing upon the north side of the Kansas.'' Clearly, the civilizing impact envisioned by William Clark in 1825 was coming to fruition.[10]

By the late 1850s, at least three groups were competing for the half-blood estates: a group of small-time operators, such as Alexander Bayne and J. E. Waddin, whom D. L. Mitchell of Lecompton had "induced" to pay him up to five dollars an acre to perfect the titles they had purchased either directly from the half-bloods in St. Louis or from other squatters; a more determined group, who organized a land-claims association as an attempt to fend off the more affluent and politically powerful land jobbers; and the big-time speculators, such as George W. Ewing of Indiana, who purchased the Joseph Butler tract for only thirty-two cents an acre, and Robert S. Stevens of Attica, New York, who claimed to be the official "half blood attorney" and who headed a group that by the late fifties had purchased more than a thousand acres of half-blood land, including one-fourth of the Julia Pappan reserve.[11]

While land jobbers and lawyers scurried between banks, courthouses, and wherever a good deal could be found, the questionable sales did generate income for a select group of half-bloods. Many of the small-time speculators believed their deeds would eventually be legalized at the minimum government price, while others assumed they simply were squatting on the public domain. But the big investors anxiously awaited a ruling by either Congress or the courts regarding the question of ultimate title and the half-bloods' power of alienation. It came on 26 September 1857, when United States Attorney General Jeremiah S. Black ruled that the lands were part of Indian country as defined by section 1 of the Trade and Intercourse Act of 1834. "Against all other individuals or combinations of individuals, their title is perfect and absolute," said Black, and intruders were to be removed by agents of the government. But the question of whether the half-bloods held the power of alienation, which was denied to the Kansa tribe as a whole, remained unresolved.[12]

It was this uncertainty that prompted William Curtis to invest in Delaware land, as opposed to the more valuable Kansa tracts. Having to contend with more affluent and politically powerful men such as Stevens and Ewing surely was an added consideration. On the other hand, the action of Congress offered some encouragement. On 26 May, President Buchanan signed into law "A Bill to Settle the Titles to Certain Lands Set Apart for the Use of Certain Half-Breed Kansas Indians in Kansas Territory," which had been introduced by Missouri's Senator James S. Green on the preceding 14 February. The bill upheld Black's ruling on ownership and heirship but went further in refusing "to give any force, efficacy or binding effect to a contract . . . heretofore made by any of the said reservees or their heirs." It furthermore required that the secretary of the interior have the final say as to any future sale by a reservee or his or her heirs.[13]

It appeared, then, that the Stevens and Ewing investments were in jeopardy and that new purchases (assuming the government's blessing) could now be made without fear of challenges regarding the issuance of clear titles to new buyers. Ewing, however, had in the meantime taken his case to the Kansas courts, in an effort to eject a group of squatters who were living on the 640-acre tract he had purchased from Joseph Butler. In 1858, Ewing filed suit in the Jefferson County court, which sustained his plea but was eventually appealed by defendant John McManamy to the Kansas Supreme Court. Its ruling, more than a year after the passage of Green's bill, upheld the ruling of the lower court. With Ewing gleefully describing Green's bill "as gotten up by disguising *Land Pirates*" and with Stevens no less elated over the implications for his own purchases, the estate of Charles Curtis once again appeared to be in jeopardy.[14]

Under Green's bill, it was mandatory that the legal heirs be determined, since some had died or were living in places unknown. In the summer of 1860 the Indian Office appointed Hugh S. Walsh to conduct an investigation to determine heirship. At her cabin across the river from Topeka, Julie Gonville surprised the government agent by informing him that she and her sisters would not testify unless their attorney, Robert S. Stevens, were present. Then Julie and several other half-bloods eagerly provided Walsh with a wealth of information regarding marriages, births, desertions, present addresses, and deaths of many of the individual reserves named in 1825.[15]

The Gonville sisters also discussed some of their own land transactions with Walsh. For example, Victoria Gonville Smith complained about how she and her sisters, as the only heirs to the estates of their deceased cousins Marie and Lafleche Gonville, the original grantees of tracts 7 and 8, had been bilked out of a fair price by certain unnamed speculators. For two full sections of well-timbered bottom land, they had received only two thousand dollars. Now they asked Walsh "if something could not be done" about recovering the deeds so they might sell to others, perhaps to Stevens, at a more competitive price. Walsh replied that this was beyond his authority, but he promised to bring the problem to the attention of his superiors in Washington.[16]

Not all of the half-bloods were as complimentary toward Stevens, which suggested that for portions of their lands the Gonville sisters had driven a hard bargain with Stevens. Two years later, this time in the absence of Stevens, other half-bloods spoke more openly about his chicanery. W. H. Coombs, whom the Lincoln administration appointed in 1862 to determine the veracity of Walsh's heirship findings and to collect additional information, confirmed that Julie, Pelagia, and Victoria Gonville had indeed "requested the Secretary of the Interior to confirm certain deeds made by them to Robert S. Stevens." The other half-bloods had not, "on grounds that they were obtained by fraud and without consideration" of the real value of the lands.[17]

The conflicting testimony was exacerbated by the failure of both Walsh and Coombs to locate some of the half-bloods or their heirs, and once again Congress sought to achieve a lasting solution. Although at first glance the resolution introduced by Senator James R. Doolittle of Wisconsin on 14 July 1862 and signed by Lincoln only three days later appeared to favor Stevens and Ewing, it in fact dealt them a severe blow by repealing the section of the 1860 law that required the secretary of the interior to serve as the final arbitrator in the determination of heirship. The 1862 law further confirmed that full and absolute title remained with the original reservees and their heirs, and nothing whatsoever was said regarding the obligation of the half-bloods or their heirs to secure governmental approval of *any* sales. Stevens and Ewing now envisaged securing their deeds without the interference of the Interior Department, but the problem was that knowledgeable lawyers—including Ewing's—suspected that the act of 17 July 1862 had vested title in the half-bloods or their heirs as of the day the law was signed and that *any* title or deed made before that day was invalid. This was confirmed in the summer of 1864, when the Kansas Supreme Court ruled in *Brown* v. *Belmard* that prior to the acts of 1860 and 1862, the half-bloods had enjoyed only a possessory right to the land and were not legally able to sell it to anyone.[18]

Ewing and the dozens of squatters who were interested in the tracts east of the Gonville reserves were now obliged to compete on the open market for the half-bloods' land. But Julie Gonville Pappan, true to her testimony to Coombs, now conveyed to Stevens a good deed for the northeastern quarter of her tract. At Mount Florence on the Delawares' railroad lands, however, the grandparents of Charles and Elizabeth Curtis enjoyed no such security. Under the 1860 Delaware treaty, the LP&WRR was required to complete a minimum of twenty-five miles of track before the Indian Office would issue any titles to land received from the Indians. At first, feelings ran high when it became apparent that the LP&WRR titles were of dubious value; then they ran to rage when it was announced, in 1863, that under the new name of Union Pacific Railway, Eastern Division (UP,ED), the line would be built west of Wyandotte, not Leavenworth. With federal troops being called in to evict all squatters until the title situation could be resolved, it is little wonder that William and Permelia Curtis looked elsewhere for a less-risky investment in Indian land.[19]

The well-being of Ellen Curtis and her two young children figured significantly in Julie Pappan's further disposal of her Kansas River estate. Her daughter Ellen was in frail health, and the uncertainty of Orren's plans to raise a militia for service with the Union pointed to a cloudy future for her two young grandchildren. A further consideration was a rumor among Julie's relatives at Council Grove that the Kaws might soon be forced to leave Kansas. Unless she and her husband rejoined her tribe on the reservation west of Topeka, they might be excluded from any future land settlement and annuities.

Julie insisted that the deeding of property to her daughter be handled as an orthodox land sale. Ellen' had no resources to make a down payment, but there was no immediate urgency from Julie's point of view. Even at ten dollars an acre (the price Julie dictated), it was a bargain, for rumor had it that a corporate successor to the LP&WRR had plans to build west from the mouth of the Kansas, directly across the plot she now had decided would belong to Ellen. Lots could be sold in the meantime, the property obviously would appreciate in value, and payments could be deferred until enough money had been realized to satisfy the original contract. The warranty deed that Julie Gonville Pappan executed on 26 January 1863 listed the grantees as "Ellen Curtis and the heirs of her body." Orren Curtis's name did not appear on the conveyance.[20]

By 1863, Julie Pappan was a powerful figure in the development of the area across the river from the Kansas capital, and her success would have an important influence in shaping Charles Curtis's views of himself as a landholding Indian. Julie's testimony before Coombs was in fact more important than the lobbying efforts of Ewing or Stevens, for there is no question that the federal investigator was impressed with what he observed on the Kaw half-bloods' tracts 1 through 6. Approvingly, he noted that on each, between fifteen and twenty acres were under cultivation. They "lived in comfortable log cabins," they wanted no governmental interference in the way they handled what they believed was their exclusive property, and, Coombs emphasized, "as they have taken more interest in these matters than the other [half-bloods] have . . . , the general reputation among them is about as good evidence as can be procured." Indeed, their progress was almost precisely what William Clark had predicted in 1825.[21]

Because the size of the individual reserves was far in excess of what the government considered ideal for yeoman agriculture, it is obvious that more was intended than the planting of potatoes, cabbage, and corn. Land was a commodity that could appreciate in value, attract towns and railroads, and then be disposed of for a profit. With her preferred status as a landed mixed-blood and with the encouragement of her French husband and her often-irresponsible but nevertheless aggressive son-in-law, Julie Pappan took well to her new role as an entrepreneur on the Kansas frontier.

On 26 January 1863, the same day that Julie conveyed the forty-acre plot to her daughter and to young Charles and Elizabeth, William Curtis purchased, for an undisclosed amount, a ten-acre tract directly east of Ellen's. He was not unaware of the LP&WRR's difficulties with the Delaware titles around Mount Florence; nor was he uninformed about the recent congressional action allowing the half-bloods to convey good titles without governmental interference. Rumors that the corporate successor to the LP&WRR might build west along the north bank of the Kansas River directly toward North Topeka were an added incentive. Even though Louis and Julie "drove a hard bargain," the investment seemed well worth the high price they demanded. On 19 May, for ten dollars an acre, or a total of $1,141, William Curtis purchased an additional 141 acres northeast of Ellen's 40-acre plot. In the meantime, probably on the advice of Curtis, Julie Pappan gave a one-hundred-foot right of way to the new UP,ED Railroad Company, to be located "in any direction" on half-blood tract number 4. The deed, delivered on 28 November 1863, was sold to Curtis and L. C. Laurent as part of still another purchase of forty-five acres along the river from Julie on 11 August 1865 and then was granted outright to the UP,ED by Curtis and Laurent on the following 28 August. Shortly thereafter, Curtis and Laurent organized the Eugene Town Company on the river-front land that abutted the forty acres that Julie had deeded to her daughter and grandchildren in 1863. Named after William Curtis's "beloved home in Indiana" and located directly across the river from Topeka, the official plat was filed on 27 May 1867, with Orren Curtis listed as one of its owners. Thus, by the ages of seven and six, Charles Curtis and his sister were heirs to land immediately adjacent to one of the most strategically positioned towns in the entire state.[22]

The route of the UP,ED was the key to the development of Eugene. B. F. Van Horn, who purchased ninety acres from Julie and Louis Pappan in November 1864 and another sixty acres in 1869, recalled the intense competition between Eugene and Topeka over the location of the track. An important factor in Eugene's favor was the action by the state legislature that moved the Shawnee County line twelve miles north, so that Eugene would no longer be in Jackson County and under what Van Horn termed "the rowdy border element" in and around Indianola. On the other hand, there were fears about flooding and concerns as to whether the unstable sand bottoms on the north side of the river could support the track bed and building construction that surely would follow. But these were only groundless rumors that were being circulated "by the Topeka crowd," said Van Horn, "who were moving Heaven and earth to get the railroad across the river." In late 1866 the railroad engineers decided "it should go on the north side and that settled it." What Van Horn failed to note was the generous right of way of nearly fifteen acres that Curtis and Laurent had given to the

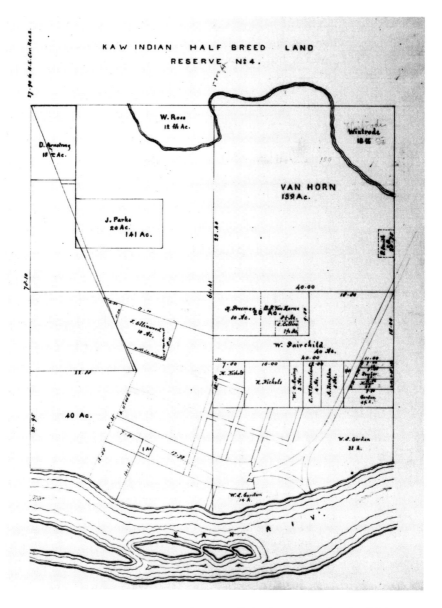

J. B. Whitaker's survey (late 1860s) of Kaw Half-Blood Tract Number 4, which was awarded to Julie Gonville (Pappan) by the Treaty of 1825. Included are the boundaries of the several sales that Julie consummated, the town plat of Eugene (North Topeka), and the railroad right of way along the Kansas River. Charles and Elizabeth Curtis inherited the forty-acre plot shown in the lower left-hand corner. Courtesy of the Kansas State Historical Society.

railroad and the detailed plans that the two had drawn up for facilities that would complement the railroad at no cost.[23]

Exactly when young Charles moved from Mount Florence to Eugene is not known, but it probably was in the summer of 1865. By then, building on the town site was well under way. As early as 1858, Orren Curtis had erected a saloon, which became a favorite attraction for the Kansas, the Potawatomis, and other tribes in the area. It was located at the corner of future Jackson and Railroad streets. In 1859, Orren erected two more buildings nearby. The arrival of the first train on 1 January 1866 was celebrated with "many bottles of champagne" and with speeches delivered by Senator James H. Lane, President R. M. Shumaker of the UP,ED, and the mayors of Wyandotte and Lawrence. William and Orren Curtis had additional construction under way, including the famous Curtis House Hotel, a livery stable, a general store, a post office, feed lots, and a "very commodious warehouse for the exclusive benefit of the railroad." Young Charles lived with his grandparents in the hotel; years later he recalled the glory of early Eugene:

Eugene or North Topeka was a most interesting place and a typical frontier town. It had a main street that ran east and west and was known as Railroad Street; the buildings erected on it faced the great depot and the railroad right-of-way. The Curtis House, the Parks House, the Antietam and other saloons and their accompanying gambling rooms . . . were all located on this street. The games of chance that were common in those days, such as poker, faro, montee, chuckoluck, etc., were always going in full blast. . . . Once in awhile "Wild Bill" would come down from the western part of the state; he always attracted a great deal of attention; he was tall and straight as an Indian, his hair was long and black and his eyes were of the piercing kind, he was a gambler and a dead shot. When he visited North Topeka the men and boys would follow him from place to place and he seemed to like the attention he attracted.[24]

B. F. Van Horn was more blunt in his description of Eugene: "Settlers came in quite fast. They organized as an independent town and called it Eugene, two or three saloons were quickly opened up and as many gambling holes, all of the riff-raff of the south side visited it, they had not respect for the law, and that element was so much in the majority that they controlled everything and we had no alternative but to annex to the south side." A few of "the more substantial citizens" like himself stood for decency and morality, continued Van Horn, and even though the roughs opposed annexation, "we had some influence in the legislature and we used it for all it was worth."[25]

Whether entrepreneur and saloon keeper William Curtis was among those whom Van Horn viewed as a substantial citizen is not known, but the joining of Curtis's town with Topeka certainly was in his best interest. From the start, Curtis had shown concern for the moral and intellectual well-being of Eugene by donating construction sites to the Baptist, Congregational, and Methodist Episcopal churches, as well as a large one for a public school. And his wife made a strong effort to wean her mixed-blood grandson from the Catholicism of the Pappans by requiring that young Charles attend Sunday School each week in the North Topeka M. E. church, of which she was a charter and devoted member.[26]

But the most exciting place for the young mixed-blood was the race course that his Grandfather Curtis built in North Topeka for the training of horses and the entertainment of citizens on both sides of the Kansas River. Apparently, Charles had learned about horses from his mother, and on his grandfather Curtis's "race-track," Charles began to develop the skills as a rider that in the future would provide him with unusual opportunities to travel and to make money years before he reached maturity. He also became acquainted with gambling, lawyers, excessive drinking, squatters, rigid Methodism, and, because his father had gone off to war, the Republican party, which was trying to contain the evil "Party of Democracy."[27]

Charles also learned about Indians, who for him posed a confusing matter indeed. His mother taught him the rudiments of the Kansa-Kaw language, which were further cultivated by his Grandmother Pappan after she moved from Mount Florence to Eugene. He learned something about the dress, the eating habits, and the leisure-time activities of his distant Kaw relatives when they came to patronize the attractions that his Grandfather Curtis provided on half-blood tract number 4. But these people lived many miles away, on a reservation, a place where the government distributed rations twice a year and where young boys like himself rode horses, danced, played games, fished, and learned to use lances and bows and arrows, as their fathers did. Somehow, he too was an Indian, but being an Indian in eastern Kansas in the 1860s was not popular, certainly not in Topeka. In Eugene, Indians, Frenchmen, trappers, traders, and railroad workers were generally welcome in the saloons and streets. But in Topeka it was otherwise, as a local reporter noted in 1868:

We have not seen the dusky forms of the noble red man of the Kaw persuasion about our streets in the last two or three days. Doubtless those sweet-scented ones that were encamped near here have gone back to their reservation. When we consider how efficient they were

Kansas Avenue in North Topeka, looking north from Curtis Street, in 1879. Charles Curtis's childhood home was approximately three blocks west of this site, on Kansas Half-Blood Tract Number 4. Courtesy of the Kansas State Historical Society.

in ''gobbling up'' the putrescent animal and vegetable matter about our fair city, we almost regret their departure. Now that these scavengers are gone, our city fathers should look to it that some other means be employed to guard the health of our people.[28]

6

A Mixed-Blood on the Reservation

"One of the most perplexing problems confronting American Indians today," a distinguished historian has recently stated, "is that of identity." Hanging in the balance might be a multimillion-dollar settlement over a legal injustice dating back to the founding fathers, the right credentials to obtain a university scholarship or free medical assistance, or membership in a corporate body that is receiving substantial income from mineral leases. Or it might involve admission into the social structure of a pueblo in the Southwest, the right blood quantum to enjoy security under federal affirmative-action guidelines, or simply the right to hunt and fish without a state license. This is not a recent phenomenon; "it has been a problem for individuals, tribes, and government administrators since the birth of this nation."[1]

In 1866, at the age of six, it surely was a problem for Charles Curtis. Born to a mother who valued her Franco-Indian heritage, taught her young son the French and the Kansa languages, and had him baptized in the Catholic faith, young Curtis had his world abruptly changed by the untimely death of his mother in 1863 and the decision to have him placed in the care of William and Permelia Curtis. Orren Curtis retained an interest in the Topeka ferry business during the Civil War years, but by then he was caught up in the heady atmosphere of land speculation and civil unrest in eastern Kansas and had little time to look after his children. Additional marital ventures, what one writer called "bad management and improvident habits," and a serious infraction of military law while he was on duty in western Missouri only further isolated Orren Curtis from his son, Charles.[2]

One person who observed Orren on the streets of Indianola shortly after he had organized a militia and had been elected its commander recalled that Captain "Jack" Curtis rode out in front of his subordinates and proclaimed, "Thar's no place where Jack Curtis dassent go." He might well have added that quick, forceful action was preferable to restraint in the treatment of the enemy, regardless of the consequences.[3]

Until near the end of the war, Curtis's military career was anything but spectacular. He was first assigned to guard duty at Fort Leavenworth and then to a brief scouting tour on the Missouri border. In the late spring of 1864, he was stationed in Topeka, "protecting the legislature," after which he was assigned to Colonel Charles R. Jennison's Seventh (later, Fifteenth) Kansas Volunteer Cavalry—the controversial Jennison Jayhawkers. Jennison claimed that Jack Curtis had displayed "instances of personal gallantry" while fighting a rear-guard action in the Price campaign in Missouri, and it was Curtis himself who presented his commander with a superb pair of ivory-handled pistols at a testimonial dinner in February 1865. On that same occasion, Curtis described Jennison as "a tried, true and fearless soldier, that original champion of human freedom." By then, however, both Jennison and Curtis had been ordered to stand trial before a general court-martial at Fort Leavenworth.[4]

Jennison was charged with general conduct prejudicial to military discipline, gross and willful neglect of duty, defrauding the Government of the United States, and the specific charge of "having in custody three prisoners of war [at Cane Hill, Arkansas], two of whom claimed to be citizens loyal to the Government of the United States, and having permitted Capt. Orren A. Curtis of the Fifteenth Kansas to hang them." On the three general charges, Jennison was found guilty and was sentenced to be dishonorably discharged, but on the specific charge of hanging loyal prisoners of war he was found not guilty. Curtis fared less well: for "executing the bushwhackers," he was dishonorably discharged on 21 April 1865 and was sentenced to one year at hard labor in the Missouri State Penitentiary. He was received at the prison on 28 April but was pardoned a month later by Major General Grenville M. Dodge, on the grounds that the court had dealt too leniently with Jennison.[5]

The pardon, of course, did not exonerate Curtis of the Cane Hill executions. Nor did it instill confidence on the part of his parents or the Pappans in regard to his ability to look after the well-being of his children. Certainly, his marital and occupational instability only served to aggravate the situation. Orren had married Rachel Funk of Jefferson County less than three months after Ellen's death in the spring of 1863. It obviously was an unsatisfactory relationship, for on 19 December 1864 the Shawnee County District Court granted Orren a divorce on the grounds of Rachel's alleged "several acts of adultery." Five days later, Orren Curtis had married Lou Jay of Olathe.[6]

After his release from prison, Orren returned to his ferry business. But competition from other similar establishments and a new pontoon bridge made it difficult to earn profits as in the past. He then tried the grocery and dry-goods business in North Topeka for less than a year, followed by a short stint as a cattle shipper out of St. Louis. By the late fall of 1868, Orren was back in the military, this time as a quartermaster sergeant in the Nineteenth Kansas Volunteer Cavalry, which had been organized by Governor Samuel J. Crawford to assist General Philip H. Sheridan with his Washita campaign against the Cheyennes and Arapahos in Indian Territory. During the 1870s, Curtis returned to cattle shipping in "many Eastern cities" and then to an abortive attempt at land speculation in New Orleans. Throughout, he claimed "he had never been confined to his bed a day with sickness since his rememberance," an obvious exaggeration in view of his official military-pension file, which in 1881 listed a three-fourths' disability from the day he was discharged from prison in 1865.[7]

For a short time, perhaps less than a month in the late summer of 1868, young Charles lived with his father and stepmother in the North Topeka home of William and Permelia Curtis. But Orren's roving habits, which culminated in his return to military life that fall, dictated that others would have to look after the welfare of the young mixed-blood. There seems little doubt that Orren's parents were agreeable to assuming this temporary responsibility, but in the meantime, circumstances involving the Kansa tribe at their Council Grove reservation, especially the influence of his grandmother Julie Pappan, provided Charles with his first and only experience as a reservation Indian.[8]

Exactly when Louis and Julie Pappan moved from North Topeka to the Kansa reservation is not known, but it probably was in 1865 or early 1866. Julie Pappan had disposed of most of her North Topeka lands by the mid sixties, and throughout her residence there, she had maintained social contacts with her tribal relatives at Council Grove. She had also sustained an interest in the economic and political affairs of the tribe, particularly through personal contacts with Robert S. Stevens, who by then had secured a lucrative federal-government contract to build permanent cabins on Indian reservations and who was also involved in land and railroad speculation on the Kansa reservation. Because of the experience that she had gained with squatters, lawyers, and governmental agents on half-blood tract number 4, she naturally was attracted to the social and economic benefits that might come her way through the treaties of 1846 and 1859.[9]

The treaty of 1846 was of particular interest to Julie. The agreement had been so worded that annuity payments to individuals were based on the fluctuating demography of the tribe as a whole. For the cession of approximately two million acres in the valleys of the Solomon, Smoky Hill, and Kansas rivers in west-central Kansas, the tribe had been awarded a thirty-year annuity amounting to $8,000 a year. The Kansas had been forced to accept a "bad bargain in 1825," said Agent Richard Cummins, and "such a liberal purchase was the easiest means of indemnifying them for the former oversight." During the thirty-year period covered by the agreement, funds were to be divided on "a *pro rata* basis, should their numbers decrease, but not otherwise," and at the end of the period, should the tribal number be less than in 1846, individuals "were to receive *pro rata* the sums paid them at the first annuity payment." In other words, a decrease in the tribe's population during the thirty-year period would mean higher individual payments up to 1876, but after that date, not more than at the initial pro-rata rate—which, on the basis of the 1845 tribal census of 1,607, came to just under fifty dollars a year per member.[10]

The long-range intent of the government was to encourage education, agriculture, and eventually, individual land ownership at Council Grove. Funding for such objectives was also included in the 1846 treaty. Demographically, it was hoped that the more than 6 percent decline in population during the previous decade would be halted in favor of a modest increase. Yet, the government failed badly in bringing epidemic disease under control at Council Grove. After an earlier unsuccessful attempt to vaccinate for the dreaded smallpox, Dr. J. Andrew Chute reported in 1838 that he had vaccinated 915 members of the tribe. Even so, because at least one hundred had been "struck down by a high fever" during the following summer, there is good reason to wonder if in fact the procedure was carried out as reported. In any case, while the mixed-bloods at North Topeka were spared, the disease struck the Council Grove villages with a vengeance in the middle of June 1855, and before the summer was over, more than four hundred additional members of the tribe had died. Four years later, a local newspaper, serving the interests of white squatters, predicted that "five more years will solve the Kaw [land] question," after the Kansa agent Milton C. Dickey reported another two hundred deaths during the previous year, which brought the tribe down to 1,037 persons. That the fatality rate continued unabated for the next two years can be seen in a March 1861 newspaper account that placed the Kansa population down to 801, a statistic that was particularly devastating for the full-bloods, because the figure now included a number of mixed-bloods who had only recently been added to the tribal roll.[11]

With the tribal population cut in half over a period of less than two decades, payments to individuals under the 1846 treaty increased dramatically and thus constituted a significant attraction for more mixed-bloods to unite or reunite with their full-blood relatives. The increasing annuity earnings of Julie Pappan confirm this, and, with added inducements provided by the Kansa treaty of 1859, suggest the most compelling reasons for her move—and ultimately that of her grandson Charles—to the Council Grove reservation.

Clearly, the demographic pattern of the Kansa tribe worked to Julie's material advantage. For example, the 1843 census, taken by Richard Cummins, listed "July Pappan" as the head of a family of four, one of them being the future mother of Charles Curtis. Based on this census and the $3,500 annuity authorized in 1825, her total income by 1846 was just over $100 per year. Four more children had been born to Louis and Julie Pappan before the 1859 treaty. If Ellen is excluded because of her marriage to Orren Curtis, Julie's total payment under the revised 1859 census of 1,037 would have increased to $617 per annum and then, under the further revised 1861 census, which indicated a tribal decline down to 802, to $798. In the meantime, the 1859 treaty went into effect, which, according to article 1, reduced the reservation from 256,000 acres to 80,000 acres, to be subdivided into 40-acre plots: one for each head of family; one for each family member; and one for each single male aged twenty-one or older.[12]

Julie Gonville Pappan had been on the tribal roll since 1825 and was thus entitled to one of the 40-acre plots. Under article 1, of the 1859 treaty, her children should have qualified in an equal manner. But jealousy and intertribal animosity, dating back to the treaty of 1825 and aggravated by mixed-blood absenteeism from the Council Grove reservation, encouraged the full-bloods to object to any further additions to the tribal roll. Nevertheless, the government's position was that the residence of mixed-bloods at Council Grove would have an exemplary effect on the full-bloods, whose resistance to farming and to Christian education remained strong. No doubt aided by pressure from Julie and her sisters to have new lands reserved for their progeny, the government included article 9 in the 1859 treaty, which in part read: "The Kansa tribe of Indians being desirous of manifesting their good-will toward the children of their half-breed relatives now residing upon the half-breed tract on the north side of the Kansas river, agree that out of the tract retained by this agreement [at Council Grove] there shall also be assigned, in severalty, to the eight children of Julie Pappan forty acres each." Similar provisions were made for the children of Josette, Pelagia, Victoria, Jo Jim, and the other half-breeds who had remained along the Kansas River in North Topeka.[13]

The treaty of 1859, which was signed by President Buchanan on 17 November 1860, gave some promise that the tribe might adjust to yeoman farming in the Neosho valley south of Council Grove. A government contract to operate a manual-labor school was signed in 1863 with the Society of Friends of Indiana, who sought to teach farming and the domestic arts where the Methodists had earlier failed; and a year later, the Kansa agent Hiram W. Farnsworth reported that crops grown by the tribe "were good, and gave them, with what they derived from hunting, a comfortable support." Even the local editor admittted that "the poor miserable race of beings" was making some progress despite many frauds perpetrated upon them by the federal government and the speculators.[14]

Farnsworth's guarded optimism was misguided, for even with the more than 175,000 acres of trust land that was made salable under the 1859 treaty, white squatters and land jobbers were not satisfied. Upon learning about plans for railroad construction through the area, Chief Istalashe wrote an angry letter to Indian Commissioner Dole on 17 July 1863, complaining about insufficient annuity payments and the illegal occupation of reservation land by whites. "White men tell us that we will be driven from the valley," he wrote through an interpreter, "but we like this place and want to stay." By then, at least three railroad companies were contemplating construction through the upper Neosho country, and Agent Farnsworth was sounding out certain Kansa leaders on their "willingness" to remove to Indian Territory. Pressure for such action increased in September 1865, when the newly organized Union Pacific Railway, Southern Branch (later the Missouri, Kansas and Texas Railway, or MKTRR), announced plans to build a line from Fort Riley to Indian Territory, across the northeastern corner of the only recently diminished Kansa reservation.[15]

Until then, there had been little incentive for Louis and Julie Pappan to leave North Topeka for the reservation. Julie had been collecting her 1846 annuities by making personal visits to Council Grove, and she was guaranteed an allotment roughly the size of the plot that she and her husband kept under cultivation on tract number 4. At least some of her grandchildren were receiving payments, and all were guaranteed a 40-acre farm on the Neosho. But rumors that the entire tribe might be removed to Indian Territory and perhaps disrupt the 1859 settlement prompted Julie and her husband to make the move to Council Grove. Besides, taking her grandson Charles with her and enrolling him in the Friends school at no cost, as a legal member of the tribe, would allow her to receive an additional $99 dollars a year on his behalf. By 1866, Louis and Julie were permanently situated at Council Grove, and shortly thereafter, young Charles came to live with them there.[16]

Prior to his residence on the Kansa reservation, there is little evidence that young Charles viewed himself as an Indian. Roaming the streets of North Topeka after the move from Mount Florence, he viewed

Indians much as he did other figures of curiosity in that frontier town. He recalled "kindly" Dr. McClease, who had a long gray beard and who carried a saddlebag full of quinine and calomel for his patients. Charles recalled "such prominent characters" as Kaw Charles, Joe Jim, Lewis Ogee, and George Young, "those leading members of the Citizen Band of Pottawatomi Indians." Then there was big Abraham B. Burnett, "a half-breed Pottawatomi but who claimed to be a full-breed," whose dimensions were so enormous "that when he rode in a lumber wagon there was no room for any other person, not even a little boy." There were the gruff and hard-drinking buffalo hunters, who during the winter would come in with the large wagons of frozen meat, and there was the notorious "Wild Bill." But from this formative stage of his life, as revealed in his later recollections, there were no admissions or comments regarding what it was like to be a mixed-blood, let alone a legal member of an Indian tribe.[17]

According to a simplistic, error-ridden biography that was released in order to enhance the Hoover-Curtis presidential ticket in 1928, young Charley was a lonely and curious figure as he came jogging across the prairie to the Kaw reservation in 1866. "How could they have guessed at that time that the shy little boy sitting on his pony would one day rank as the greatest of all the Kaws? That he . . . was destined, perhaps, to occupy a position next in importance only to that of the President?" He had come to the reservation, wrote the author, Don Seitz, because the hotel in which he had been living in North Topeka "was not considered a suitable home for little Charley." Curtis himself recalled that he went to live with Julie primarily to attend the Friends Mission school on the reservation, "his grandmother Pappan being a member of the tribe."[18]

Life at Council Grove was vastly different from that on the streets of North Topeka; as young Charley recalled, it was "an experience among the Indians never to be forgotten." Among his most vivid memories were his visits to the lodges and to the three different villages, the dances and feasts that lasted for days, the government's "cattle issues," and the sweet "squaw corn and buffalo jerky" that the women prepared for winter consumption. He witnessed the full-bloods burying their dead in the branches and trees or on the side of a hill, with great rocks piled on the graves as protection from wild animals. "It seems that even now I can hear some of the wailing that went up in early morning from those poor people whose loved ones had been taken," he recalled. Thanks to his mother, young Charley could converse in the Kaw language, and he took part in the games played by boys his age—racing, wrestling, swimming, fishing, and riding. "I had my bows and arrows . . . and joined with the other boys in shooting arrows at nickels, dimes, and quarters which visitors would place in split sticks." He even attended tribal council meetings, where questions regarding annuities, treaties, the hated Pawnees, and possible removal to Indian Territory were discussed.[19]

The degree of tribal acculturation that Curtis experienced at this time was marginal, but surely it included some awareness that the Kaw presence in Kansas was soon to end, which certainly was a major topic of discussion at council meetings between 1866 and 1868. As early as the fall of 1866, Agent Farnsworth reported that the Friends school would close because the full-bloods refused to support it, and in early 1866 a Kaw delegation to Washington agreed to a draft treaty that provided for the sale of all unsold trust lands, as well as the diminished reservation itself. Included also in the tentative agreement was a provision for the funding of more than a hundred thousand dollars worth of Kaw script, authorized by an amendment to the 1859 treaty, that was designed to compensate ejected squatters who had illegally erected cabins and other improvements on reservation land. The treaty was not ratified, mainly because the squatters and the railroad interests were pulling at cross-purposes over the reservation spoils. But with railroad construction begun just north of Council Grove by the fall of 1867 and with tribal indebtedness to the traders being irreversible, it was a foregone conclusion that removal to Indian Territory would be the best solution to "the Kaw Question."[20]

The seven-year-old Charley only vaguely perceived the details of such problems. Yet, land ownership and use, some dictated by non-Indians such as his Grandfather Curtis in North Topeka or by lawyers and public officials in Topeka and distant Washington, provided the young mixed-blood with an awareness of the impermanence of reservation life. Empty-handed hunters, returning from the plains of western Kansas, sometimes with accounts of bloody confrontations with the Pawnees or the Southern Cheyennes, only fortified this sense of impermanence. An encounter with the latter was what presented Charley with his most profound experience as a reservation mixed-blood.

Western Kansas during the months and years after Colonel John M. Chivington's senseless attack on a Southern Cheyenne village at Sand Creek, Colorado Territory, in November 1864, remained tense. The treaty of the Little Arkansas in the fall of 1865 brought some temporary relief, but a mindless demonstration of military power by Major General Winfield S. Hancock west of Fort Larned in the spring of 1867 only excited the Cheyennes and their Arapaho allies, as did the steady westward construction of the UP,ED. Angry warrior bands harassed outlying white settlements and made hunting on the plains a dangerous undertaking for weaker tribes such as the Kaws. A late winter raid in 1867 netted the Cheyennes more than forty ponies and at least one Kaw scalp from a Kaw hunting party. That fall, while en route to the Medicine Lodge treaty grounds in southern Kansas, the Kaws lost an additional thirty-four horses and several lives to an Arapaho party that was hunting southeast of Fort Larned. In late November, the Kaw hunters retreated to Plum Creek, at the Great Bend of the Arkansas near Fort Zarah, hoping that some game could be found in the vicinity.[21]

It was an unsound and tragic decision. No game could be found, and in early December a party of Cheyennes came to the Kaw camp, offering "to discuss difficulties existing between the two tribes." The talk, which was ostensibly friendly, lasted for several hours and seemed to be productive for a peaceful understanding. Minutes after the Cheyennes had departed, however, they fell on a lone Kaw herder, whom they killed and swiftly scalped. In a frenzy, the Kaws retaliated, and within four hours, they had driven the Cheyennes from the area. Two Kaws and fourteen Cheyennes lay dead on the field; more were badly wounded; and both sides lost a substantial number of horses. Convinced that their enemies were rushing to obtain reinforcements, the Kaw hunters fled to Council Grove, where they arrived on 25 December in a destitute condition. Sixty more had died of exposure or wounds during the retreat. Additional horses had been lost, so that the number of mounts for the entire tribe had been reduced to less than 150. A return to the buffalo plains the following spring would have been both dangerous and materially impossible.[22]

The excitement and anger that were prompted by these events constituted a further inducement for the Kaws to consider a move to Indian Territory, because unless they could dispose of the reservation for badly needed funds, they would remain at the mercy of insufficient support from the government or, more likely, continuing credit against their annuities that the Council Grove merchants were only too eager to provide. For Charles, it represented a frightening, vivid example of the "savage" Cheyenne nomads' challenging a beleagured reservation tribe that was attempting to make the adjustment to the sedentary life. It would also lead to renewed intertribal conflict, which abruptly terminated the young mixed-blood's brief tenure as a reservation Indian.

The conflict was renewed on the afternoon of 3 June 1868, when approximately one hundred Cheyenne warriors appeared at the Kaw Agency just south of Council Grove. White squatters and a few Kaws who were living on the fringe of the reservation were certain that they would be witness to Indian brutality at its worst. Apparently, there had been advance warning of the Cheyenne attack, for a number of Kaw warriors had armed themselves, had painted their faces and bodies, and were displaying their warring bear claws around their necks. The Kaw children, including young Charles, were ordered to take cover at the Friends Mission school, while the older men and women were ordered to take cover in an abandoned barn near the agency.[23]

The actual encounter, however, was merely ostentatious. A few scattered shots were fired, much shouting and charging on horseback occurred, but no one was injured or killed. With governmental officials standing by, confident that if need be, military assistance was available from nearby Fort Riley, the incident was more on the pattern of a medieval joust than of an unrestrained, savage battle. For the Cheyennes, the encounter was largely ceremonial, a demonstration of power and a means of regaining prestige against an enemy on unfamiliar ground. In fact, the entire affair lasted no more than four hours and gained for the Cheyennes a small amount of plunder from two neighborhood farms, some sugar and coffee from the townsfolk of Council Grove, a few goods from a trading post near the reservation, and eighteen cattle from a party of Texas drovers who happened to be in the vicinity. Later, at Fort Larned, the Cheyennes told their agent that they wished to have the cost of their booty deducted from their annuities. Nothing at all was taken from the Kaws.[24]

In his later years, Curtis never wearied of recounting the supposedly heroic role he had played during the encounter and the ensuing difficult circumstances that had led to his departure from the Kaw reservation. In 1929, for example, when delivering a political speech at Council Grove, he discarded his prepared notes and rambled on and on about his famous "cross-country run" from the reservation to Topeka. Because Curtis was "lithe and active" and could speak "good" English, the chief of the tribe allegedly had ordered him to walk and/or run the nearly sixty miles to Topeka, to warn the people about the Cheyenne threat to Council Grove. Others, having heard Curtis's version, embellished the story in a manner befitting James Fenimore Cooper's Hawkeye himself. A reporter for the *New York Times* wrote:

Few knew the way to Topeka, or what to do after getting there, while Charley Curtis was perfectly familiar with the road and had a father and Grandmother Curtis living there. "I offered to go," he said, "and slipped out alone at dusk to travel on foot with the star as a guide." There was no telling which way the Cheyennes had gone. He might run right into them. But little Indian boys are not taught a great deal about being scared, and no doubt Charley welcomed the chance to be something of a hero. He stuffed his pockets with buffalo meat and slipped softly out of the barn as the night was coming on. Soon his little moccasined feet were moving rapidly along the Santa Fe Trail. . . . No doubt the wind rustled among the leaves as if some one were hiding there waiting for him. But the little moccasined feet did not falter. They must have kept moving pretty steadily, for the next afternoon Charley came walking into Topeka.[25]

Curtis's own statement, made some forty years later, was less poetic, but it outdid other accounts by recalling that he had arrived in Topeka at noon, which would have required averaging about four miles an hour with no intervals for rest. Curtis conceded that upon his arrival in the state capital, word had already been received that the Cheyennes no longer posed a threat, but he refused to deny the awesome responsibility that the leaders of his tribe had supposedly assigned to him:

> It was thought best that some one should hasten to Topeka and notify those along the way that the Cheyennes were coming. I volunteered to make the trip. When we heard the Cheyennes were coming, the horses and ponies were driven to pasture, some distance from my grandpa's [Louis Pappan's] home, so there was no horse or pony to ride. I, therefore, started out on foot, traveling during the night . . . and I arrived in Topeka, I think, about noon the next day.[26]

These words were followed by a statement clearly indicating that Charles did not travel alone: ''It was a very exciting time for the others as well as for me, but being accustomed to frontier life, I did not mind the trip.''[27]

Still another version, certainly a more plausible one, was that of Kansas' governor, Samuel J. Crawford. Crawford, who later made a personal inspection of the Kaw Agency and discussed Indian affairs with governmental officials there, stated that he had received intelligence regarding the situation at Council Grove at seven in the evening on the day of the raid. His informant was the Kansa interpreter Jo Jim (Joseph James), who had been dispatched to Topeka by the Kaw agent E. S. Stover. Jo Jim—as a son-in-law of White Plume, who under the name of Kyhegashinga (Little Chief) had signed the 1825 treaty and who had been named a recipient of one of the prized half-blood tracts near North Topeka—was well acquainted with Julie Pappan and hence, with her grandson Charles. Julie had obviously entrusted Jo Jim with young Charley's safety, and when the Cheyennes appeared at Council Grove, Jo Jim had made certain that the young mixed-blood traveled with him back to North Topeka.[28]

In North Topeka, young Charles became an instant celebrity and no doubt provided his father and his paternal grandparents with considerable information about the Cheyenne danger to the Kaws. Indeed, Orren Curtis's enlistment in Crawford's Cavalry for service against the Cheyennes shortly thereafter may have been greatly influenced by his son's account of the flight from the reservation at Council Grove. Certainly, William and Permelia Curtis were persuaded that young Charles should not return to the reservation, especially since it had been announced that the Friends school there would be closed and that the entire tribe might be removed to the area south of Kansas. Legally, young Charles Curtis was still a member of the Kaw tribe in 1868, but circumstances dictated that he now find his place in the more hospitable "civilized" setting of Topeka. In this, he would be successful beyond his wildest dreams.

7

The Mixed-Blood Mounted

"Charley" Curtis, as he came to be known among his playmates and kinsfolk at the Council Grove reservation, returned to Topeka a few months before his father enlisted in a volunteer regiment organized to campaign against the Southern Cheyennes south of the Arkansas River. For the first time since the death of his mother, Charley was reunited with his father and was introduced to his second stepmother and his three-year-old half-sister, Permelia (or "Dolly") Jay Curtis. In the North Topeka hotel owned by William Curtis, where Orren and his fourth wife were living, Charley listened to his father's version of dealing with the hated bushwhackers, the injustice of his confinement in a dirty Missouri prison, and the necessity of chastising the "savage nomads" who only recently had struck at Council Grove. Hotel guests who had grandiose plans for homesteading and speculating in Indian land west of Topeka discussed their plans for reducing the Indian country to a garden, and the daily arrival of merchants and traders from Kansas City, St. Joseph, and St. Louis added to the excitement of young Charley's new environment. Certainly, it was a dramatic change from life on the Neosho River reservation.[1]

Orren Curtis's bellicose views about the Cheyennes and their Arapaho allies were typical of those held by white residents in Topeka and eastern Kansas. Certainly, they were relieved when the Kiowas, the Comanches, a small band of plains Apaches, and the Cheyennes and Arapahoes met with representatives of the United States Peace Commission at Medicine Lodge Creek, in October 1867. For substantial annuities, the right to hunt buffalo south of the Arkansas, and more concentrated reservations in Indian Territory, the five tribes relinquished all claims to the area between the Platte and the Arkansas and promised not to obstruct the construction of railroads on lands outside the reservations' borders.[2]

76

But Governor Samuel J. Crawford was categorically opposed to such "coddling" concessions. To Kansas' Senator Edmund G. Ross, Crawford wrote: "Congress might with equal propriety and justice have forwarded a train of supplies . . . to the rebel army after the first Battle of Bull Run, as to expect hostile Indians to stop the war by giving them annuities." At Medicine Lodge, Crawford demanded severe punishment for "the savages," rather than presents to reward them for their duplicity. After the Cheyenne raid at Council Grove and reports later in the summer about scattered atrocities that were attributed to Cheyenne-Arapaho war parties in the upper Smoky Hill and Solomon valleys, Crawford bombarded War Department officials with requests to enlist state volunteers to end the Indian menace once and for all. General Philip H. Sheridan, who was then planning a campaign to force all the tribes onto their new reservations, reluctantly agreed by authorizing the enlistment of the Nineteenth Kansas Volunteer Cavalry. Crawford immediately resigned the governorship in order to take command, and the enlistment of the regiment was accomplished on a farm just outside of Topeka. Included in its rank was Quartermaster Sergeant Orren Arm Curtis.[3]

With young Charley once again in the care of his paternal grandparents, his father eagerly returned to the battlefield—this time to fight Indians. But his experience was even less rewarding than against the rebels in Missouri. Until mustered out less than five months later, the Nineteenth Kansas participated in no important battles and in fact was plagued by short supplies, sickness, bad weather, and incompetent scouts. Worst of all, certainly from Crawford's perspective, was the regiment's late arrival at Camp Supply, which prevented it from taking part in Brevet Major General George A. Custer's attack on Black Kettle's village on the Washita on 27 November. For Charley's father, the entire Cheyenne campaign was a humiliating experience, mainly because, as a quartermaster, he was forced to deal with woefully inadequate rations. Ninety men deserted, and more than two hundred horses were lost. Custer received all the glory, and General Sheridan was anything but pleased with Crawford's performance. When Orren Curtis returned to Topeka, about all that he could tell his son was that he had survived a major blizzard on the Great American Desert and that he had been an official participant in a military action that had resulted in the most severe defeat of the Cheyennes since Colonel John M. Chivington's attack at Sand Creek four years earlier.[4]

Charles Curtis made no mention of his father's Washita campaign in his recollections some sixty years later. But inserted between his lengthy description of the Cheyenne attack at Council Grove and his new life as a non-Indian in North Topeka was a strong testament to the midwestern pioneers who brought civilization to Kansas, a testimony that more befitted a white politician on the stump than a young mixed-blood with increasingly ambivalent views regarding his own Indian-ness: "We, the sons and daughters of the pioneers are proud of the work of our fathers and mothers. They came to Kansas to help free it and to reclaim what was known, when they came west, as a desert. They have transformed the plains into the garden spot of the world and have, in Kansas, created one of the greatest states in the entire union."[5] No reference to Indians; no reference to the reservation that, at this point in his recollections, he only recently had abandoned; and certainly no reference to the increasingly important role the mixed-bloods of several emigrant tribes were playing in the government's removal plan in Kansas.[6]

It was an instructive time for the young mixed-blood to be ap-proaching his adolescent years. While leaders of his own tribe were fighting a losing battle against the railroad and squatters at Council Grove, Charley once again came under the tutelage of his white grandparents. His sister, Elizabeth, and his half sister, Dolly, were sent to live with Dolly's uncle in rural Shawnee County, while Charley remained in North Topeka. Following his return from the Washita campaign, Orren Curtis tried farming in nearby Jackson County, but in this he was no more successful than he had been as a soldier or as a retailer. His primary interest lay in securing legal control of Ellen Curtis's share of half-blood tract number 4.[7]

After Ellen's death in the spring of 1863, Orren assumed he had a legal claim to at least half of the 40-acre plot that Julie Pappan had sold to Ellen three months earlier, even though the actual conveyance listed the grantees as "Ellen Curtis and the heirs of her body" only. Nevertheless, Orren was encouraged by the Doolittle resolution, signed by President Lincoln the previous July, which invalidated all Kansa half-blood trans-actions before that time and prohibited any future governmental inter-ference with any land sales that the half-bloods or their heirs might wish to negotiate. Ellen had died intestate, and as the de facto guardian of the surviving children, Orren apparently was confident that the local courts would uphold his assumed claim to all of Ellen's property. Less than a month after Ellen's death, Orren sold twenty acres of the estate to Samuel Brandon, and on 8 December 1863, he sold additional acreage to George W. Anderson.[8]

Whether William Curtis was fully informed regarding these ques-tionable sales is not known, but there is no doubt that by the time young Charley returned to Topeka from the Kaw reservation, relations were strained between Orren and his father—mainly over his marital in-stability and his failure to look after his children. After his brief attempt at farming near Topeka, Orren left Kansas for the next eight years, working as a cattle broker "in all the largest Eastern cities, but doing most of his business out of St. Louis." In 1879, he moved to Arkansas as a wood shipper; this was followed by a short stint with the Missouri Pacific Railroad in Nebraska; and then he came back to Kansas as a laborer for the LT&SW Railroad. In March 1882, he journeyed to Florida and New Orleans to promote a "5,000 acre land deal which did not prove to be a success." Later that same year, he returned to Topeka to "work in the interest of prohibition," a cause that was becoming increasingly fashionable among Kansas' Republican leaders, who by then were displaying considerable interest in the political charisma of "Indian" Charley Curtis. Orren was never one to articulate pride in his son's mixed-blood heritage until he had begun to make a mark in local and state politics, so it is ironical that the benevolence that the younger Curtis later bestowed upon his father was in large measure based on the very Indian estate that Orren had unsuccessfully attempted to wrest from his son and daughter in 1863.[9]

In view of Julie Pappan's experiences with her reserve on the Kansas River, it is not surprising that she was distressed when Orren disposed of the 40-acre tract in North Topeka. Ellen had been dead less than a month; the land had been deeded to her and the two minor children; and Orren had remained aloof from his immediate family and from the mixed-blood culture that they represented. Moreover, as recipients of tribal annuities and as official members of the Kansa nation in residence at Council Grove, young Charley and Elizabeth were, from Julie's perspective, the social, if not the legal, responsibility of the extended family. In 1825 the property had been given to Julie as an instrument of civilization, and now, in 1863, she determined to make the most of it. Ignoring Orren's deals with Brandon and Anderson, she sold the very same property to Ora O. Kelsa. There the matter rested until Charles left the reservation in 1868 to live with William and Permelia Curtis in North Topeka.[10]

From 1868 until William Curtis's sudden death five years later, it is difficult to overstate the influence that he had on Charles Curtis. Attracted to the lower Kansas valley by his son's marriage to the daughter of a landed mixed-blood, William was sixty years old when he located his claim at Mount Florence. By frontier standards in 1860, he truly was a senior citizen, for nearly 90 percent of the white settlers were under forty years of age, and more than 40 percent were between twenty and forty. But like the thousands of younger hopefuls who came to Kansas before it became a state, William Curtis was attracted by land and little else. He opposed slavery, but like the majority of white settlers in Kansas, whether from the North or from the South, he viewed the institution more as an obstacle to economic development than as a burning moral issue. As for Indians, what concerned him most of all was the realty that they controlled and, he hoped, would relinquish under pressure from the national government.[11]

Like his fellow settlers, William Curtis considered towns and railroads to be the engines of progress on the Kansas frontier. Certainly, his purchase of a substantial tract of land from Julie Pappan for ten dollars an acre in 1863 would be difficult to understand had he not been confident that a railroad would be built from the mouth of the Kansas River to his land across from the state capitol, and when the first passenger train arrived in North Topeka on 1 January 1866, it was a time for celebration. R. M. Shumaker, president of the Kansas Pacific (the corporate heir to the UP,ED) was there; so were the mayors of Topeka, Wyandotte, and Lawrence, as well as Senator James H. Lane of Kansas, who presented "one of his usual characteristic speeches." After the "vast crowd assembled to celebrate the completion of the first railroad to the capitol of the state" had dispersed, it was time to proceed with development.[12]

Not far from the site where his son had attempted to promote a settlement during the late fifties, the senior Curtis moved ahead with the building of Eugene. With the land that he had purchased in 1863 as security, he borrowed $2,000 for development purposes, secured a platting deed, and in the spring of 1867 had the land surveyed for lot disposal. According to one account, lots sold "all the way from $200 to $400 each"; less desirable locations were "given away left and right." At the corner of Railroad and Van Buren streets, the two-story Curtis House Hotel was erected, not far from Eugene's first hotel, the Antietam. Bars were included in these hotels to accommodate the travelers and especially the "riff-raff" from across the river in Topeka, where it was not possible to obtain a legal drink. Curtis also established a grocery business, and along the railroad track he erected a large warehouse for the storage of goods brought in by the railroad. He gave free land to the Methodist, Congregational, and Baptist churches, in addition to one hundred dollars to each, to aid in the construction of their edifices. He hired and paid for a teacher in the school that he constructed with his own funds, and with E. G. Moss, he organized a bank in "his Eugene," opposite Topeka. Curtis was, according to his attorney, a man of "liberal views, a temperance man but no prohibitionist; one who scorned hypocracy and admired sincerity and integrity." Others described William Curtis as "a very useful and esteemed citizen." While he was not a member of any church or secret society, he nevertheless was tolerant of others, "a generous, kind-hearted old man greatly respected by the community."[13]

To eight-year-old Charley Curtis, the excitement of Eugene in 1868 offered a profound contrast to the reservation life that he had been experiencing for the past two years. Most of all, the young mixed-blood was attracted to the race course that William Curtis built in Eugene "for the training of horses and the entertainment of the people." If the account of a twentieth-century biographer can be believed, Charles had been given a mount called Kate when he was only one year old, and by the time he was three, he could ride bareback "at some speed." A more plausible explanation for his early skill as a rider was his residence on the Mount Florence farm of William Curtis, where a number of horses were kept, and the subsequent sharpening of his equestrian skill while he was on the Kaw reservation at Council Grove. Horse racing was very popular among the Kaws; it usually involved considerable betting against the mounts of the Osages and the Potawatomis and those of white settlers at the various county fairs in eastern Kansas.[14]

Charley was an accomplished rider by the time he had returned to North Topeka, as Eugene had come to be called by the late 1860s; and because of Charley's light weight for his age, his grandfather saw in him an opportunity to make money while keeping the boy busy with an activity that he obviously enjoyed. In his autobiography, Charley recalled in great detail the satisfaction and excitement of this first formal race at the age of nine, which he attributed to his experiences with the "Kaw ponies" at Council Grove:

> While on the Reservation I had ridden all kinds of Indian ponies and had ridden in a number of important pony races and was considered a good and fearless rider. . . . In the fall of 1869 I rode my first race in North Topeka. . . . It was a regular frontier crowd that gathered and the betting was not very heavy because of the rumors of the speed of the other horse. The starter and judges were soon selected; we riders were lifted to our mounts, we both rode bareback, and the horses were soon ready for the word "go." Flatfoot [Curtis's horse] took the lead and held it until the crowd at the lower end was reached. The shouts for the leading horse were loud and long but were too much for him and he broke from the track and before I could get him back the other horse was in the lead and won by a neck. . . . It was the beginning of a riding career which lasted until 1876, and the next year I became a full-fledged jockey.[15]

William Curtis, of course, was greatly impressed with his grandson's performance and winnings, which over the next three years averaged fifty dollars a month, according to the contract with the manager of the racing tour, plus 10 percent of the purse. During the summer of 1870, with a new and much-faster horse named Carrie, Curtis took his grandson on a tour of Western Kansas as far west as the notorious cattle town of Ellsworth. Here Charley and Carrie won a very profitable race, and the young mixed-blood became an instant hero with the cowboys, saloon keepers, and prostitutes—"all the way from the fresh young girls just starting out . . . to the experienced madames who managed the 'places' and knew the business from 'A' to 'Z.' '" Charley recalled:

> I never knew how much money our crowd actually won but I know it was a very large sum and the gamblers and the madams [sic] insisted on taking me to her house and then up town and bought me a new suit of clothes, boots, hat and all, and the madam had a new jockey suit made for me. I was proud of my good luck, the suit was a good one. They gave me money and bought me candy and presents and they came to our camp every day. . . . I had never been so petted in my life and I liked it.[16]

For Charley, the experience obviously was exhilarating, and it contributed substantially to the growing ego and the self-reliant posture that he would display in the months and years ahead. Continuing as a jockey during the following summer provided him with a different but no less important experience in his quest for identity between the worlds of Indians and whites.

The occasion was the county fair on the racing circuit at St. Marys on the Potawatomi reservation west of Topeka, where in 1860, Ellen Pappan had had the infant Charley christened at the Catholic mission there. In 1861, in a treaty engineered mainly by the LP&WRR, the Potawatomis had legally separated into a minority Prairie Band faction, which was opposed to the treaty, and a larger Citizen Band, which supported the treaty in return for an allotment in severalty and future financial support from the government. By 1867, most of the Citizen Band allottees were destitute, and another treaty was arranged to remove them to Indian Territory, on a pattern not unlike the one that Curtis's relatives were experiencing at Council Grove. It was not until 1870 that the Citizen Band finally agreed to a reservation on the lower Canadian River, and in the summer of 1871 the final payment for the ceded land in Kansas was to be made.[17]

A number of the Potawatomis had married members of the Kaw nation, including several mixed-bloods, and as part recipients of the final payment, these Potawatomis were of particular interest to Charley. The total that was due the Citizen Band was more than $166,000, certainly an enormous sum to a young boy of eleven. In his own words, the payment was an experience "he could never forget." It was also a time of great excitement, with "the Indians, the traders, gamblers, horse men, and spectators all there in great numbers." Moreover, in comparison to the recalcitrant Prairie Band—whose members continued to occupy a diminished reserve north of Topeka—the Citizen Potawatomis could now occupy a 900-square-mile reservation deep in Indian Territory. One day, it, too, would be allotted, Curtis was told, and these "progressive-minded" Indians would be comfortably independent and economically secure.[18]

In short, by the time Charley Curtis was approaching his adolescent years, he had been exposed to certain basic tenets of the government's Indian policy in Kansas and the trans-Missouri West. More in company with adults than with children of his own age and influenced by a white grandfather and a mixed-blood grandmother, who themselves were heavily involved in the development of Indian land, the young Curtis was beginning to understand that the allotment of reservations was the wave of the future for those Indians who might successfully make the transition from barbarism to civilization. Land ownership by individuals and profitable stewardship were the keys to assimilation, and mixed-bloods such as he could play a positive role in the process, which dated back to the treaty of 1825. Although Curtis did not know this at the time, it was not insignificant that when he witnessed the Potawatomi payment at St. Marys in 1871, the commissioner of Indian affairs in Washington was a mixed-blood Seneca who had risen to the rank of brevet brigadier general in the United States Army and who had had the pleasure of having a future president, Ulysses S. Grant, serve as his best man at his wedding. Truly, Ely Parker, as the ranking individual in the Indian Office, was proof that mixed-bloods could rise to high and responsible stations in the United States.[19]

Curtis also came to understand the important role that lawyers and the courts played in the transfer of land in eastern Kansas to private ownership, whether Indian or white. The literal swarm of white land seekers who invaded Kansas during the territorial and early statehood periods encountered a confusing array of allotments, floating allotments, Indian trust lands, and tribal reserves that were still intact but were well on their way to dissolution. In eastern and southern Kansas, the Homestead Act of 1862 and previous legislation in regard to the public domain were of little help, since by the mid 1860s nearly eleven and a half million acres had already been allotted to individual Indians or their heirs or had been sold in trust for the alleged benefit of Indians and therefore were not legally included in what many speculators imagined as part of the public domain.[20]

Conflicts were especially pronounced in areas where major railroad lines were planned (with governmental assistance); where town sites, rail terminals, and county seats were to be located; and of course, where the state capitol was to be established. After the passage of the Doolittle resolution in the summer of 1862, sales of tracts belonging to Kansa half-bloods could be negotiated without the permission of the federal government, and almost immediately the twenty-three prized tracts became a veritable lawyer's paradise. Initially, the litigation involved suits over titles or possession. These fell into four general categories: (1) suits brought by half-bloods or their heirs against other half-bloods or their heirs; (2) suits brought by half-bloods or their heirs against white squatters or speculators of various ethnic backgrounds; (3) suits brought by white squatters or speculators against half-bloods or their heirs; and (4) suits brought by white squatters or speculators against other whites. The majority of these suits, which numbered well over a dozen, were tried between 1862 and 1865, after which the more commonplace action was the simple suit over quiet title. In the spring of 1871, the latter type marked the formal beginning of Charley Curtis's legal education and the framework for his subsequent views regarding individual property and the American Indian.[21]

Several factors prompted William Curtis to file a quiet-title suit on behalf of his mixed-blood grandchildren. Orren Curtis was a partner with his father in the Eugene Town Company, which was formed on 29 March 1867 and was annexed to Topeka on the following 9 April. Orren's sale of his children's inheritance to Brandon and Anderson may initially have been viewed by William Curtis as a potentially profitable move. By the late sixties, however, it obviously was contrary to law. The 40-acre tract was located immediately south and west of the town site, and thus it was strategically positioned for future expansion, especially after the railroad had reached the area. Julie Pappan's sale of the same property to Kelsa, however, caused the elder Curtis considerable concern, as did a court ruling shortly thereafter involving inheritance rights to half-blood tract number 9, which had been awarded to Laventure, the son of Francis Laventure and a Kansa woman. In *Brown v. Belmard* (1864), the Kansas Supreme Court reaffirmed not only that under the Congressional Act of 1860 the half-bloods could not convey property without the approval of the Interior Department but also that the children of half-bloods—whether the children were legitimate or not—were the sole legal heirs to the twenty-three tracts. As the guardian of his children's property, Orren Curtis had violated his trust, and, difficult as it may have been for William Curtis to sue his own son, he decided that Charley and his younger sister deserved their day in court.[22]

Under the advice of Aderial Hebard Case, one of the most respected and experienced attorneys in Kansas, William Curtis filed a quiet-title suit against his son on 2 March 1871. Named also as defendants were Ora O. Kelsa and Louis and Julie Pappan. The petition asked clear title for Charley and Elizabeth Curtis to "the S.W.¼ of Section 4, of the Kansas Half Breed Lands . . . amounting to forty acres, more or less." The summonses issued in the late spring of 1871, and the defendants' answers had been submitted by the end of June 1872. Because of the untimely death of William Curtis on 3 March 1873 and because of the scattered residences of the several defendants, the case was continued until 26 July 1875, when the Shawnee District Court waived a trial by jury and issued a judgment in favor of the plaintiff, to wit, that "the defendants had not at the commencement of this action any right, title or interest in and to said last described tract of land . . . and that the same was the sole property of Elizabeth and Charles Curtis, minor heirs of the said Ellen Curtis, now deceased." It was further ordered that the decision of the court be entered as of the date of the original hearing, 12 July 1872.[23]

From that date forward, then, Charles and Elizabeth Curtis were legal owners of some of the most valuable pieces of real estate west of Kansas City and, certainly, one of the most prized portions of the half-blood reserves granted in 1825. Even though Charley was only twelve years old when he became a Topeka landowner and though his inheritance was encumbered by unpaid taxes, he was being schooled well in the value of real property and the rudiments of how it had become his by way of the white man's policy of benevolent paternalism. Being an Indian, for him, was likewise becoming a matter more of litigation than of the life he had only recently experienced in Council Grove.[24]

There is no doubt that William Curtis was genuinely fond of his mixed-blood grandson and that his plans for young Charley went well beyond the development of his talents as a jockey. The title suit marked William's final break with his son Orren, who shortly thereafter left Kansas and his children for the cattle business in St. Louis. Meanwhile, by clearing title to the forty acres adjacent to his own property in North Topeka and by having himself appointed the legal guardian for both Charles and Elizabeth, William concluded that his grandchildren's interests would be best served while his own could be expanded by the development and sale of their land directly west of his own. He had, in short, accomplished for the two young mixed-bloods what their father, Julie Pappan, and outside speculators had not—the development of their tribal inheritance into a profitable, urban enterprise.

Whether Charley understood the precise details and implications of the suit that his grandfather brought is not known. Certainly, he was close to William Curtis, and surely he must have understood, even at the age of twelve, that family property of considerable value was at stake. He spent the summer of 1872 racing successfully at fairs around Topeka and Kansas City, and he was developing a business acumen that must have been the envy of racers and trainers who were easily twice his age. And ironically, it is possible that the very track at which Charley trained his horses in North Topeka may have been on the property that was then under litigation on his behalf.[25]

William Curtis's plan was to terminate the 1872 racing season at Independence, in southern Kansas, so that his grandson could return to school in Topeka, as he had done the previous year. But because "the horses were doing so well," William decided to send them south for the winter, to the Indian country and perhaps to Arkansas or Texas as well. William believed that at these more distant places, Charley's talents for riding and the speed of the horses would be less known and thus would be more likely to attract larger purses and generate even greater profits. A team of draft horses and a large wagon, fixed for travel and camping, were purchased in Independence; a manager, a trainer, an assistant trainer, and a cook were hired; and while William Curtis headed back to look after his affairs in Topeka, the young jockey and his entourage headed south.[26]

Even for that time, when young males often were cast into the adult world well before maturity, Charley's experiences bordered on the remarkable. In the company of men twice his age and living in a setting that routinely was characterized by gambling, heavy drinking, grasping for the first chance, and often operating in an illegal or quasi-legal manner, the young mixed-blood displayed remarkable maturity, while at the same time earning a not-inconsequential sum of money. From Independence, the party traveled to the Kansas border town of Baxter Springs, then a boisterous center for cattle and for Indian trading. Crossing onto the Quapaw reserve in the northeastern corner of Indian Territory, the party moved southeast through the Cherokee Nation to Fort Smith, Arkansas, and southwest to the booming railroad town of McAlester, Oklahoma. Even father south, they raced successfully at Stringtown, just north of the newly designated Choctaw capital at Atoka. This was followed by an eastward diversion across the Red River to Texarkana, then south to Waco, Texas, by way of Sherman and McKinney, back north to Fort Worth and Denison, and then northeast across rain-swollen terrain to Pine Bluff, Arkansas. Here, in early March 1873, the expedition was abruptly terminated when a mixed-blood Cherokee resident of Topeka brought the sad news that William Curtis had died of smallpox.[27]

The widely broadcast slogan "There is no Sunday west of St. Louis—no God west of Fort Smith" was, of course, exaggerated by

comparison to many other lawless areas of the trans-Missouri West of
that time. But in the wake both of the devastation that the Civil War
wrought among the Five Civilized Tribes and of the government's
punitive treatment of these nations during the early years of Radical
Reconstruction, few areas of the country experienced greater torment as
a motley but determined horde of cattle thieves, whiskey merchants,
squaw men, town promoters, prostitutes, and brawling railroad construction crews invaded Indian Territory. So-called tribal progressives—
such as Elias C. Boudinot of the Cherokees, who murdered the editor of
the *Tahlequah Telephone* because he published an unfavorable editorial,
and squaw man Robert L. Ream of the Choctaws, a full-blood white who
specialized in ferries, toll bridges, and investments in mining around
McAlester—fueled the conflict as corporate America moved into Indian
Territory and exerted enormous pressure for allotments and the destruction of tribal sovereignty.[28]

In his twentieth-century rendition of his 1872/73 travels, Charles
Curtis emphasized the heroic nature of the trip: how he had dealt
successfully with horse thieves; gamblers; unprincipled racers, who had
drugged one of his favorite mounts; bad roads; bad weather; irresponsi-
ble "half-breeds," who advised, "Wathchum horses bad men take
um"; the pathetic little Indian settlements; various temptations of the
purse and flesh and how one day he would contribute mightily to
improving the lot of the natives who had been forced to reside in Indian
Territory against their wills. Curtis later recalled: "I little thought when I
was traveling in the old Indian Territory, as a boy, in 1872 and 1873, that
twenty-five years later, I would be in Congress drawing up a measure to
settle the affairs of the members of the Five Civilized Tribes . . .
intended to protect the interest of the people of the Indian Territory."[29]

His key phrase was "interest of the people," which at the young
and impressionable age of twelve-going-on-thirteen meant little more
than gazing in awe at human destitution as a result of the first phase of
white intrusion into the region south of Kansas but which, from his
adult perspective years later, would mean welcoming—indeed, ap-
plauding—the march of white America against tribal sovereignty in
Indian Territory. At the mining town of Krebs, Oklahoma, for example,
young Curtis had the occasion to observe the power of industrial
civilization in the heart of Choctaw country. Nearby, and extending all
the way from the Quapaw reserve down to Texas, town promoters of
both white and mixed blood were involved in the very kind of enterprise
that his Grandfather Curtis was advancing in North Topeka. The
MK&TRR, which began near the Kaw reservation in Kansas, had by
then built its rails through Cherokee country, had reached McAlester,
Atoka, and Caddo in the Choctaw nation, and was aiming toward a port

on the gulf. Although young Charley was not there, he surely would have been impressed with the words of Robert S. Stevens, by then an employee of the MK&T, on the occasion of Elias C. Boudinot's hammering the first MK&T spike on Cherokee land:

> It is with feeling of no ordinary interest that we meet on this spot considered by many as on the verge of civilization—on the line which divides the red man from the white man. This gathering augurs that the two civilizations which meet and commingle here today are to be *blended into one* [emphasis added] and that line which separates them to be blotted out. . . . Nor shall we stop here. . . . We shall not pause till our engine stand panting in the palaces of the Montezumas and halls of the Aztecs.[30]

The news of his grandfather's sudden death was a shock to Charley, and he returned to Topeka as quickly as possible. "I cannot describe how greatly Grandfather Curtis was missed," he recalled; "he was a wonderful man, a real leader among men and his death seemed to change everything." Indeed, it did. Attorney Case recalled that William Curtis had always conducted his business in a "precise and terse way" and that in his will he insisted that all of his debts be paid promptly, with the remainder of his property to be divided equally between his wife and his fourteen children. But the real estate that he had purchased from Julie Pappan was heavily mortgaged, and after a public auction to sell the race horses and after the settlement of the estate, there was little left for the security of Permelia Curtis and her household. Pending the outcome of the title suit that William had filed two years earlier, the contested 40-acre plot in North Topeka was sold for taxes to T. P. Thompson in 1871 and then to John A. Moss three years later. In the meantime, the Shawnee County Probate Court appointed Daniel M. Adams of Topeka as the legal guardian of Charles and Elizabeth, and on 5 March 1874, the court ordered a deed for the property from the estate of William Curtis "to the minor children of Ellen Curtis, deceased, Charles and Elizabeth Curtis." The final action in *William Curtis* v. *Orren Curtis et al.*, rendered in the Shawnee County District Court on 26 July 1875, confirmed that young Charley and his sister were the legal owners of the land that their mother had purchased for them in 1863.[31]

Even though Charley was now a landed mixed-blood and even though he had been absent from the Kansa reservation for several years, his name remained on the tribal roll, and his Grandmother Pappan continued to receive his annuity payments under the treaty of 1846. Charley was now an official member of what the Indian Office termed "the Half-Breed Band of Kaw Indians," in effect a subdivision distinguishing the more "progressive" Kaws from the full-blood Picayune, Kahola, and Rock Creek bands, who were opposed to moving to Indian Territory. Little wonder, then, that young Curtis lost interest in affairs on the Council Grove reservation and began to think seriously about attending the white man's schools in Topeka and, perhaps, about his future as a lawyer and a politician.[32]

8

"Our Charley"

The death of William Curtis in the spring of 1873 was a turning point in the life of young Charles Curtis. Except during Charles's short stay on the Kaw reservation at Council Grove, William Curtis had exerted a profound influence on him since the death of his mother a decade earlier. Under the tutelage of his paternal grandfather, young Charles came to appreciate the importance of towns and railroads in frontier economic development. He was subjected to the rudiments of the white man's law and courts in defense of individual property, particularly as it related to Indian land, and he was able to observe at first hand the techniques needed for survival in the often harsh economic setting of Kansas during the period following the Civil War. His undisguised approval of his grandfather's efforts to reduce the wilderness to a garden was a veritable litany of traditional white pioneer virtues:

> Every fall he [Grandfather Curtis] made full preparation for the coming winter, the hog killing, always ten or twelve, the smoking and curing of the meats, the rendering of the lard, the making of lye hominy, the moulding of the candles, the making of soft soap, the drying of apples, peaches and wild grapes, the sweet corn, the red peppers, the pounds of potatoes, cabbages and turnips. The making of sauerkraut and sausages, the gathering of walnuts, hickory and hazel nuts, the making of applebutter, the putting up of jellies and preserves and lots of mincemeats and various kinds of pickles, the cribs of corn and stacks of hay and fodder. These *wise* preparations for the winter months were always made under the watchful eyes and careful direction of Grandfather and Grandmother Curtis.[1]

By contrast to this bountiful cornucopia, the situation among Charles's Indian relatives at Council Grove was one of starvation and despair. In July 1866, two years before the Cheyenne raid, the government assured the tribe's removal when it granted to the Union Pacific, Southern Branch Railroad (later, the MK&TRR), a land grant from the junction of the Republican and Smoky Hill rivers near Fort Riley down the Neosho valley to the southern boundary of Kansas. The main obstacle was a ten-mile stretch across the northeastern corner of the diminished Kaw reservation. A treaty in 1867 to accommodate railroad investors from Boston and New York, the latter group headed by Robert S. Stevens, was challenged by local white squatters who were determined to have these final Kaw lands on their own terms. Complicating the situation was the fluctuating value of thousands of dollars worth of Kaw land scrip, issued under an amendment to the treaty of 1859, which constituted speculative paper that could be traded as cash to compensate squatters who had improved the Indian land that now constituted the diminished reserve. As proposed, the treaty included the cession of the entire reserve, the recognition of the railroad's land grants, and a governmental guarantee to fund, out of the contemplated sale of the reserve, $120,805 worth of Kaw scrip at face value plus interest.[2]

After the 1868 Cheyenne raid, the Kaws were unable to return to the buffalo plains, so they became dependent on the credit provided by traders who were no less determined to have the treaty ratified. But the Senate turned it down, mainly because the contending groups were pulling at cross-purposes. So destitute were the Kaws by 1869 that Congress was obliged to authorize an emergency appropriation of $25,000—an action that prompted an immediate trader claim of $27,718 by Spencer and Mead Company of Council Grove. In that same year a final effort by the railroad to buy the entire diminished reserve for fifteen cents an acre, with six "government chiefs" being offered a quarter section each for their cooperation, was acceptable to the Indian Office but was turned down by Secretary of the Interior Jacob D. Cox. By then, according to the Kansa agent, the tribe was wholly disillusioned, "having been so badly dealt with in former years—that they now have but little confidence in white men of any class."[3]

With railroad crews breaking down its fences and destroying its crops and with squatters overrunning its lands with impunity, the tribe was resigned to removal by the spring of 1872. A congressional act, necessitated by the end of the treaty procedure the preceding year, provided for the tribe's removal to a 100,137-acre reservation immediately south of Kansas and east of the Arkansas River, to be purchased from the Osages at seventy cents an acre and to be paid for with the proceeds from the final sale of their Kansas lands. In his last speech in Kansas, Chief Allegawaho denounced the government for its duplicity, but to no avail. The movement of the Kaws began on 4 June 1873 and was completed when 533 of them arrived at the confluence of Beaver Creek and the Arkansas River fourteen days later. Louis and Julie Pappan were among those who went south, less than a month after their grandson had returned to attend the funeral of William Curtis in Topeka. Young Charles Curtis was still on the tribal roll.[4]

After the settlement of William Curtis's estate, Charles spent the remainder of the summer training horses for various owners, including Colonel Charles Jennison of Leavenworth, his father's former commander during the Civil War. Charles also rode several other horses, mainly at the Topeka fairgrounds. In the fall, he returned to school, where he remained until the end of the term in June 1874. By his own account, he sold apples and peanuts during the noon hour at the North Topeka railroad station and worked as a bookkeeper on Saturdays to make ends meet. The summer of 1874 was again spent racing, at Lexington, Council Grove, and Wichita, followed by a return to school in the fall. Then came what Charles Curtis later recalled as a pivotal event in his life, one that determined the future course of his Indianness.[5]

Not long after school had begun in the fall of 1874, Louis and Julie Pappan arrived in Topeka from Indian Territory in company with several other members of the Kaw tribe. They had come to visit relatives in Topeka and in the nearby Potawatomi reservation. In Topeka, Curtis recalled, "the men folks of the tribe induced me to go to their reservation in the Indian Territory." He was advised that "under an old treaty provision the government was issuing free rations to all members of the tribe." Without hesitation and apparently without consulting Grandmother Curtis, Charles rounded up the little brown mare that had been given to him by his deceased mother in 1863, packed his few belongings in a flour sack, and joined the covered-wagon train that was headed back to the Kaw reservation. But at Six Mile Creek south of Topeka, one of the Kaw women gave birth to a child, which halted travel for several days. On the day before the train was to depart, most of the men made a return visit to Topeka, and young Charles was left behind with his Grandmother Pappan. The moment of decision had arrived:

She asked me to come to her wagon and when I arrived she was the only one there. She talked to me awhile and asked why I wanted to go to the Indian Territory. When I told her of what the men had said she told me she would like the best in the world to have me at her home but she told me what I might expect on the Indian Reservation and that I would likely become like most of the men on it; that I would have no schooling, would put in my time riding race horses or ponies, and become a reservation man with no future, and that if I ever expected to make anything of myself I should return to Topeka and start to school again—that as much as she wanted me, because of my dead mother and her love for me, yet for my own good she wanted me to return to Topeka where I could attend the public schools and make somebody of myself. I took her splendid advice and the next morning as the wagons pulled out for the south, bound for the Indian Territory, I mounted my pony and with my belongings in a flour sack, returned to Topeka and school. No man or boy ever received better advice, it was the turning point in my life.[6]

Julie Pappan's words were no more important than certain details that she omitted from her conversation with her grandson in 1874. When the Kaw men had advised Charles about the free rations that were available in Indian Territory, they were referring to the thirty-year annuity provision included in the treaty of 1846. Only two more payments remained in 1874, and in Indian Territory, the Kaw agent was authorizing payments only for those Indians who resided on the new reservation—hence, the pressure on Charles to come south to claim his share. Julie Pappan had collected her grandson's payments while they were at Council Grove, and she knew full well that the subsidy would soon run out. Moreover, after visiting Topeka, she was aware that the title suit that William Curtis had filed was going against her and the other defendants. The contested property that Julie had sold to her daughter in 1863 would shortly be awarded to Charles and his sister, and the young mixed-blood needed to remain in Topeka in order to protect his interest. Conditions in Indian Territory, on the other hand, were in fact not much better than they had been at Council Grove, and with a white man's education and clear title to valuable land across from Topeka, young Charles would indeed be able to make something of himself. Even though Julie Pappan had returned to reservation life, she was a shrewd and influential individual in the increasingly powerful ''Half-Breed Band.'' With her experiences at Kawsmouth, Topeka, and Council Grove, she knew the worlds of Indians and of whites, and when she talked to her grandson at Six Mile Creek about ''a reservation man with no future,'' she meant an Indian without property—a shiftless traditionalist who spent his time hunting, dancing, gambling, and riding the ponies—ironically, some of the same activities that William Curtis had encouraged.[7]

In contrast to her late husband, Permelia Curtis was an ardent Christian, a charter member of the North Topeka Methodist Church, which had been organized by P. T. Rhodes in 1870. Permelia, who was physically strong and was affectionately known as one of the most benevolent and unselfish women in North Topeka, exerted an enormous influence on her fourteen children after the death of her husband. Years later, Charles's half-sister recalled:

> She ruled the family. . . . Not that any of us wished to oppose her; if we strayed momentarily, by accident or inadvertence, from the fold of her orthodoxy, she needed only to remind us of our allegiance, which lasted to her death at the age of ninety-six. . . . She was a Methodist. She was a Republican. I think she regarded being both a Methodist and a Republican as essential to anyone who expected to go to heaven.[8]

Charles agreed. At a political meeting in a North Topeka church in 1884, when he was seeking his first public office, Curtis confirmed his half-sister's appraisal. Pointing to Grandmother Curtis, who had proudly taken a seat on the front row, he openly confessed:

> I want to tell you folk here tonight that whatever I am, and all that I have in the way of success, I owe to that little lady seated there—my Grandmother Curtis. She helped me get an education, she clothed me and fed me when I was too young to fend for myself. Her precept and example have helped me, and her teachings have been a safe-guard in time of temptation. No mother could have done more for her own child than my Grandmother Curtis has done for me![9]

In Topeka, then, Charles Curtis experienced the full force of what were the dominant powers in post–Civil War Kansas: the Methodist Church and the Republican party. At the time of statehood, Methodists in Kansas numbered more than the total of Baptists, Congregationalists, Presbyterians, Episcopalians, Catholics, and Jews; and by then, Kansas was clearly the political preserve of the Republican party. Plagued by factions that initially were controlled by the state's first governor, Charles Robinson, and by Senator James H. Lane, the Republicans could bicker over patronage, railroad development, and Reconstruction policy, but "waving the bloody shirt" and insisting that the people "vote the way they had shot" held the Republicans together against the hapless Democrats. All, however, could agree that the Indians must be forced out of Kansas. Just after the war, for example, the Indian commissioner Lewis V. Bogy wrote to the House Committee on Indian Affairs that his object was to remove all Indians, because "their present location is of great injury to the white race." By the time that Curtis had decided to make Topeka his home, the Osages, Kickapoos, Delawares, Shawnees, Miamis, Ottawas, Sacs and Foxes, and most of the Potawatomis had been forced to join the Kaws on new reservations in present-day Oklahoma. Excluding three small reservations in the northeastern corner of Kansas, a few allottees who had relinquished their tribal membership, and an even smaller number of mixed-bloods who, like Curtis, had stayed in Kansas while retaining nominal membership in the tribe, Indian Kansas was no more.[10]

Under the watchful eye of his grandmother, Charles finished elementary school in 1875 and augmented the family income by working in a local livery stable. During the summer months of 1875 and 1876, he continued to follow the county-fair racing circuit, and he was so successful that in the fall of 1876 he was offered a contract to race at the Philadelphia Centennial and then to follow the southern racing circuit. The pay was good—$50 a month and 10 percent of the winnings—but Permelia Curtis said no. William Curtis was no longer there to support Charles, and so he "bade the men and the horses goodbye," returned to his grandmother's home, and prepared to enter Topeka High School the next morning.[11]

It was a difficult adjustment, for in school, Charles became embroiled in many fights, mainly because his classmates ridiculed him as the "Indian race rider" or as "the French apple seller." He also experienced financial difficulties, so he found it necessary to drive a hack in the evenings and on Saturdays and Sundays. His hack was an ancient vehicle which a local livery owner called Noah's Ark, but when businessmen who needed transportation from the North Topeka railroad depot to downtown Topeka learned that the young mixed-blood worked hours that other hacks did not and that he was using his earnings in order to finish school, they went out of their way to patronize him. "I soon began to take in from two to six dollars a night," Curtis recalled, "and had all the money I needed." During the summer months, he supplemented his income by painting carriages. In short, the environment provided by Permelia Curtis encouraged a sense of individual accomplishment and financial responsibility, qualities that William Curtis had also sought to instill, albeit in the more exciting milieu of the race track.[12]

Charles did well in school, so well, in fact, that at the end of his third year he was selected to represent his class at the annual graduation exercises. For his oration, he selected Daniel Webster's address "The Duty of a Chief Magistrate," which conformed well with Curtis's involvement in the school's debating society. And because he was "part-Indian," he naturally was chosen to act in the theatrical perfor-

Charles Curtis at the age of fifteen in a tableau from Hiawatha, *presented by Topeka High School in 1875. Curtis is on the left. Courtesy of the Kansas State Historical Society.*

mance of "Hiawatha." By his own account, he would have graduated if, on his way home after giving his oration on Webster, he had not been accosted by the wife of attorney A. H. Case. When she asked him what he planned to do with his life, he replied that he had not yet made up his mind. Mrs. Case responded by suggesting that her husband might need someone in his office and that Charles might be the very kind of young man he was looking for. After discussing the matter with Grandma Curtis, Charles called on Case the following Monday morning. So impressed was Case with the young man's ambition that Charles was given a job as a custodian and handyman about the office. In his spare time, he began to read William Blackstone's and James Kent's *Commentaries*, while serving as a bill collector and assistant for routine cases before the police court and the justices of the peace. It was good experience, both intellectually and politically, and in June 1881, at the age of twenty-one, Charles Curtis was admitted to the Kansas Bar.[13]

Charles's almost meteoric rise from Indian jockey to mixed-blood attorney in Topeka seemed not unlike Harry Walton's performance in *Risen from the Ranks*, by Horatio Alger, Jr., which was copyrighted in the same year that Charles bid his Indian grandmother a sad farewell at Six Mile Creek. Not only had Charles shrugged off his Indian heritage and turned his back on the world of racing; he had secured professional status in the non-Indian world of eastern Kansas and had the requisite credentials for moving ahead in the even more exciting arena of local and state politics. Along the way he had worked hard, had made the right choices (with the advice of his grandmothers), and had proven to his detractors that a mixed-blood could make it in the competitive world of the majority culture. Above all else, Charles Curtis loved to recall his response to attorney Case, who had cautioned him "that there were too many poor lawyers at the bar in Topeka." Curtis's response was, "I asked him if there was not room at the top."[14]

But unlike Alger's hero, who advanced without benefit of family assistance from the lowly station of printer's devil to the ownership of a newspaper, Charles had the not inconsiderable advantage of his inheritance in North Topeka. He insisted that he had not learned about it until after he had gone to work for Case in the spring of 1879. Yet, the final decision in *Curtis* v. *Curtis* was issued on 25 July 1875, and "Hib" Case (as he was known in Topeka social circles) had served as William Curtis's attorney from the original filing in 1871. Case had also served as the family's attorney after William's death in 1873, and apparently Case had been involved in the several guardianship actions involving Charles and his younger sister. Case aided Charles in securing his right of majority in 1878 and certainly was aware of the value of the 40-acre plot in North Topeka. Indeed, it is likely that Hib Case's employment of Charles Curtis in 1879 was less the consequence of his wife's intervention than of longstanding ties with the family and the known potential of the estate on the north bank of the Kansas River.[15]

In the same year that he was awarded his majority and the right to manage his own legal affairs, Charles Curtis's legal membership in the Kaw tribe was terminated. Annuity payments under the treaty of 1846 had expired in 1876, and two years later, "because he never moved to or resided on the [Kaw] reservation," the Osage agent Laban Miles, on the recommendation of the Kaw subagent Cyrus Beede, removed Curtis's name from the Kaw roll. Curtis's only remaining legal tie to the tribe was his part heirship to the relinquished Kaw lands at Council Grove that still remained unsold. At the time, the action went unannounced in Topeka, even though many still called him Indian Charley or the Indian racer. Never very open about his own Indianness, Curtis saw fit not to mention this important event in his twentieth-century recollections. In fact, he was more concerned with his new profession as an attorney, the possibility of going into politics, and, of course, the management of his property in North Topeka.[16]

Recalling that a land speculator had secured a quit-claim deed which the courts had judged worthless, Curtis obtained a power of attorney over his sister's half interest in the property and then moved ahead with the development of his inheritance, dating back to the treaty of 1825. Back taxes, land-survey costs, administrative costs, and loans to guardians appointed by the court had contributed to build a debt of more than $5,000 on the property. Charles attempted to negotiate a new loan, but he was turned down. Undaunted and with the support of Hib Case, he arranged to sell lots and to pay his mortgage holders in installments of money from these sales. In the southwest corner of the tract, he sold a quarter of a block to a distillery and, as a bonus, gave the company an extra quarter of a block at no cost. Nearby, he made the same deal with a brewery company—all this in the face of mounting prohibitionist sentiment in Topeka and most of Kansas. "After this was done," he reported, "it was easy to sell additional lots on monthly payments and I turned the payments over to the bankers and soon had the mortgage and back taxes paid and after this was done I began to build small houses on the lots." And in the tradition of his late grandfather's community benevolence, he allowed the Freedman's Relief Association, which was then trying to locate homes for refugee black Exodusters in Topeka, to use the native timber on his property to build houses and rude dugouts. Although the action was eventually blocked by less sympathetic white Topekans who claimed that the settlement was a danger to public health, the fact is that it placed Charles Curtis in favorable political circumstances with the substantial black minority that chose to remain in the capital city.[17]

As a partner in the firm of Case and Curtis, Charles made criminal law his specialty. He was a young man of great energy, and he had been admitted into partnership primarily to handle cases in the towns and rural communities surrounding Topeka. In time, he formed his own firm, Curtis and (David) Overmeyer, and, in 1889, the even more successful firm of Curtis and (Henry) Safford. In 1884, Curtis married Anna E. Baird of Topeka, whose parents, devout Baptists, had come to Kansas from Altoona, Pennsylvania, in 1869. Anna and Charles had one son, Harry, and two daughters, Permelia and Leona, who were six-teenth-blood Kaw Indians but probably were not aware of this until the question of Kaw allotment came up years later.[18]

By the late 1880s, the mixed-blood Charles Curtis was comfortably integrated into the legal community of middle-class, Republican, white Topeka. Only occasionally did he let his guard down regarding his views about Indians. While prosecuting a white man who allegedly had murdered a mixed-blood Indian in Belleville, Kansas, Curtis reminded the jury "that had Kennedy [the victim] been other than an Indian half-breed, his murderer would have thought twice before he killed him," but this deference to native ferocity and presumed savage invulnerability was probably more for jury sentiment than a concern for Indian welfare. Certainly, a local paper treated the matter in this fashion: "His [Curtis's] allusion to his people, the Indians, driven by the relentless white man from the Atlantic to the far west, driven until only the scattered remnants of once powerful nations remain, brought tears, but in any other place than a court room would have brought cheers from an appreciative audience."[19]

Certainly, the difficult circumstances that the Kaws were then facing in Indian Territory and the important shift that was taking place in national Indian policy were of little interest to Curtis. The flight of Dull Knife and Little Wolf across the plains of western Kansas in 1878; Standing Bear's escape from the Ponca reservation and the legal maneuvers that led to Judge Elmer Dundy's 1879 ruling in *Standing Bear v. Crook*; and Standing Bear's subsequent speaking tour in the East seem not to have captured Curtis's interest. Neither did the killing of Agent Nathan Meeker on the Ute reservation in Colorado later that year and the beleaguered position of Secretary of the Interior Carl Schurz in the wake of the scandals that beset the Indian Office in December 1879.[20]

What consumed Curtis's interest was politics. His Grandfather Curtis had recommended strongly against this, as had Hib Case, who advised, "Keep out, at least so far as being a candidate." But with Grandma Curtis's strong encouragement, it was love at first sight, and when asked to join the popular Topeka Republican Flambeau Club in 1880, Curtis could not resist. "I joined and with the other young Republicans, put on an oil cloth cap, carried a torch and helped shoot off the fire works." Immediately, he became active in ward politics. He cultivated friends and acquaintances who dated back to his years as a jockey and as a hack driver, and with the blessing of Grandma Curtis— who seemed to have the last word on everything—he soon delighted in the political appellation "Our Charley." Of course, some of the old Civil War veterans preferred "ol' Cap. Curtis's boy," while others now turned "the Indian jockey" into a laudatory title. But to Curtis it really did not matter. He adored attention, he became a solid organization man almost overnight, and he quickly gave notice that he was far more interested in names, faces, families, and friends than in ideas and nostrums for the smoldering political issues of the times. William Allen White, who knew Curtis well, concluded that he was a Republican "by inheritance" and an attractive politician at that:

He [Curtis] appeared at the city and county conventions, in those first days of the eighties in Topeka, with the names of hundreds of farmers at his tongue's tip. He was handsome, slight, with the jockey's litheness, with affectionate, black, caressing eyes that were

hard to forget; with a fine olive skin, and a haymow of black hair
and a curling black mustache. Add to that a gentle, ingratiating
voice, an easy flow of innocuous conversation unimpeded by
pestiferous ideas, and you have a creature God-sent into politics.[21]

The issue that propelled Charles Curtis into his first political office
was prohibition, even though he himself was a social drinker and
apparently was opposed to the absolutist approach toward solving the
problem of a state that one observer described as being "awash in
liquor." The stern and unbending abstinence of Permelia Hubbard
Curtis surely was a factor, but conditions that Curtis had observed as a
young boy also contributed to his disdain for abusive drinking.[22]

On the Kaw reservation in the mid 1860s, Charles had had ample
opportunity to observe whiskey peddlers such as J. L. French, who had
managed "a grocery joint" adjacent to the reservation and who, in the
face of a federal law prohibiting the sale of liquor among Indians,
nevertheless submitted a substantial depredation claim requesting that
the government compensate him for whiskey that allegedly had been
stolen from him during an altercation that had led to the deaths of seven
Kaw men. In Topeka, it was not much better. Under the bylaws of the
Topeka Town Association, which were adopted in March 1855, the sale
or purchase of liquor was banned on real estate that had been deeded by
the association. The result was the rapid growth of the saloon industry
across the river in North Topeka. Both Charles's father and William
Curtis had operated saloons there. In 1866, a saloon operated by J. S.
Dowdell reported an average sale of two thousand drinks a day during
the first five days it was open, and throughout the decade of the sixties,
various Indian tribes camped at or near North Topeka to drink and play
poker after their government "payday."[23]

In November 1880, by a vote of 92,302 to 84,304, Kansas voters
adopted an amendment to the state constitution which provided that
"the manufacture and sale of intoxicating liquors shall be forever
prohibited in the State, except for medical, scientific and mechanical
purposes." The important medical loophole was widely abused, however. In Topeka, for example, it was reported in 1885 that no fewer than
11,866 "whiskey permits" were issued by a score of druggists in an two-
month period. This caused one wag to suggest: "It must be admitted
that this is the sickest town of its size on top of God's green earth."
Likewise, saloon keepers continued to ply their trade and then pay the
modest fines imposed by the local legal system, which was not especially enamored with the new dispensation. Rescinding the amendment
became the call of the "resubmissionists," whose ranks included

Charles Curtis. In fact, his law firm was retained by the liquor interests in Topeka at a monthly fee of $500.[24]

Personally, Curtis conceded that ''liquor broke men down, took away their pride, made wrecks of them [and so] I left it alone.'' Yet, he insisted he ''had no high-flown moral principles against drinking,'' and the fact that he had a brewery and a distillery on his own property endeared him to the resubmissionists, who viewed him as a ''safe'' candidate for the post of Shawnee's county attorney. They gave him their solid support, and after a particularly bitter contest in which it was reported that both candidates shook hands with every voter, ''Our Charley'' was elected to that post in 1884.[25]

Then, in a stratagem that almost overnight gave him a regional and state reputation as an effective law-and-order prosecutor, Curtis turned the tables on his supporters. He enforced the prohibition law to the letter, and within the first thirty days of his tenure in office, he had closed every one of the more than eighty ''open saloons'' in Shawnee County. One local newspaper noted, with not a little wonder: ''The rapid manner in which our Charley has put the forces of the saloonists to flight must be surprising to a good many people who anticipated something else.'' Another reporter said: ''The stories will soon be told, the jokes all exhausted, and these law-breakers will realize that there is a serious side to their present situation. It will dawn upon them gradually that being in jail . . . is not at all funny and that a very few people in the community are helping them laugh.'' In criminal prosecutions, Curtis was equally successful. During his first term in office, Curtis secured convictions in all but 5 of 108 cases, and in his second two-year term, every criminal case that was brought before him resulted in a conviction.[26]

Given his record, his penchant for long hours and hard work, and what editor White called ''his blessed gifts as a hand-shaker, a palaverer, the indefinable thing called charm which binds men to one forever,'' it was inevitable that Curtis would seek higher office. In 1888, his friends wanted him to run for an unprecedented third term as county attorney, but he refused, insisting that he simply wanted to return to his law practice. In fact, his political ambition could not be contained, especially in 1889, when Congressman Thomas Ryan of Kansas' Fourth District resigned to become minister to Mexico.[27]

Curtis lost the nomination by one vote, and in an uncharacteristic outburst of anger, he castigated the delegates before the entire convention. Because of an expected Farmers' Alliance landslide, reflecting midwestern and Kansas agrarian discontent in 1890, Curtis sat out the election that year, but he came back with an intensive campaign in 1892

Charles Curtis in 1884 at the age of twenty-four, when he was first elected as Shawnee County's district attorney. From Don C. Seitz, From Kaw Teepee to Capitol: The Life Story of Charles Curtis, Indian, Who Has Risen to High Estate *(New York: Frederick A. Stokes, 1928), following p. 150.*

to win the Fourth District in an election that saw Kansas go for the Populist presidential hopeful, James B. Weaver of Iowa; the election of a Wichita groceryman, L. D. Lewelling, as the first Populist governor of Kansas; and the handing over of the majority of its congressional seats to the Populists. Truly, this was a remarkable victory for the conservative Republican Curtis; it was also a testimony to his exploitation of the personal, human side of politics. White explained: "Issues never bothered him. His job was to fight the Farmers' Alliance. He had a rabble-rousing speech with a good deal of Civil War in it, a lot of protective tariff, and a very carefully poised straddle on the currency issue [which White was certain, Curtis simply did not understand]. I never saw a man who could go into a hostile audience, smile, shake hands, and talk before and after the meeting so plausibly that what he said on his feet was completely eclipsed as a human being." No doubt about it, White concluded, Curtis "was a wonder with his winning ways."[28]

There was another side to Curtis's popularity, however, one that was largely ignored by the political pundits of the time. It had to do with his uncertain Indianness, what some called that "confusing mixed-bloodedness." White alluded to it, but without reference to the larger picture: "His enemies made the mistake of stressing his Indian blood in ignominy. When he appeared in a little town the people turned out to see the Indian. What they saw was a gallant young Frenchman, suave, facile, smiling, with winning ways and a handshake that was a love affair itself." But fused to the Indian and the French was yet another component—the stern New England heritage that he took from his Grandmother Curtis. Writing to Curtis in the mid 1920s, White suggested: "Looking over your career in a rather cold-blooded way, I should say, externally, you have a lot of the French and Indian, but internally your governing spirit has been New England. Your efficiency comes out of New England. Your industry . . . for combining the interests of men . . . is a talent that comes out of a clear, hardfibered brain, the heritage of New England."[29]

The larger picture that eluded White was President Grover Cleveland's signing, on 8 February 1887, of the General Allotment Act, which marked the nation's acquiescence to the program of forced assimilation for Indians. This law provided for the allotment of Indian lands in severalty and for conformity to Anglo-American "civilization," not a blend of Indian ways and white ones. Senator Henry L. Dawes of Massachusetts and his supporters were convinced that the private ownership of land, in concert with schooling, agricultural instruction, and United States citizenship, would contribute to the improvement and the survival of Indians. Westerners, such as Kansas' Senator

Preston B. Plumb, were less optimistic. Proper policy, Plumb argued, should consist simply of breaking up the reservations, making the Indians self-supporting, and getting them "off the hands of Government." Similarly, Senators George Vest of Missouri and Richard Coke of Texas demanded the end of reservations, with no concern regarding assimilation: give Indians their rightful allotments, open up the surplus lands to white farmers, "and let nature take its course."[30]

In Kansas during the 1880s and the early 1890s, the Social Darwinist appeal about the "Vanishing American" seemed to be in the process of fulfillment. Medicine Lodge and Council Grove were by then the havens for white farmers; Dull Knife's raid had been consigned to history; and agrarian unrest and worries about the money supply had replaced Indians as the *bête noire* of Kansas society. Even though Indian culture seemed to be disappearing in the transition from barbarism to civilization, Indian *individuals* were not disappearing, certainly not mixedbloods such as Charles Curtis, who, as a rising politician, was succeeding at the most visible level of the democratic process.[31]

On the Kaw reservation in Indian Territory, the mixed-bloods outnumbered the full-bloods by the mid 1880s, thus adding credence to John Wesley Powell's 1885 prediction that within just three generations it would be difficult to find a single drop of pure Indian blood in all of America.[32] A report that was submitted by the Kaw Agency's physician in 1886 (quoted here unedited) confirmed the tragic details of the decline in the number of full-bloods:

Since my arrival here one year ago last May, there has been 5 births & 22 deaths among these people as a steady increase of the halfbreeds with a decrease of the full-bloods—out of that no. only one of the births was a full-blood and 20 deaths. This may be attributed to the following facts. First. The mixed-blood w'th scarcely an exception are free from veneral infections. Second. Tuberculous affections, heretofore &C are found no more frequently among them than among a corresponding no. of whites. Third. Sterility is almost unknown among them. Exactly the opposite conditions exists with the full-bloods. Tuberculous affections & the different forms of veneral diseases are very prevalent among them & as a result sterility is the rule & not the exception—with but few births to offset the deaths it may readily be seen that the total no. of the tribe decreases rapidly. To what may this distinct difference of conditions be attributed? I think their manners or habits of living, a total disregard of all hygenic laws may be considered the one actiological factor of their condition. Of loose morals venral diseases are rapidly propotated. . . . Their hygenical surroundings & habits are such as

to not only develop but invited every other disease that may be
lurking in the vicinity. . . . They are also deteriorating as a tribe
from close intermarriage of families & at the early age at which they
marry their daughters. . . . White who marry into this tribe invari-
ably choose from the mixed-bloods. Mixed-bloods seldom marry
full-bloods and other tribes scarcely ever marry into this one.[33]

In short, unless conditions could be altered dramatically or unless
individuals such as Curtis and other mixed-bloods who had been
dropped from the tribal roll could be reinstated, the Kaw tribe appeared
to be headed for extinction. Like their Osage relatives, the Five Tribes,
and several smaller tribes in Indian Territory, the Kaws had been
exempted from the allotment provisions of the Dawes legislation. Yet,
there was no legal impediment to additional legislation that might
accomplish for these tribes what the Dawes Act had prohibited. With
few exceptions, the mixed-bloods in all of these tribes favored such
action and could count on the strong support of the land boomers in
Kansas, who were led by David Payne. More than a hundred thousand
acres of prime unallotted Kaw land lay just south of the Kansas border,
and it was this, not the physical well-being of the full-bloods or the
integrity of the Kaw nation, that encouraged the mixed-bloods to have
their names placed back on the tribal roll.[34]

On 1 June 1888, the acting Osage agent C. H. Potter was advised
that the Indian Office in Washington had received a letter from ''a Mr.
Charles Curtis, requesting to have himself and his sister Elizabeth Curtis
(now Elizabeth Layton) enrolled as Kaw Indians. Please return the
enclosure with such information as you may have, or can obtain in
regard to these applications.'' Clearly, Curtis was cognizant of the
implications of the Dawes legislation for his future as an Indian allottee,
and although there was no immediate decision regarding the application, his movement into the national political arena was bound to help
his cause.[35]

In that same year, however, problems developed in Congress for
aspiring nontribal mixed-bloods such as Curtis. Senate Bill 928, ''Marriage between White Men and Indian Women,'' introduced as an
administration measure in the spring of 1888 and signed into law on 10
August, was designed to answer the concerns that the commissioner of
Indian affairs, John D. C. Atkins held regarding the large number of
white men who had married Indian women in order to escape the white
man's laws and courts, while at the same time securing a valuable
interest in Indian land. Excluding the Five Tribes, section 1 of the law
prohibited white men who had married Indian women from ''acquiring
any right to any tribal property, privilege, or interest whatever to which

any member of such tribe is entitled.'' Section 2 made the Indian wife of a white man a United States citizen, without impairing her right or title ''to any tribal property or any interest therein''; and section 3 provided that ''whenever the marriage of any white man with any Indian woman, a member of any such tribe of Indians, is required or offered to be proved in any judicial proceeding, evidence of the admission of such fact by the party against whom the proceeding is had, or evidence of general repute, or of cohabitation as married persons, or any other circumstantial or presumptive evidence from which the fact may be inferred, shall be competent.''[36]

Property rights, both tribal and nontribal, for white husbands and Indian wives were thus unambiguous, as was the Indian wife's right to United States citizenship. Less certain was the circumstance of the mixed-blood children, whom Congressman Abraham Parker of New York called that ''degenerate progeny.'' While conceding that nothing in the legislation could bar the Indian wife from becoming a citizen, Parker asked if the same right then extended to her children as well. Congressman John Rogers of Arkansas, the principal sponsor of the bill, replied in the affirmative. But could mixed-blood children inherit property—say, for example, annuities or an allotment under federal law? Could these children inherit tribal property through the maternal line?[37]

Because the law was silent on this point, Rogers evaded the question. Noting that ''the bill is fraught with a great deal of philosophic wisdom,'' he simply responded: ''I think the tendency and effect will be to keep white men out of the Indian Territory . . . and will likewise . . . prevent to a very large extent the intermarriage of these Indian women except for the purpose of obtaining a head-right.'' But George Adams of Illinois pressed: ''Are not the children of such a marriage likely to be a little nearer to civilization—which we hope to be the ultimate outcome— than the children of a full-blood marriage?'' Absolutely not, responded Congressman Samuel Peters of Kansas:

Some of the worst characters, the vilest outlaws, men who violate every law known to humanity as well as to Christianity, are the children of white men who went among the Indians and intermarried with them. I would rather trust my life or my property today in the hands of a full-blood Indian than trust it in the hands of a half-breed who has been raised in the midst of the barbarous influences that surround many of these tribes.[38]

The question of whether mixed-bloods had inheritance rights remained unanswered, although the tenor of the debate provided the secretary of the interior with considerable leverage to rule in the negative. But to do so would be to discourage the mixed-bloods as instruments of civilization, which had been a strategy of the Indian Office since the early nineteenth century, and it certainly was bound to excite the wrath of the freshman Indian congressman, Charles Curtis of Kansas.

9

Whispering in Washington

From 1892 until January 1907, when the Kansas legislature selected him to fill out the term of Senator Joseph R. Burton, who had resigned after he lost his appeal on a conviction for having accepted a bribe from the Rialto Grain and Securities Company of St. Louis, Charles Curtis represented Kansas from the Fourth and First districts in Congress. Although a "standpat" Republican, he nevertheless displayed remarkable dexterity in weathering the storms of populism and progressivism in Kansas and, at a more personal level, a keen ability to outmaneuver such Kansas GOP strongmen as Cyrus Leland, Chester Long, and William J. Bailey.[1]

In 1897, with unexpected Republican support, the Populists erred mightily when they gerrymandered the First Kansas District to include Shawnee County, a Curtis stronghold. Their intent obviously was to provide Bailey with a distinct advantage over Curtis. Undaunted, Curtis took to the hustings with his usual energy and confidence. Shaking hands, slapping backs, kissing babies, and making friends with many a farmer, but suggesting no remedies for the agricultural crisis, Curtis made significant inroads north of Topeka, even in Bailey's own backyard near the Nebraska border. Clearly, the personable, hard-working law-and-order mixed-blood was a political force to be reckoned with.[2]

At the convention in Horton, the Republicans became almost hopelessly embroiled in a deadlock between Curtis, Case Broderick, and Bailey, and it was not until 701 ballots had been taken that the infamous "Horton Agreement" was allegedly forged: national committeeman Leland would release his delegates for a Curtis nomination in return for Curtis's promise that he would retire in 1900 and support Bailey for the same seat. When the time came, however, Curtis reneged, claiming that the political broker Marcus A. Low was the only individual who was authorized to carry out such a bargain and that because Low had made no formal deals with Leland, Curtis was free to run for reelection. This he did successfully, thereby precipitating a decade of intense factional struggle among Republicans in the First District and providing the "boss-busters" in Kansas with considerable fire for their cause.[3]

Nonetheless, Curtis made a bid for the United States Senate on the basis of his personal popularity and his disdain for reform. Some went so far as to suggest that his native Indian stubbornness urged him on. The direct election of senators, which Curtis always disliked, still lay in the future; according to law, the election of senators was still in the hands of the legislature. After only two caucuses, it became apparent that this time, Curtis was pitted against a strong combination of Governor William Stanley and Chester Long from Wichita. With bitter recollections of the Horton Agreement, Stanley reluctantly threw his support to Long, thus causing Curtis's defeat and his continuation in the House until the embers of Republican factionalism in Kansas had ceased to smolder. In the 1903 campaign, however, Curtis did not alter the strategy that had worked so well for him in the past. It was as if nothing had changed, as a Topeka reporter observed:

> For instance, this is the way Mr. Curtis greets a short grass statesman, who has just arrived in Topeka: "Why, hello Jim, how are you? How are the folks? And your uncle, old Fred Siftings, who lived down in the bend of the creek, how is he? . . . Your wife was looking especially well when I last saw her, and I hope she is still hearty and good looking." And he goes on this way until he has threshed over the pedigree of the whole family, and all the time he is holding on to the representative's hand and looking into his eyes with that piercing gaze, which could convince a stone image of his sincerity.[4]

Curtis did not change his style in Washington. According to one account, he received fourteen hundred letters from his constituents in one twenty-four-hour period, and with the help of his half sister and a battalion of secretaries, he answered every letter within the day. "As part of my duties as secretary," recalled his half sister Dolly, "I began to keep systematic records for campaign use—books filled with the names of Kansas voters, the citizens of every county and town. . . . A short biography of each voter, with his achievements, sometimes with a description of his personality." It was an awesome system, one that, with the passing of time, prompted ridicule from the media. On the eve of the 1928 Republican convention in Kansas City, for example, Oswald Garrison Villard wrote: "Senator Curtis [a contender for the presidential

nomination] is as faithful and as devoted to his party [and his constitu-
ents] as he is dull and dumb." In Kansas, however, William Allen
White, who knew Curtis more intimately, wrote in 1924: "Our Charley
was a figure in Kansas, by reason of his brains. For it takes as much
brains of just as high an order, to remember ten thousand names and
faces in a district . . . as it does to remember tariff schedules or the
relation between the price of wheat and pig iron or bar silver in a given
month for half a century."[5]

As a freshman congressman, Curtis quickly displayed his strategy
of ingratiating himself to others. When the Fifty-third Congress con-
vened in 1893 and the various members partook in the lottery that
determined where their seats would be located, it was found that
Nelson W. Aldrich, Jr., of Rhode Island, the veteran chairman of the
Ways and Means Committee, had lost his front seat to one far in the rear
and that Curtis of Kansas had drawn the one to which Aldrich was so
greatly attached. "Curtis, pleased with his luck, sidled up to Aldrich
and told him that he, as a cub, had no particular use for the seat, and
that he would be delighted if Mr. Aldrich would exchange with him."
Aldrich never forgot this little courtesy, and thereafter he returned many
important favors to Curtis.[6]

Even though a recent study of the Kansas Progressives has suggested that Curtis was only a moderate opponent of reform during the
Progressive Era, it is nevertheless true that many of his contemporaries
believed that for Curtis the trinity was "the Republican Party, the
protective tariff, and the Grand Army of the Republic." As a Republican
regular who refused to stake his political future on what he considered
to be the whims of the reformers, Curtis took great pride in his
protectionism; this included the much-maligned law that he guided
through Congress, which provided the egg producers with protection
against Oriental dried eggs—hence the occasional appellation of "Egg-
Charley." Similarly, he supported or sponsored high duties against
English horses, Mexican cattle, gypsum, and swine. Securing military
pensions was one of his most effective means of garnering support at
election time. One newspaper reported in 1922: "In his docket are the
names of more than 10,000 veterans for whom he obtained aid. That is
one of the main reasons his enemies couldn't end the Topekan's political
career." And when it was rumored in 1897 that the Topeka Pension
Office might be moved to St. Louis, Curtis blocked the action by
reminding Secretary of the Interior Cornelius N. Bliss that during the
Civil War, Kansas had supplied more soldiers per capita than any other
state.[7]

Still another weapon in Curtis's political arsenal was his personal
endorsement. In response to a request for a message of hope to be

included in Christmas greeting cards from a Boston publisher shortly after the stock-market crash in 1929, Curtis obliged with this offering: "Our economic ills are an effect, not a cause. The cause is widespread spiritual illness of our people." His name was printed on thousands of ink blotters that were distributed free of charge to the public schools, and he achieved not a little notoriety by having his name included in a Lucky Strike cigarette advertisement, much to the distress of Lillian M. Mitchner, president of the Kansas Woman's Christian Temperance Union, W.C.T.U. In August 1927, Mitchner wrote to Curtis that her organization had helped promote the ink blotters but now could no longer support him and that his endorsement of Lucky Strikes "would cost him thousands of votes." How wrong she was became apparent fifteen months later, when Curtis was selected as Herbert Hoover's running mate for the presidential race of 1928.[8]

In the House and in the Senate after 1907, Curtis was a dedicated committee man and an indefatigable servant of his fellow solons. A Topeka reporter in Washington in 1896 observed that Curtis "was almost worn out with work on the Indian appropriation bill" and that "he came up from the committee room with enough papers to fill a bushel basket." Curtis's committee assignments in the House were Ways and Means, Public Lands, and Indian Affairs. He also served as chairman of the subcommittees on Indian Territory Legislation and Expenditures in the Interior Department, and by 1903 he had advanced to the chair of the powerful House Committee on Indian Affairs. In the Senate, he also served on the Indian Committee, chaired the subcommittee on Indian Depredations, became party whip in 1915, and after Coolidge's victory in 1924, was elevated to the distinguished post of majority leader. So dedicated was Curtis to the responsibilities of public office that on the eve of the 1928 election a New York paper insisted that for years, Curtis had not missed a word spoken in the Senate.[9]

Regarding his philosophy toward good public performance, an Indian Territory newspaper quoted Curtis in 1900: "Single out a few of the most vital points, agree on them *absolutely* and then work for those alone. For goodness sake do not undertake to get everything at once by putting all manner of pet theories up for experimentation." Thirty years later, in a speech to the graduating class of the Pierce School of Business Administration in Philadelphia, Curtis provided a more detailed outline on how to be successful:

1. Do not become mentally lazy.
2. Honesty, with yourself first.
3. Use common sense.
4. Rely on yourself.

5. Have a definite action in mind.
6. Don't fret or worry.
7. Believe in 'God's plan of human progress.'

And he might have added, as was his most effective finale while on the stump, take pride in yourself: "I'm one-eighth Kaw Indian and a one-hundred per cent Republican."[10]

As one who preferred to work behind the scenes, Curtis came to be known as a whisperer, even from the lofty heights of Senate majority leader. In the summer of 1928, when he was considered a serious candidate for the presidential nomination, analyst after analyst commented on the silent Indian from Kansas. One said:

> He has been called—and is—the greatest whisperer in the United States Senate. When most Senators whisper, they are merely telling what Pat said to Mike; when Curtis whispers, he may be arranging a deal with the opposition, or telling how the next vote in the Senate will result, or conveying some message he had received from the White House—conveying just as much of it as he thinks his listener ought to hear.[11]

And another analyst said:

> As a Republican leader following the death of Henry Cabot Lodge, Charley came to be known as the greatest whisperer in Congress. Whenever he took his favorite pose with a short fat arm coiled around another Senator's shoulders, the Press Gallery got busy. It is a sure sign that something was doing. "Talk, talk, talk," he would complain to the reporters about the endless Senate deliberations. . . . It is his firm belief, borne out by extensive experience, that everything can be fixed by friendly and confidential getting together. . . . As a fixer Charley is truely one of the best in the business.[12]

Whence sprang this extraordinary talent? Was it simply the expected performance of a shy country lawyer, a hayseed from the heart of agrarian America, a regular Republican functionary who chose not to bother with the intricacies of the tariff, the workings of the monetary system, the new imperialism, or the plight of the Cubans? Was Curtis afraid of displaying his ignorance on the congressional floor? Was it because of shoddy deals from which he might profit personally? Were there too many nefarious IOUs that might come back to haunt him? Was he, as Bill White from Emporia suggested, a profound student of human behavior, a social scientist who manipulated people very much as the analytical chemist works the elements and compounds? Or did he simply relish the title of public palaverer number 1?[13]

That "Indian Charley" was a country lawyer—a rather good one at that—no one disputed. That he comprehended only the most simplistic notions regarding the domestic economy and the emerging forces of imperialism in the late nineteenth century nearly everyone could agree. And that he was dedicated, honest, and hard-working seemed equally beyond dispute. In 1920, after fifteen years in the House and nearly a dozen in the Senate, one of his hometown newspapers proudly reported: "In the whole course of his political career no charges of self-seeing, crookedness or graft have been made against him, even by his enemies, nor has he trailed off after false political gods or spent time on junkets." White insisted that Curtis "was an honest agent; he did not lie; he did not steal; he did not blab." He simply stayed on the job, working hard for his slight commission, "just places for his friends."[14]

Such testimonies, however, were oversimplifications. Early in his congressional career, Curtis came to understand that the real powers in his district were those who profited by shaping the trends and direction of state and national politics. In his district, the Santa Fe, the Rock Island, and the Missouri Pacific railroads exerted significant power, in fact to the degree that in party caucuses their employees were sufficiently persuasive to dominate the county conventions. In Topeka, it was the Santa Fe; in Horton, it was the Rock Island; and in Atchison, it was the Missouri Pacific. As a lawyer and a very practical man, Curtis naturally made friends with the railroad attorneys who "generally took care of the railroad vote." In turn, Curtis made friends with the people in Washington who instructed the Kansas railroad lawyers. The same technique worked well with the Grand Army of the Republic. Thus, with the railroads and the veterans behind him, he could, as White knew, "defy the world in his district." O. G. Villard, writing in the *Nation*, agreed: "His [Curtis's] god is the Process of Elimination and Kansas knows that Curtis is a great man. . . . As Senator, not one has kept his political fences in better repair."[15]

This is not to suggest that Curtis was incapable of using his public position to further his private interest, particularly when opportunity came knocking as the "natural result" of his contribution to government. In the interim between filling out Burton's senatorial term in 1913 and his return to the Senate on 4 March 1915, Curtis returned to his Topeka law firm. Business was slow at first, and he lamented that "a man who had been out of practice for a number of years would have to build up so slowly." Fortunately, a call came from the oilman Theodore Barnsdall to look after some legal business in Washington, D.C., and in

Oklahoma. Barnsdall, who many believed was in the pay of Standard Oil (which had loaned him $7 million), held a 55,660-acre sublease on the Osage reservation near Bartlesville. Like such oil magnates as J. M. Guffy and George Getty, Barnsdall had negotiated his sublease with the Indian Territory Illuminating Oil Company (ITIO) of New Jersey, the well-financed successor to the Phoenix and the Osage oil companies, which earlier had experienced difficulties in meeting the lease requirements stipulated by the Interior Department.[16]

In 1906, during hearings before the House Committee on Indian Affairs over the Osage leases, the committee's chairman, Charles Curtis, admitted that he had written the clause attached to the Indian appropriations bill which relinquished the leases to the ITIO and, by extension, to Barnsdall, Guffy, and Getty. But Chairman Curtis insisted that he was not well informed about the leasing of Indian land to a non-Indian corporation. A committee colleague, who was well aware of Curtis's reputation as a fixer, replied that "the chairman of this committee is not excelled by any other member of Congress in drawing bills where he does not have knowledge of the subject." At that, the committee broke out in unrestrained laughter. As politics, this was Curtis at his best, but at the remunerative level the association proved invaluable, for during the nine months after he went on retainer with Barnsdall, Curtis earned more than six thousand dollars. In addition, it brought him in touch with other individuals and firms that were working oil leases in Indian Territory, and Curtis recalled, "I soon had quite a business from Tulsa, Bartlesville, and other towns in Oklahoma."[17]

Certainly, Curtis's dealings with Barnsdall and the other oil companies added credence to the assertion of a Muskogee newspaper in 1900, when it claimed that the representative from Kansas was by far the most powerful political broker in Indian Territory and that one day he would exert similar power in the Senate. The same paper marveled at the deference that his legislative colleagues granted to Curtis on matters dealing with Indians. In so doing, they were pointing to an important aspect of his political power that has gone largely unnoticed by students of federal Indian policy from the Dawes Act to Oklahoma's statehood in 1907.[18]

This had to do with his Indianness, and Indianness that went beyond that perceived by the so-called "friends of the Indian" during the closing years of the nineteenth century, beyond that understood by the ethnologists who were increasingly confident that the mixed-blood population was nothing to fear, and certainly beyond those writers who have viewed "Our Charley" as a kind of sideshow curiosity in Washington. It was power, sheer political power, conceived and nurtured by an ambitious mixed-blood who was determined to prove the truth of the assimilationists' dream.[19]

Not that Charles Curtis was ignored as a rather curious specimen in the nation's capital. One need only consider House Speaker Thomas B. ("Czar") Reed's initial response to "the Indian" for the format of the side-show phenomenon. The time was just after Curtis had arrived in Washington, and the setting was a caucus of prominent House leaders who were struggling mightily with the gold-standard question. Like a stumbling country bumpkin, Curtis inadvertently wandered into the chamber where Reed and his colleagues were making but little progress on the momentous question. Curtis, a little abashed at interrupting the distinguished assemblage, had withdrawn to a window space on the south side of the Speaker's room, when the "Czar" hailed him:

"Indian," said the Speaker, "what suggestion have you to make regarding this committee to draw up a gold bill?" Congressman Curtis thought a minute. "Since you ask me, Mr. Speaker," he replied, "I would suggest that you appoint a committee no member of which is a member of the Committee on Coinage, Weights and Measures, the Committee on Banking and Currency, or the Committee on Ways and Means." A roar went up from the assembled statesmen. "Just what do you mean by that?" asked Reed, a bit puzzled. "I mean just this," replied Curtis boldly, "that if you put these specialists on that committee, each with a bill of his own in mind, you won't get anywhere and you won't have any bill. Neither one will yield to the other and you won't make any headway. You had better let the thing out to fellows who may not know so much about currency but who will bring in a bill." Reed shot a glance at the audacious Indian from Kansas, but said nothing. A few days later the committee was appointed, and none of the currency stars were on it. In fact, the committee was enlarged from ten to eleven, and Curtis of Kansas was the eleventh man. It was this committee that framed the Gold Standard Act of 1900.[20]

This was just plain no-nonsense compromise—what was needed to overcome the demands of the gods and the egos of men. Understand people, and the issues become manageable. Work behind the scenes, explore feelings and frailties, and politics becomes the art of the possible. One observer wrote, after Curtis had become vice-president: "He isn't much to look at. A little, fat, saffron-skinned man, with a round seal-lion-like visage. True, there is no affectation or culture of learning about him, but he is worth a dozen austere and disdainful [Henry Cabot] Lodges for fixing things up."[21]

But beyond that were the forbearance and the wisdom of the Native Americans, the noble savage incarnate; one observer said: "He has all the wisdom of his aboriginal ancestors. He thinks first and when he speaks he has thrashed and winnowed his thoughts of all the chaff." Another one said: "The pure possession of his ancestral qualities—the Indian tendencies toward taciturnity and general powers of self-repression and control—have something to do with the career of Curtis."[22] With these ancient tools, he had invaded non-Indian society at the highest levels and had demonstrated that the assimilationist strategy was no pipe dream of the misguided idealist. Certainly, he was living proof that giving handouts to Indians who called on the Great Father was a bad habit that was contrary to sound policy, as one critic was only too happy to point out:

> Curtis is an Indian in many ways, albeit there are some features of "Lo" that have been toned down. . . . He looks like an Indian, a sort of Fenimore Cooper Indian and has coal-black hair and a copper colored complexion and all those Cooper attributes, and certainly does not resemble the pigeon-toed braves that come on from the West every year to see the Great Father in Washington, and spend the money which the kind and loving Indian Commissioner gives them.[23]

Curtis was, in short, a self-made man, a progressive Indian who could parade and be paraded before the public as proof that allotment and the assimilationist strategy were working. In 1925, Indian Commissioner Charles Burke, who earlier had served with Curtis on the House Committee on Indian Affairs and who in 1906 had authored a bill allowing Indian allottees to secure citizenship and titles to their allotments prior to the twenty-five-year minimum that had been required by the Dawes Act two decades earlier, selected the career of his good friend Charles Curtis as one for all children—but especially Indian children—to emulate. In a pamphlet that was widely distributed by the Interior Department to Indian schools throughout the country, Burke characterized Curtis as a self-reliant, hard-working, loyal, honest, and "self-made man in the highest sense." Unwavering adherence to such noble principles, said Burke,

> has led to the high positions and the wide public confidence bestowed upon this stalwart character in our national affairs, whose added responsibilities are now those long entrusted to so eminent a statesman as Henry Cabot Lodge. Thus passes to one from the primitive people of the great plains this high command released by the death of him whose cultured lineage was linked with the first white settlements of America, and marks both a fulfillment and an assurance of the Red Man's progress under the influence of a civilization in which he shall become an enduring power.

To which Curtis added a resounding confirmation in the form of a question for *all* young boys to consider: "Since this journey has been possible for me who started so obscurely and who had so many early handicaps, is there any reason why any boy anywhere should not consider that to him all things are possible?"[24]

The fact is that Charles Curtis used his celebrated Indianness with considerable finesse. The *Nation* could ridicule his "rotund historical phrases," such as, "Mr. President, I suggest the absence of a quorum; Mr. President, I ask a roll-call; Mr. President, I rise to a point of order," and then try to appease him with the offering that his whispering sprang naturally from "those stoical chiefs who were his ancestors." But underlying the bluster of the "Indian Charley" gibes was a patronizing deference to Curtis as *the* Indian expert in Congress, a deference that with few exceptions crossed party lines and provided the mixed-blood from Kansas with significant power in the assimilationist program that had been established during the 1880s. Curtis, after all, was an Indian. He had lived on a reservation. He had relatives and close friends in the Indian country whom he visited regularly. He understood Indian traditions as well as the Anglo-American law that was his professional expertise. He had walked the paths of both the red man and the white man and, having opted for the latter, was comforting proof that progress was possible.[25]

The Indian Office's files and congressional records are replete with the details of how Curtis attended to the interest of Indian individualism while he was in Congress. In 1908, for example, he wrote to a field agent in Kansas: "David Puchkee, whose Indian name is Mezhes, tells me he desires to sell his land and that he is sure arrangements can be made with the man who holds the lease, to give it up, in fact thinks this man will buy the land. Please look into the case—I think it will help this young Indian." He promoted the construction of a free wagon bridge across the Arkansas to aid Indians in the northern part of Indian Territory gain better access to white towns and markets, and he helped the Kiowas expel squatters who tried to overrun the lands that had been allotted to the Kiowas by the Jerome Commission in 1892. He pressured the Indian Office into having revenues from coal and asphalt pay for the operation of schools among the Five Tribes, and he introduced numerous bills for the construction of railroads that would connect Kansas, Arkansas, and Texas with Indian Territory. He wrote letters of introduction for merchants who were attempting to sell goods and services on reservations; he made numerous recommendations for teachers who were interested in working in the reservation schools; he took great interest in expanding the federal court system into Indian Territory, and he responded sympathetically to Indian individuals who pressed claims against the government. In fact, he made so many junkets to Indian Territory that in later years he often was referred to as Oklahoma's third senator.[26]

The underlying strategy of these actions was to encourage reservation Indians to reject communal life and to reap the rewards of individual enterprise. Relentlessly and with little ballyhoo, Curtis labored on committees, fixing and refining the details of allotment legislation and then, with his legal expertise and his remarkable command of parliamentary procedure, defending such legislation with great effectiveness on the floor of Congress. Never one to disguise his abilities in such matters, Curtis was not far afield when in 1900 he said to Secretary of the Interior Ethan A. Hitchcock: "I have done more to secure legislation for the Indian Territory than all the others put together since the 54th Cong. in 1896." In Indian Territory, there certainly were those who agreed. Noting with approval that the Indian legislator from Kansas supported single statehood for Oklahoma and a comprehensive public-school system for Indians, a Muskogee newspaper stated: "Charles Curtis has had more to do with the shaping of legislation affecting the Indian Territory than any other member of the lower house in Washington."[27]

Working behind the scenes, which was always his most effective tactic, Curtis used his position to influence the appointment of Indian Office personnel who would be agreeable to his politics. At Greyhorse and Hominy on the Osage lands, he insisted that trade licenses and inside information regarding land sales be granted to conservative Republicans. He did the same on the Potawatomi reserve north of Topeka. Responding to a complaint filed in the Indian Office in Washington regarding a banker of sound Republican persuasion who had been given special considerations in the purchase of the lands of deceased Indians, Curtis simply advised that the matter would be "carefully looked into," while assuring that the alleged culprit was "an honorable man fully interested in the well-being of the Indians." He tampered freely in the certification of tribal attorneys, and he encouraged the appointment of tribal councilmen who promised to cooperate with the government's assimilationist program. As for patronage, a Guthrie newspaper lamented in 1903 that because of Curtis's influence, "Kansas has the lion's share of the federal jobs in the Indian Territory— fully one-third more than any other state in the Union."[28]

To Curtis, the business of non-Indians in Indian Territory was business, and he consequently supported the unfettered invasion of corporate America into the region. In 1897, he applauded Indian commissioner William A. Jones's decision to support the investments of more than two hundred thousand whites in the territory, for "they have made improvements worth millions of dollars and to talk of ejecting them and confiscating their property is sheer nonsense." Three years later, in commenting on a pro-oil amendment, proposed by Curtis, to the Cherokee allotment bill, a newspaper in Indian Territory suggested "that Standard Oil truely has a champion in Congress." Several weeks later, the same paper noted, "Curtis has again overridden the report of the sub-committee and has introduced a section . . . protecting Standard Oil in the Cherokee nation." Evidence was also brought forth indicating that Curtis had used "questionable legal tactics," to prevent the courts from tampering with other oil firms that were after Indian land, and while Curtis reportedly was "singed" in the Teapot Dome scandal of the twenties, he was able "to escape the holocaust." One of his closest friends, a regular campaign contributor, was Harry F. Sinclair, who eventually gave Curtis's son a job with the firm that Sinclair headed in Chicago.[29]

After the passage of the Curtis Act of 1898, which, among other matters, gave the Interior Department final say in the awarding of mineral leases on tribal land, a spokesman for the Cherokees rose to eloquent heights regarding Curtis and Indian oil. D. W. C. Duncan, writing under the pseudonym Too-qua-stee, predicted that with Curtis's help, Indian Territory eventually would be pocked with "oil leases, asphalt leases, stone leases, marble leases, granite leases, air leases, and possibly the very blessed light of the sun (should it prove capitalizable) may be captured and monopolized by some shrewd speculator under one of Charley Curtis's wonderful lease-traps."[30] Indeed, so blatant were Curtis's actions that in 1906 the Interior Department, in an angry memorandum to President Theodore Roosevelt, stated that eighty-one leases—underwritten by Standard Oil and certified by Congressman Curtis, amounting to 6,648 acres in Cherokee country worth in the vicinity of $8 million, were patently illegal.[31]

But Curtis managed to escape his tormentors. In 1906, while presiding over the House Committee on Indian Affairs, he elicited only coarse guffaws and backslapping for having authored a bill to give the ITIO a lease to half of the Osage reservation. On the surface, it may have appeared to be a treacherous undertaking, but Curtis was comforted that his good friend Frank Frantz, a former Osage agent who in 1906 was the Republican governor of Oklahoma Territory, had escaped indictment for having taken a bribe from James Glen, vice-president of the ITIO. In that instance, as Curtis knew well, President Roosevelt had intervened. Recalling the good old days when Frantz had served with him in the Rough Riders in Cuba, Roosevelt dismissed all the talk about Indians and oil as simply "vicious gossip." Roosevelt, too, was concerned about the future of the Republican Party in Indian Territory—a place that

Curtis described as "having about 400,000 people and something like 399,999 Democrats"—and saw no reason for pursuing the Cherokee charges against an Indian congressman of his own party.[32]

Curtis also took comfort in the inconsequential outcome of charges that the Indian Rights Association brought against the Dawes Commission (or Commission to the Five Civilized Tribes). Beginning with the Choctaws and the Chickasaws in 1897, and followed by the Seminoles in 1898, the Creeks in 1901, and the Cherokees in 1902, Congress had passed forced allotment laws, and it was the commission's responsibility to determine which Indians were entitled to free homesteads and a share of the surplus lands. S. M. Brosius, a special agent for the Indian Rights Association, reported in 1903 that members of the Dawes Commission were enriching themselves by organizing trust companies to lease lands. The leases, in effect, constituted agreements to sell to oil corporations, once the allotted land had been cleared for sale. The chairman of the Dawes Commission, Tams Bixby, for example, was also vice-president of the Muskogee Title and Trust Company; lesser officials were involved as well, including Indian inspectors, commissioners, recorders, judicial officials, and what one writer has termed a vast "corps of clerks" who were involved in partitioning the communal domain of the Five Tribes. Brosius blamed all the trouble on the House Committee on Indian Affairs, especially its chairman, Charles Curtis of Kansas, for providing places for his friends "where the corruption has grown." Officials of the Interior Department were shocked by the charges, and in Kansas the situation was no better for Curtis.[33]

Taking advantage of the bitter struggle that was prompted by Curtis's bid for a Kansas seat in the Senate in 1903, a Leavenworth newspaper fired a broadside at the whispering mixed-blood. Noting that Brosius was headed for the Pawnee Agency to check charges of brutality and financial extortion against George I. Harvey, the superintendent of the school at the Pawnee agency, the paper reported, "Brosius is the man who uncovered the land frauds on the Indians in Brown and Jackson counties, Kansas, [which] involved Congressman Curtis and his coterie of close political friends." The frauds involved the attempted sale, in 1898, of certain Potawatomi and Great Nemaha allotments at half their true value. This, according to the newspaper account, had prompted Curtis to make a hasty trip to Washington to cover up his involvement in the attempted sales. For his part, Harvey smugly boasted on the streets of Pawnee that he had the ear of the assistant secretary in Washington and "the friendship of Congressman Curtis of Kansas" and "that no matter what kind of report is sent in, he would not be fired." The Leavenworth paper said that Curtis "was dancing on a coal-bank" to keep all the charges from getting out of hand.[34]

After it was announced that Charles H. Bonaparte, a Baltimore lawyer who was a member of the Board of Indian Commissioners, had been authorized to conduct an investigation of the Dawes Commission and any governmental officials who had been accused of fraud in Indian Territory, the Leavenworth newspaper renewed its attack on Curtis:

> No man connected with Indian affairs is so heartily cursed in the Indian Territory as Curtis. . . . He is blamed for the appointment of a lot of carpetbaggers who are to blame for the present investigation and for the corruption that is found. . . . To cite one case. A year ago Congressman Curtis held a council with the Creek Indians. He was there to further the interest of a select few friends regarding land and oil leases. From the council in company with one William Higgins he went to the town of Sapulpa, where Higgins then canvassed the town for campaign funds for Curtis. . . . Curtis's assertions that he is in favor of dismissing dishonest Indian employees is simply not borne out by the fact or his actions. If he was so disposed, he could do more toward clearing up the charges of fraud and speculation in the Indian Territory than any other man in the country, for he is fully informed regarding all the rotten business. . . . But he will not do so. He is afraid to do it.[35]

Because of Curtis's powerful political position, however, the same paper conceded that he held the upper hand: "Congressman Curtis is looked upon as an authority of *all* Indian matters, and is part Indian himself." This, plus his membership on the Indian Committee of the House, made him "a stronger man today on Indian matters than any other person in government." Curtis himself urged this view when he told the El Reno paper in October 1903 that "he had done more for the Oklahoma Indians than the entire Dawes Commission since 1893." The Bonaparte investigation resulted in nothing more than a prohibition that in the future, officials of the Interior Department could neither lease nor speculate in Indian land and the requirement that all money that was appropriated for Indian Territory be withheld from any federal official until that official had taken an oath that he had no financial interest in Indian land. Sins of the past would be forgotten, while in the meantime, Curtis regained the initiative by picturing the Dawes Commission as a permissive, cumbersome bureaucracy that complained a great deal about corruption but had not the will nor the capacity to do anything about it.[36]

This became evident during the congressional debate over single statehood for Oklahoma in April 1904. By 1894, the Dawes Commission had concluded that corruption could have been prevented if the mixed-bloods and adopted whites had not cooperated to the fullest extent with the non-Indian land jobbers. But Curtis had reference to a particular type of mixed-blood, the mixed-blood who voted the opposition and who sought to create a separate Indian state—a prospect that was anathema to conservative Republicans. They were the ones who were responsible for all the corruption; they were the ones whom the Dawes Commission had not been able to control. "I want to tell you," he boomed forth at the Democratic opposition, "the kind of men in the Indian Territory that are anxious for double statehood are some of the chiefs, the leading men who have been controlling the affairs of these people and living fat off them for the last fifty years." And who had saved the Five Tribes from oblivion? Curtis, of course, who knew more about Indians than anyone else in Washington. "I want to say," he continued on the House floor, "that the very bill I introduced in 1898 was introduced to prevent the passage of the bill recommended by the Dawes Commission, the bill that would have wiped the Five Civilized Tribes off the face of the earth without their consent."[37]

The 1898 bill was the Curtis Act, the most important piece of Indian-policy legislation between 1887 and 1934. There is no doubt that Curtis took pride in its authorship and in his ability to have it signed into law where the Dawes people had failed. A few months before it was enrolled in the statute books, Curtis boasted to a newspaper in Oklahoma Territory that "the passage of this bill will be the beginning of a new era for that country, and I expect the *Natural* result to follow: the union of the Indian Territory with Oklahoma, and the formation of one of the grandest states in this union." Two years later, however, the same newspaper announced: "The Curtis Bill is not a document to be proud of, as it contains more incongruities than perhaps any other measure passed by Congress in a decade." Another paper reported: "The Indian Territory has, since passage of the Curtis law, been treated exactly the same as Cuba and Puerto Rico and with less cause. But none of the political speakers up to date have had the courage to admit the fact."[38]

Before 1898, Curtis had complained about the Dawes Commission's intent unilaterally to abrogate time-honored Indian treaties, but in fact this was precisely what the bill that he wrote accomplished. By abolishing tribal courts, by instituting civil government for Indian Territory, by requiring that tribal individuals submit to allotment regardless of the consequences, and by providing the guidelines for political union with the state of Oklahoma, the act was far more radical than the one that the Dawes people envisaged prior to 1898. The very title of the law, "An Act for the *protection* [emphasis added] of the people of the Indian Territory and for other purposes," was a clever deception, designed to give the impression that the exploitation of the Oklahoma Indians was a thing of the past.[39]

Informed people knew better. In Guthrie, the capital of Oklahoma Territory, bold headlines announced, "It Will Revolutionize the Indian Territory!" Earlier, the same newspaper had noted that white speculators, in anticipation of the passage of the act, were "greatly elated but the squaw men were not." In fact, the latter had put in "big money to defeat the Curtis Bill." After passage, Robert L. Owen, the mixed-blood Cherokee president of the First National Bank of Muskogee, told an Indian Territory reporter what the real outcome of the bill would be: "The Bill is what is apparent on its face—a drastic political measure, intending and accomplishing the utter destruction of the tribal governments of the Indian Territory." The elderly Too-qua-stee agreed, although he voiced his objections in more eloquent terms:

> Now, while it is not unreasonable to imagine that the effects of such a dereliction could really pervade the congressional membership to much extent, it is nevertheless pretty certain that, in the Indian Committee of the lower house, where the bill originated, it provided to be the occasion for giving the measure more clearly something of the nature of a penal sentence. . . . It had not the moral courage to repudiate, in terms, all the treaties with the Cherokees; it simply proceeded as if they never existed.[40]

Over and above its many stipulations for the individual development of former tribal land (which covered, in the federal statutes, nearly twenty-five pages of text), the core of Charles Curtis's most prized legislation was tribal destruction. The devices were the unilateral abrogation of tribal courts and tribal law and the implementation of federal authority over all residents of Indian Territory, regardless of race or previous tribal affiliation. The act that prompted Curtis to boast that he had done more for Oklahoma Indians than any other legislator in Washington was, as one Oklahoma historian has recently suggested, "a sort of organic act for Indian Territory." Similarly, a scholar of federal Indian policy has described the Curtis Act as "practically an organic act for the establishment of the long-sought territorial government," the instrument that laid the groundwork for Oklahoma's statehood less than a decade later.[41]

Neither historian, however, commented on what it meant for *individual* Indians. After nearly a decade of practical experience under the Curtis Act, Too-qua-stee addressed this question. In Washington, this time to testify on why it was impossible to survive on a governmental allotment, the Cherokee sage asked: "What am I to do? I have a piece of property that doesn't support me, and is not worth a cent to me, under the same inexorable, cruel provisions of the Curtis law that swept away our treaties, our system of nationality, our very existence. . . . I think, gentlemen, when you investigate the case fully you will find that these people have been put off with a piece of land that is absolutely inadequate for their needs.''[42]

10
Easy Allotment

The decade and a half in which Charles Curtis served as a congressman from Kansas, 1892 to 1907, was a difficult time for most Native Americans in Indian Territory. Like the more populous Five Civilized Tribes, the Cheyennes, Arapahos, Kiowas, Comanches, Pawnees, Tonkawas, Poncas, Otoes, Missouris, Kaws, Osages, and Wichita and Affiliated Tribes fell under the allotment hammer during the period, and a massive amount of former tribal land was soon appropriated by non-Indians. On the Indian side, difficult problems arose in regard to alienation, taxation, interest on debts, town development, the leasing of mineral resources, and especially, inheritance rights. As a member and then as chairman of the Indian Committee in the House, Curtis was involved with all of the tribes, but his greatest attention was directed toward the Five Civilized Tribes—clearly, the most obstinate when confronted with sectioning off their communal lands.

By the time the allotment rolls of the Five Civilized Tribes were closed in 1906, 101,506 individuals had been enrolled, including 1,572 full-blood whites who had married into the tribes, and a massive number of mixed-bloods with varying quantums of Indian blood. The best estimate of the time was that there were only about 18,000 full-bloods in all of Indian Territory in 1906, most of whom refused to have anything to do with allotment, even though individual lands had been assigned to them by the Dawes Commission. Nevertheless, a number of congressmen sought to eliminate all distinctions between full- and mixed-bloods on the important question of land alienation and thus to make the allotments free game for all. Curtis opposed this strenuously, and in a bill that he sponsored in 1906, he succeeded in retaining the restriction that the full-bloods could not alienate their allotments without the government's approval for a period of twenty-five years.[1]

Curtis's action was a strong reminder that mixed-bloods enjoyed a commanding lead over the full-bloods in terms of their capacity to deal with individual property, and as expected, he articulated a vitriolic response to an amendment that contemplated the obliteration of any distinction between the two native groups. Citing his personal acquaintance with Chitto Harjo, the recalcitrant full-blood leader of the Crazy Snake band of Creeks whose more than two thousand members had refused allotment, Curtis recalled how, in a personal audience with President William McKinley, the Creek leader had vented his opposition "against all treaties and agreements of any kind." Harjo's followers, Curtis insisted, required as much supervision as the most primitive blanket Indian of the high plains, "and certainly the gentlemen [of the House] will not say that members of the Crazy Snake band are fit to handle their own business and that all restrictions should be removed from their hands."[2]

The amendment was easily defeated. Even Congressman John Lacy of Iowa, who wanted to distribute all tribal funds without considering the blood quantum or the degree of assimilation, conceded that Curtis's "knowledge of the situation down there [in Indian country] is worth a great deal to all of us." Six months later, in the legislative maneuvering that led to the passage of the Burke Act, Curtis played an important role as well, and in the Osage enrollment hearings of 1908 his intricate knowledge of the social and genetic relationships between the several tribes of northern Oklahoma was instrumental in the defeat of a few proposals to add names to the final Osage allotment roll.[3]

During the Osage hearings, Curtis vigorously supported the federal courts as the only proper place for dealing with allotment appeals and the determination of legal tribal membership, as opposed to legislative fiat and/or the rulings of the Department of the Interior. As an attorney by profession, this was to be expected. But for Curtis it was also a very personal matter that dated back to 1878, when he and his sister had been dropped from the Kaw roll upon the recommendation of the Kaw agent Cyrus Beede. The reason given then was that he and his sister had refused to reside with the Kaw tribe on their new reservation in Indian Territory. But because other mixed-bloods and even some no-bloods (or squaw men) who did establish their residence on the reservation had also been dropped from the roll, other considerations were obviously involved.[4]

Heading the list of considerations was the shocking numerical decline of the tribe after 1873, especially among the full-bloods, and how this downward trend had affected the tribe as a whole. The total number of Kaws who had moved onto the reservation in June 1873 was 523—of which approximately 10 percent were mixed-bloods. The move was no trail of tears, and the Kaw agent Mahlon Stubbs happily reported:

Soon after arriving at this place the half-breeds selected home-steads, built cabins, and moved into them, and have fenced from five to forty acres and planted corn. . . . All the half-breeds and a number of Indians have traded ponies, or other articles, for hogs, and will, in a short time, with proper encouragement, raise their own meat. A day-school for the half-breed children was kept up four months, with an average attendance of twenty. Religious meetings and Sabbath-school have been kept up at the agency regularly since its establishment here . . . at which we have generally found a willingness to hear gospel truths.[5]

Stubbs complained about Indians who were committing depreda-tions against other Indians, and he requested that a native police force be established to prevent such activity. On an even more somber note, he called for a law to prevent white men from taking small parties of Indians through the eastern states and abroad for show and quick profits. Fifteen Kaw full-bloods had been hired to engage in such demeaning activity during the spring of 1873; they were gone from the reservation for nearly a year. "They were cheated out of part of their wages," complained Stubbs, "and came down with syphilis, which is now spreading rapidly through the tribe and doing incalculable damage."[6]

As late as 1886, it had been reported that the mixed-bloods, with scarcely any exceptions, were free from venereal infections, and hence it was the full-bloods who suffered the brunt of the deadly contagion. By 1880 the tribe had been reduced to 300, consisting of 250 full-bloods and 50 mixed-bloods. One year later, the mixed-blood population had remained constant, but another 50 full-bloods had died. The Kaw agent reported: "Most of the full-bloods are diseased, and traces of their common enemy is plainly noticed, even among the children. Their habits are against them and from chronic disease and disappointment they have lost their courage and now look to the Great Father like children, confidently expecting that all their wants will be supplied."[7]

Not surprisingly, the full-bloods were disturbed about the increas-ing ratio of mixed-bloods among their ranks, especially about the prospect of having the mixed-bloods receive a greater amount of land should the reservation be allotted. The political power in the tribe was shifting into the hands of the mixed-blood faction as well; and this caused the full-bloods to pressure their agent to maintain a better balance between the two factions. Dating back to the mid 1870s, similar pressure from the neighboring Osages and other tribes of the Central Superintendency had finally prompted Superintendent William Nichol-son to order that "no citizen of the United States can claim, by virtue of adoption into any Indian tribe or by intermarriage with a member of

The Kaw full-bloods Josiah Reece and Bacumjah, his wife, in traditional dress about 1895. Courtesy of the Kansas State Historical Society.

any tribe [of the Superintendency], the right to receive either rations or annuities due to said tribe." The Kaw agent Cyrus Beede further recommended that the right of membership in the Kaw and Osage tribes be more explicitly defined and "that a provision be made by law for ridding the Indian country of men (whether possessed of Indian blood or not) who persist in leading the Indians off the reservation." Beede was also concerned about the liquor traffic across the border into Kansas, and he singled out several mixed-bloods for their involvement in the traffic. The mixed-bloods were also fomenting political strife, which seemed to be playing into the hands of the government's forced allotment program.[8]

By the time that Charles and Elizabeth Curtis were dropped from the tribal roll in 1878, the Kaws were irrevocably divided into mixed-blood and full-blood bands. The full-blood leadership that had tried to direct affairs on the Council Grove reservation in Kansas was disintegrating and was being replaced by what the Indian Office recognized as four distinct bands: the full-blood Picayune, Kaholas, and Rock Creeks bands and the dramatically increasing "Half-Breed" band. At stake was not only the 100,141-acre reservation that only recently had been purchased from the Osages but also the income from the sale of more than 200,000 acres of former reservation land in Kansas. Understandably, then, the mixed-bloods and the no-bloods who had been dropped from the tribal roll were concerned about their nontribal status, particularly because there appeared to be no recourse for judicial appeal.[9]

"General" W. E. Hardy's response to the purging of the Kaw roll in 1878 is a good illustration of the challenge that the purge posed. Born a full-blood white in 1815, Hardy was employed by the American Fur Company, and in 1845 he was working for the Chouteau brothers at Kawsmouth. As a purchasing agent, he made regular visits to Frederick Chouteau's trading post at the Mission Creek villages west of present-day Topeka, and it was here that he met Joseph Vertafault, a French trader also in the employ of the American Fur Company at Kawsmouth, who was to become his father-in-law.[10]

As was the case with other Kansa mixed-bloods, the consequent social relationships were complex. Vertafault had married Elizabeth Carboneau, one of the twenty-three half-bloods who had been awarded a section of land under the 1825 treaty. She and her younger brother Pierre, also a recipient of a half-blood reserve, were the children of Ahsingah, a full-blood Kansa female and Pierre Brisa, an independent French trader who sometimes used the surname Revalette. Apparently, Brisa was a roving man; therefore, as infants, Elizabeth and Pierre were placed in the home of Pierre Carboneau at Kawsmouth and took the name of Carboneau, instead of Brisa. The younger Pierre died in infancy, so that Elizabeth and her husband, Joseph Vertafault, became legal heirs to more than twelve hundred acres of half-blood land not far from the tracts awarded to Julie Gonville and her sister in 1825. Then, in 1834 or 1835, Ahsingah had borne a third child, Wahshungah. Brisa may have been the father; if so, Wahshungah would also have been a mixed-blood—even though in later years the majority of the Kaw tribe viewed him as a full-blood. General Hardy, who married Elizabeth and Joseph Vertafault's daughter Victoria in 1860, was certain that Wahshungah was a mixed-blood, as is evident in an affidavit that he prepared in order to guarantee the future leadership of the Kaw tribe in 1911. Hardy testified:

> That he was well acquainted with Joe Vertafault and his family, for they were both employed by the "American Fur Company,"; That Elizabeth Vertafault was the wife of Joe Vertafault; That he at this time made the acquaintance of Washunga's mother and was well acquainted with her for years, but her Indian name he cannot recall; Ah-sing/gah, he thinks was her name. But as to her name he is not absolutely positive; That Elizabeth Vertafault and Washungah were brother and sister [not *half* brother or *half* sister]; That Ah-sing-gah held out and claimed Elizabeth and Washungah to be her children . . . and they were so accepted by the Tribe.[11]

Hardy, who had moved south with the tribe to the Indian Territory reservation and had continued to live with his quarter-blood wife, Victoria, until her death in 1901, nevertheless had been dropped from the tribal rolls in the same year that Charles and Elizabeth Curtis had been expelled. Wahshungah, however, had remained on the roll, claiming full-blood status and cultivating a following among both the mixed-bloods and the full-bloods that by the turn of the century contributed to his emergence as the principal leader of the Kaws. In the meantime, Hardy and his wife had successfully litigated a suit against several other mixed-bloods who claimed ownership of the 640-acre tract that had been awarded to Elizabeth Carboneau Vertafault in 1825. By the late 1870s, then, Hardy and Elizabeth's only other surviving child, Pay-lage, were sole heirs to that tract and the one that had been awarded to Elizabeth's brother Pierre in 1825. On the other hand, because of being ousted from the tribe, Hardy could no longer share in the annuity distribution that he had been receiving since 1860, when he had married Victoria Vertafault.[12]

Clearly, Hardy was determined to obtain his share of the Kaw tribal estate. In his affidavit he also testified that he had served as the official secretary of the tribe since 1867 and that by an action of "the Chiefs and Braves," he had retained this important position after the tribe had been relocated. He had been with the tribe since 1858 and had even taught in their government school from 1858 to 1860.[13]

On 4 February 1881, Hardy seized the initiative. In a blunt letter to Secretary of the Interior Samuel J. Kirkwood, Hardy had demanded that he be immediately restored to the Kaw tribal roll. "The full bloods of the tribe deny my rights," he complained, "notwithstanding the fact that former Superintendent of Indian Affairs Enoch Hoag and Agent Mahlon Stubbs agreed at the time of removal [to the Indian Territory] that I and other members for whom I speak should be recognized as members of the tribe &c." In a letter to the Osage agent Laban Miles in Pawhuska, where local jurisdiction over the Kaws had been established, the Indian commissioner Hiram Price rejected Hardy's demand on the grounds that Hardy had failed to provide specific reasons for his reinstatement, that he had failed to indicate his Indian-blood quantum, and that he had failed to explain why he had been dropped from the roll in the first place.[14]

Agent Miles was opposed to Hardy's being reinstated, although Miles reported that Hardy was married to a mixed-blood Kaw woman and had been living with her and the tribe for some time. Commissioner Price, who was opposed to having full-blood whites enjoy tribal subsidies and legal rights "unless they were the 'right' kind of white men," modified his position: he took the view that Hardy might indeed measure up to a civilizing responsibility on the reservation. He therefore ordered that the final decision be left to the tribe itself, "expressed in council and in such a manner as may be customary among them in settling their tribal affairs, a certificate of which must accompany the roll if he [Hardy] appears thereon."[15]

Thus the stage was set for a confrontation over the power of the mixed-bloods to control the affairs of the Kaws and, more specifically, over the reinstatement of Curtis and Hardy. But they were not alone. In fact, at least thirty additional mixed-bloods or no-bloods had been dropped in 1878, and by the early 1880s, they were exerting pressure to return to the fold. With Hardy as their leader, a petition for "re-enrollment" was presented to Miles on 13 September 1883, under the signatures of Little Louis Pappan, Benjamin Fronkier, and Joseph James—all mixed-bloods. Former "treaty chiefs" and the full-bloods Nopawarra and Allegahwahu also penned their Xs on the document, as did Wahshungah, Hardy's chief spokesman from within. Of the thirty individuals who were requesting admission, Hardy's name was the twenty-fifth on the list, and among the six who were designated as "not here at present" were "Libby and Charley Curtis."[16]

Although blood quantum, the right to receive governmental payments, and a stake in the Indian Territory reservation were important factors in the 1878 expulsion, the land issue in Kansas was equally critical. Under the 1872 appraisal, the sale of Kaw trust lands in the Neosho valley had languished, and by 1876 only 3,023 of the more than 200,000 acres had been sold. With pressure exerted on all sides—from the Osages, who demanded payment for the reservation that had been sold to the Kaws; from Eastern investors, who had speculated in Kaw land scrip; from traders, who had extended too much credit at Council Grove; and from the government itself, which had advanced funds for surveys, emergency stores, and the cost of removal itself—the Indian Office insisted that the only alternative was a new, a lower, appraisal. But to this the full-bloods were opposed. The government then turned to the mixed-bloods and to Wahshungah. The technique that was used is reminiscent of the 1825 treaty and is well documented in a letter marked "private," written by Uriah Spray, a Quaker teacher at the Kaw Agency, to agent Beede, in May 1877 (quoted unedited):

> I have been talking the affair of reappraising the Kaw lands to the Chief and some of his men. I think we can induce them to sign the bill. Jo Jim, Big and Little Louis Pappan, Chief Washungah, Shagainha, Isawiah: I think are willing if thee favour the plan. I will bring those men over to talk with thee and if it will do for them to sign in the absence of their people it can be done this way. Elickmahu has not been consulted as we know will raise a row as he has always stood to it they were to have 600 thousand dollars for their lands: My own opinion is we had best use a little stratigens in order to get this signature with the exception of him they will all ring in; we had best settle the affair soon if it does not suit to bring them over: Thee could come here as I should like to have thy assistance and support in obtaining this as I think desired object.
>
> Very respectfully,
> Uriah Spray
>
> P.S. I have my doubts whether they would sign in the presence of their people but are willing to take our advise in the case please give me thy opinion.[17]

The "stratigens" might very well have worked had they not been compromised by Miles's expulsion of the mixed-bloods a few months later, including several who had agreed to "ring in." In the meantime, an election for a new tribal council was demanded on the basis of a petition submitted by the mixed-bloods who had been expelled. It was held on the reservation on 16 November 1883, and of the tribal total of

265 (including 50 mixed-bloods), 225 votes were actually cast. The outcome was a surprising victory for the full-bloods. By-passing Wah-shungah and his followers, those who voted chose Keboshliku (44 votes), as the principal chief, and as councillors, Pahhanegahli (42 votes), Nehujohinkah (39 votes), Benjamin Fronkier (38 votes), and Keboshliku Kahola (29 votes). Hardy and the mixed-blood petitioners had been dealt a severe but, as it turned out, not fatal blow.[18]

Members of the new tribal council took office on 4 January 1884 and were to serve until the next election one year later. This election, however, was deferred until 19 March 1885, mainly because in the meantime, General Hardy had gone to Washington to file a complaint regarding fraud in the election of 1883. On official governmental stationery, apparently supplied by the Indian Office, Hardy insisted that only "100 or 102 votes had been cast in 1883 and that Wahshungah and the old and recognized chiefs and braves" had been elected by a slight majority. In fact, claimed Hardy, Wahshungah and his group were declared "elected" by the Kaw agent, but two weeks later it was learned that Agent Miles in Pawhuska had officially sanctioned Keboshliku and the full-bloods as the official council. "I come here as a representative of the Kaw tribe," declared Hardy, "to protect against any further recognition of this said fraudulent council and to ask that the old treaty chiefs and braves be recognized as constituting the only court or tribunal of the Kaw other than what is derived from and through the Government of the United States."[19]

Whether Curtis was aware of Hardy's trip to Washington is not known. At the time, Curtis was county attorney in Topeka and was fully aware that he had been dropped from the Kaw roll. He certainly knew Hardy, who on several occasions referred to Curtis as "my Charley" and once as his grandson—a Kaw custom that indicated close affection of an elder for a younger member of the tribe. And it is certain that Curtis was determined to get back on the Kaw roll. Years later, after Curtis had gone to Congress, the Republican notable Cy Leland wrote: "Curtis was an Indian. He represents Shawnee County and the Indians, and his only use for Shawnee County is to help him get this graft on the Indians. Why for years he has spent one-third of his time with his relatives of the Kaw Tribe in the Indian Territory. He is making a good thing out of it."[20]

The fact is that Hardy's complaint to Commissioner Hiram Price was a fabrication, for the official tally that agent Miles submitted to the Indian Office on 16 November indicated that Wahshungah and the mixed-bloods had been soundly defeated. For the future, however, it really did not matter. Hardy and the mixed-bloods had made it abundantly clear they were receptive to allotment and that they were

Seated is Sojumwah, aged seventy-two, the oldest surviving Kaw full-blood in 1925. To the left is A. W. Stubbs, the son of the former Kaw agent Mahlon Stubbs; to the right is the Kaw full-blood Barclay Delano, aged fifty-seven. The photograph was probably made at Council Grove, Kansas, at the commemoration of the hundredth anniversary of the Kansa Treaty of 1825. Courtesy of the Kansas State Historical Society.

more than willing to negotiate a quick settlement over the lands in Kansas. Moreover, disease was continuing to take a frightening toll among the full-bloods, so that by the turn of the century, there remained only 97 out of a tribal total of 217. No record has survived to indicate whether an official investigation was made of Hardy's spurious charge, but because the government soon reinstated all mixed-bloods except the half dozen who were not permanent residents of the reservation, his action accomplished his goal. In the Kaw tribal election of 19 March 1885, Wahshungah was returned to office, and the pendulum of power had swung back in favor of the mixed-bloods.[21]

In 1880, two years after Curtis had been dropped from the tribal roll, the acting commissioner of Indian affairs, C. W. Holcomb, informed agent Stubbs that Stubbs and Superintendent Enoch Hoag had exceeded their authority in promising citizens of the United States equal rights with members of the Kaw tribe and that Beede had done the right thing in dropping individuals such as Curtis from the roll. "Persons not Indians," said Holcomb, could not have any legal status unless they had been explicitly adopted by the tribal authorities or had been made legal members by treaty or a special act of Congress. Those who had married and were living with their spouses on the reservation could remain there, but only "if their presence there was not detrimental to the peace and welfare of said Indians."[22]

Confident that the mixed-bloods were sympathetic to his cause, on 1 June 1888, Charles Curtis submitted an application for himself and his sister "to be enrolled as Kaw Indians." The Indian Office in Washington communicated the application to the Osage Agency in Pawhuska, along with instructions to obtain "such information as you might have on the applicants in question"; and within a year, agent Miles had enrolled the two as legal Kaw Indians. Whether Miles consulted with the Kaw Council is not known, but with Wahshungah and his group in power, the outcome was not in doubt. In a 1903 interview with a Kaw City newspaper, Hardy stated that Curtis was voted into tribal membership just before the 1902 allotment bill was passed; so it may have been that agent Miles acted on the Curtis application without consulting the tribal council in 1881.[23]

As a legal Kaw Indian in Congress, Curtis displayed no great interest in the difficult circumstances of the full-bloods, nor was he concerned that the best reservation lands had been preempted by the mixed-bloods. With other so-called progressive legislators, he supported the awarding of large pasture leases to non-Indians, leases that payed low rental fees and discouraged the traditionalists from farming and competing with the more aggressive mixed-bloods. Curtis was interested in railroads, towns, natural resources, allotment, and—

always—the political gains that he could derive from his contacts in Indian Territory.[24]

As chairman of the House Committee on Expenditures in the Interior Department, for example, his correspondence provides interesting details of the "Indian business" south of Kansas. Writing to his close friend the Indian commissioner W. A. Jones in 1897, Curtis reported,

> I have just returned from a trip to the Osage Reservation. At Greyhorse there are about four hundred Indians, mostly full bloods, who trade at the stores at that place. There are two stores, one run by Florer and Stick and the other by Huffaker. These gentlemen are Republicans and I am reliably informed contributed to the Republican campaign in the 3rd Kansas Dist. and in the O.T. At Hominy there are about two hundred Indians, mostly full bloods, who trade at the stores, there are three traders Price & Co. who are Democrats, Reed and Pabst, Republicans, and who contributed to the campaign fund mentioned above. There is a new trader there by the name of Smith, who has goods in a tent and I understand intends to build. I am informed he is a Republican. . . . I hope you will not disturb the Republican traders, as they are all active and have helped out in Kansas and Okla. Ter. I wrote you some time ago about Mr. Hiatt, a Republican and you answered Sept. 14. I would like to see him have a license and as Sander & Co. have not had their's renewed why cannot he be substituted for them?[25]

Curtis also informed Jones that many Indians were making their selections of land and that he had advised them to do so "until every one of them had a home." But on the Kaw reservation, the full-bloods remained opposed to allotment, and there was the further problem of the Dawes legislation as it related to the Kaws. Section 8 of the General Allotment Act excluded the Osages from allotment, and because the Kaws had purchased their lands from the Osages, who in turn had purchased them from the Cherokees, who also were excluded from the Dawes settlement, the government was obliged to use other means to secure a division of the Kaw reservation. As a device to prevent litigation in the future, the government established allotment commissions to negotiate contracts with the excluded tribes: the Dawes Commission was to deal with the Five Tribes; and the Jerome Commission was to deal with the Osages, Kaws, Pawnees, Tonkawas, and Otoe-Missouris. The latter commission was headed by a former governor of Michigan, David H. Jerome; its other members were Alfred M. Wilson and Warren G. Sayre.[26]

Beginning on 23 June 1893 the commission visited the Osage Agency for nearly a month, but with no success, and in the meantime, it sounded out the Kaws on allotment. One report had it that the Kaws would negotiate only if their Osage "brothers" did so as well, whereas another indicated that the Kaws might come to an agreement on their own. In 1903, however, a year after allotment had been made final, a local newspaper recalled: "At the time [in 1902] the sentiment against allotment was almost unanimous, both among the full and mixed factions. Any persons even talking allotment was considered an enemy to the best interests of the tribe."[27]

How, then, was allotment carried out with so little difficulty in 1902, fully four years before the Osages capitulated to the Jerome Commission? How was it that a tribe that was divided between 97 full-bloods and 120 mixed-bloods would soon be singled out as a model of easy allotment and acquiescence to the government's program of tribal dissolution? Any why was it that as early as December 1900, Commissioner Jones said to a delegation of Kaws in Washington: "I wish to say to you that it is a very novel experience to me to have Indians come here and ask to have their land taken in allotments. Usually Indians come here and protest against allotments, but wish to have their tribal relations maintained. It tends to show what a wonderful progress toward civilization your people have made, and I am very glad to find it out, and I wish to encourage you as much as possible."[28] Jones, who was Indian commissioner from 1897 to 1904, certainly was no friend of the reservation system. In 1902 he described it as having been "conceived in iniquity" and as being "vicious in practice." Indians simply could not be "civilized" until they looked and behaved like white men. He therefore issued directives that required Indians to obtain licenses from their agents before getting married and to have young Indian boys shorn of their braids and given short haircuts, similar to white youths. No Indians were to participate in public exhibitions that in any manner recalled what Jones viewed as the "barbaric glories" of their past. Blankets and traditional garb were to be discouraged, as were the painting of faces and traditional dances, which Jones characterized as "subterfuges to cover degrading acts and to disguise immoral purposes." Agents who were sympathetic to the acceleration of the allotment program, particularly among the more recalcitrant tribes, were to be appointed; and Republican congressmen who needed political accommodation could expect Jones to place their valued friends in unclassified positions in the Indian Office bureaucracy or to give them lucrative contracts for governmental services to the Indians.[29]

"The request of a Senator goes a great way in the department," Jones admitted on one occasion. A memo in this vein—of which there were many—was penned to Congressman Charles Curtis in September 1902: "I have a vacancy here paying $1,000, but had hoped that you could give me a man with some little legal training. But if Mrs. Bland is a good copyist I can use her; if not, I would prefer that you send a man for the position. . . . As soon as I hear from her I will endeavor to have the appointment made, especially as it seems to be of interest to you in your campaign."[30]

Through Jones, Curtis was also instrumental in getting Oscar A. Mitscher appointed to replace William A. Pollack as the Kaw/Osage agent in 1900. Mitscher, a firm champion of allotment who recalled that "after being on the reservation a short time I came to the conclusion that it would be best for the Indian and best for Oklahoma to open this land for settlement," was expected to succeed where the Jerome Commission had failed in 1893. Once in office, he proved to both Jones and Curtis that he could operate well behind the scenes, a style that was clearly agreeable to Curtis. With General Hardy as the secretary of the tribe, with Wahshun-gah as the tribal "governor" under an alleged lifetime appointment in 1899 by no less a person than Secretary of the Interior Hitchcock, and with Charles Curtis as the architect who was operating from the power base of the House Committee on Indian Affairs, the expeditious allotment of the Kaw reservation was virtually guaranteed.[31]

By contrast to the situation among the Osages, where the mixed-bloods were viewed with disdain because they "lie around . . . instead of being a help to their less fortunate tribesmen," mixed-blood Curtis was determined to vidicate his type not only to his less-blessed Kaw and Osage brethren but to the outside world as well. Thus, from 1898 through 1902 he demonstrated his political power and the finer techniques of easy allotment.[32]

Curtis spent the first six months of 1898 guiding through Congress his bill, which was signed into law on 28 June. Then he went back to Kansas and to the Kaw reservation in late November, where the situation was anything but encouraging. With winter approaching, many of the Indians were suffering because of a lack of adequate clothing, and some were on the verge of starvation. As the result of a hasty meeting with the Kaw Council, a memorial to the Indian Office in Washington was drawn up, requesting "that all monies accrued to us as annuities or [grants] be placed to the credit of our Agent and distributed per capita to us as soon as possible." Back in Washington by early December, Curtis wrote to Commissioner Jones: "I visited this Tribe several weeks ago and am wholly satisfied that quite a number of them are in very needy circumstances. Hoping you will grant the request of the Council, I am, Yours very truly, Chas. Curtis." The setting for more concerted action was thus established.[33]

The interest on Kaw annuities had dwindled drastically, and the annual income from the thirteen pastures amounted to less than three cents an acre. No settlement had been reached in regard to the reservation lands in Kansas, and there seemed to be no prospect for a settlement in the immediate future. In February 1899 a Muskogee newspaper reported that Wahshungah, Little Louis Pappan, Hardy, and an unidentified chief had boarded a train in Arkansas City for Washington, "to see the great father on the subject of selling their lands." Hardy claimed that the action was to the entire satisfaction of the tribe, but it was an unauthorized trip, and it apparently was never completed.[34]

Curtis returned to the reservation in the late summer of 1900, fully determined to move ahead with allotment. Under his guidance, the Kaw Council unanimously passed a resolution requesting that Wahshungah, councilman Forrest Chouteau, interpreter Achan Pappan, and W. E. Hardy be allowed to visit Washington, at the tribe's expense, to discuss "certain interests peculiar to the Kaw Tribe both of land and money." The request was quickly granted after Curtis personally endorsed the resolution to Commissioner Jones on 10 September.[35]

On the reservation, Mitscher executed his part in the plan with dispatch. He forwarded a petition, which allegedly was from the tribe as a whole, to Washington, and in late October, Secretary Hitchcock granted approval for the visit. By late December, the group was in the nation's capital, where Congressman Curtis had planned its itinerary. In company with Curtis and in full traditional dress, Washungah met with President McKinley and made speeches before Secretary Hitchcock and Commissioner Jones. The speech to Hitchcock was not recorded, but to Jones, Wahshungah stated that he wanted 160 acres for each of his children, with the remaining land "to make a settlement with the government." Wahshungah complained: "There have been so many treaties made . . . and we ought to be rich, but we are not. My people are now in debt and I would like to have you help them out." Then, in a direct reference to Curtis, Wahshungah stated: "I have been wanting to come here a long time, and now I am glad that I am here. I have always said, when asked to come, that we had one of our own men here to represent us who would do all that could be done for us." With an understanding smile, Commissioner Jones agreed: "Your matters have been carefully looked after by your representative in Congress."[36]

This meeting was followed by one with Vice-President-Elect Theodore Roosevelt, who suggested that the Kaws be granted blanket citizenship regardless of acculturation and that this very important "test case" be used as a model for future tribal allotments. When the delegation returned to the reservation in mid January, however, support for allotment had deteriorated dramatically. One source has suggested that the meeting in Washington was "difficult to assess" but that the visit seems to have been "the proper prelude to events of the next three years." In fact, the trouble was over the premature and arbitrary selection of allotments. Mitscher reported in 1901 that nearly all of the Kaws had made their selections, and later that same year, the governor of Oklahoma Territory proudly reported that "the Kaws are anxious for allotment and have asked for it" as a tribe. But trouble over the selections had been brewing well in advance of the delegation's visit to Washington.[37]

As early as August 1901, Curtis reported that there was much trouble over Hardy's continuing to act as tribal secretary and that the problem was over his role in the selection of allotments. Hardy had threatened to resign, said Curtis, "but it would be wise to keep him on until after the selections are made." Then followed a letter to the Indian Office marked "Personal," in which Curtis insisted that because many of the Kaws could neither read nor write English, it was essential to retain Hardy and grant Wahshungah's request for an immediate return trip to Washington. Wahshungah, through Hardy, had written to Curtis: "I made up my mind long ago to travel the white man's road but I can't go without help—Now my Grandchild, you must get me help, some Police and an Interpreter." Another letter followed in early 1902, again in Hardy's words, in which Wahshungah emphasized the proper strategy to be followed: "My Dear Friend—I very much prefer a delegation to go to Washington rather than attempt a settlement here, for to submit matters here would only delay our purpose—So I ask that a delegation of 7 representative Kaw Indians be allowed to come and treat with the Government for the final disposition of our matters."[38]

From this point onward, Curtis provided the basic direction of Kaw life for the future. Allotment was absolutely essential for the development of farms, towns, railroads, mineral production, and the ushering in of the new dispensation. Agent Mitscher cooperated to the utmost. On 14 January 1902, he signed an agreement granting the Blackwell, Enid and Southwestern Railway a right of way across the reservation. By then, a subsidiary of the Santa Fe had completed plans for a line from Newkirk, just west of the reservation, to Pauls Valley, south of Oklahoma City. Oil had been struck on the nearby Osage lands, and Curtis was well entrenched with Standard Oil and the ITIO. Land values were appreciating, and Kay County, adjacent to the reservation, was reporting the highest land values in all of Indian Territory. On 21 January, Curtis hand-picked the allotment delegation that was to go to Washington, assuring Commissioner Jones "that the various elements in the tribe will be fully represented." But this was hardly the case. Included in Curtis's list were Wahshungah, Forrest Chouteau, Wahonokoeke, William Hardy (General Hardy's son), Mitchel Fronkier, Achan Pappan (interpreter), and of course, the council secretary, General Hardy. With the exception of Wahonokoeke and perhaps Chouteau, the delegation was sympathetic to the immediate division of the reservation.[39]

In fact, the agreement had been prepared in advance by Curtis and Mitscher and as drafted by them, it was signed without change by the delegation on 8 February and was made into law the following 1 July. Each of the 247 individuals who were listed on the final allotment roll received a 160-acre homestead, plus an equal share of the surplus land and of the annuity funds that remained in the tribal accounts. In addition, each would also share equally in a future settlement for the former reservation lands in Kansas. A quarter section was reserved for the agency headquarters, school, cemetery, and an eighty-acre town site near the agency headquarters, appropriately named Washungah. Unlike the Dawes legislation, this act permitted the immediate leasing of allotments, but allotments could not be taxed until the allottees had been declared competent by the secretary of the interior.[40]

Curtis, it will be recalled, had been returned to the Kaw roll by the agent Laban Miles in 1889. While this qualified Curtis for rations, schooling, annuity interest, and the like, his reinstatement did not automatically attach his name to the allotment roll. Yet, Curtis was granted an allotment, as were his sister and her husband. Curtis's three minor children were also placed on the roll, so that with his children's homesteads and surplus lands, Curtis was the owner of 1,676 acres of Kaw land in 1902. And with his children's share, he received $22,136 from the settlement over the Kansas lands in 1904.[41]

Curtis may have sought a Kaw allotment as much for the political prestige and vindication of the mixed-bloods as for immediate economic gain. His close association with Commissioner William A. Jones points in the former direction. Responding to the expansion of the plenary power to allot reservations without tribal approval, which on 5 January 1903 was upheld by the Supreme Court in *Lone Wolf* v. *Hitchcock,* Jones approvingly told the House Indian Committee, ''Supposing you were the guardian or ward of a child 8 or 10 years of age, would you ask the consent of a child to the investment of its funds? No; you would not.'' Why, then, should not a distinguished mixed-blood such as Curtis be applauded for having led—indeed, pushed—his childlike brethren along the road to progress? After all, as Frederick Hoxie has recently pointed out, allotment programs after *Lone Wolf* were no longer shackled by the assumption that native ownership was guaranteed by treaties or traditions of the past. Congress could initiate the destruction of reservations and ''would no longer be insulated in their responsibilities by layers of bureaucracy.'' Curtis, in effect, had accomplished precisely that.[42]

The Kaw Allotment Commission in 1902. Standing, left to right: *eighth-blood William Hardy; half-blood interpreter for the commission, Achan Pappan; quarter-blood Mitchell Fronkier; no-blood secretary for the Kaws, "General" W. E. Hardy.* Seated, left to right: *full-blood Forrest Chouteau; full-blood Wahonokoeke; full-blood(?) Wahshungah; the Kaw agent O. A. Mitscher. Courtesy of the Archives and Manuscripts Division of the Oklahoma Historical Society.*

For his part, General Hardy worried about having Curtis function openly as an Indian in national political life. Hardy—himself an allottee, as were his quarter-blood wife and their six children—said as much in an interview in the Guthrie newspaper on 14 September 1903, which was reprinted in a Wichita paper on the following day. Three days later, Hardy's admission of Curtis's good fortune appeared in the Kaw City newspaper, under the headline, "Curtis Gets Allotments: He and His Children Accounted Indians." Said the no-blood Kaw secretary:

> Since Curtis had been in congress he had done great things for the Indian, not only the Kaws, but the Indian everywhere, whenever an opportunity offered. When the Kaw lands were allotted the general council of the tribe voted unanimously to place his name on the Kaw rolls of citizenship, together with those of his children, allowing him to share equally with us our land. In this manner we made him an honorary member of the tribe and only in part repaid him for the work he has done for the Indians.[43]

With obvious pride, Hardy also described Curtis as a quarter-blood and as his beloved nephew. But between the Guthrie interview and the statement that appeared in the Kaw City paper, Hardy came to regret his candor. Curtis may have scolded him in the meantime, for the Kansas congressman was then trying to recover from the defeat he had experienced in his quest for the Republican senatorial nomination at the Wichita convention earlier that year. In any case, Hardy demanded a retraction, which was printed in the same issue of the Kaw paper that carried the Guthrie interview. Titled "Bogus 'Thunder,'" it read:

> Gen. W. E. Hardy informs us that the above purported interview is purely bogus and that he gave no interview whatever to the *Wichita Daily Eagle* reporter. He also states that the statement showing Curtis and his family as owning 1,800 acres of fine bottom land in the Kaw Reservation is wholly without foundation and did not come from him. This report was concocted and published to be used as political thunder against Congressman Curtis.[44]

Hardy's attempted retraction failed to mention that the *Eagle* story was a verbatim account of the original Guthrie interview, nor did he mention that in Guthrie he had gone so far as to label the allotment bill as the Curtis Act. But a greater threat to publicity regarding Kaw allotment was Wahshungah. His name had been given to the first town on the former reservation. Both of his adopted children, Lucy and Emmett Tayiah, were given allotments, and he himself was appointed a lifetime chief by Secretary Hitchcock. On the surface, Wahshungah appeared to be jovial and outspoken, and he seemed to enjoy his status as one of the most powerful full-bloods. In Washington at the time of the allotment talks, he joked with President Roosevelt and later told a reporter that he was 207 years old. In Arkansas City, in company with a fellow tribesman, Charlie Red Horse, he was observed charging "five dollars a head" to shake hands with the wives of a group of Shriners who were traveling from Chicago to Texas—after which the two were seen heading for a local bar to purchase "some of that joy-producing beverage." L. A. Smith, the prominent cigar manufacturer, jumped on the bandwagon by naming his finest product "The Washungah," and Smith delighted the Kaw dignitary no end by placing the chief's photograph, with cigar in mouth, on each box containing the popular cigars. "Old Wash," as his fellow Kaws and close associates called him, was becoming a legend in his own time.[45]

Yet there was a more serious side to Wahshungah, a side that became a cause for concern after the affairs of the Kaws had been settled. As an assumed full-blood, but more likely a mixed-blood, his cooperation in the final agreement had been essential, and for this, Wahshungah insisted on being paid in kind. In an interview at Pawnee, shortly after Hardy's interview with the Guthrie newspaper, the more serious side of "Old Wash" came to light: "His knowledge of men and measures is extensive and his unvarying rule is to husband his information and use it exclusively for the benefit of his tribe and his personal advancement—the latter consideration, he claims, having been suggested by his long association and familiarity with his white brethren."[46] Agent Mitscher knew this. Commissioner Jones knew this, and certainly, the Indian Congressman Charles Curtis had known this long before the Pawnee interview.

After the passage of the Kaw allotment bill, a festive atmosphere prevailed on the former reservation. In May 1903, some fifteen hundred Osages, Otoes, Poncas, and Kaws congregated at Washungah for what outsiders described as a "carnival" celebration. Dancing and feasting went on for an entire week. "The Indian is a fading factor in the life of the world," noted the Kaw City newspaper, "but while he stays he proposes at least in these parts to enjoy himself to the brim." Several months earlier, it had been announced that the Kaw allotments would soon be ready for sale to "those sturdy white farmers and homemakers" who for so long had been determined to get title to Kaw land. Then, on 3 March 1905, it was announced that a congressional act had been passed which authorized the payment of $155,976.88 for the former reservation lands in Kansas. After deducting the 10 percent fee of attorney Samuel J. Crawford—the former governor of Kansas, who was a good friend of Curtis's and had been his father's commander in the Washita campaign back in 1868—the settlement came to just over $5,500 per allottee. The full-bloods tried to hold out for a higher payment, but Curtis and Crawford advised them that the sum seemed the best that could be had. In that same year, the first of the allotted lands in Indian Territory were sold by the Kaw Indian Albert Taylor at fifteen dollars an acre. Nearby, General Hardy had taken his titles and was busy promoting a new town that would bear his name, and no fewer than forty allottees had been declared competent to manage their newly awarded estates. Noncompetent Kaws, mainly in the full-blood band, leased their land to non-Indians, and across the river from Washungah, no less than five saloons in Kaw City were doing "a very lively business," which prompted one federal attorney to style the town as the "worst place for booze in all of Oklahoma." Chief Wahshungah was one of the more regular customers at these establishments.[47]

Other problems confronted the ostensibly emancipated tribe. Contrary to the anticipation of many white merchants in the vicinity, payments for the final settlement of the Kaw accounts did not come in a lump sum; they were prorated, with adults receiving only ninety dollars a month and with minors receiving less than a third of that amount.

Debts that had been incurred in advance now plagued many of the Kaws. "They did not need to go to the banks to cash their checks," it was reported, for "the buzzards stood ready for the carrion and cashed the checks as fast as they were presented." Many Kaws simply refused to receive their checks at Washungah and, instead, traveled forty miles to Pawhuska to obtain their money and thus evade their creditors. By October 1906 the situation was so bad that the Indian Office advised Newkirk merchants that they could not expect any assistance in collecting credit accounts and that permission from the commissioner of Indian affairs was required for individual Kaws to receive more than ten dollars a month from the tribal treasury. In the meantime, the head of the Kaw Training School at Washungah reported that there was not enough lease and land money to fund the school operations that were required by the Allotment Act of 1902.[48]

Years later, from his office in the Senate Office Building, Charles Curtis wrote to the clerk in charge at Washungah: "I, like you, am sorry the Kaws have sold so much of their land. I had agreed with Chief Washungah that I would let my titles remain as they were during the twenty-five year competency period, so as to set an example." Unbeknownst to the clerk, J. W. Clendening, and certainly to the majority of the tribe, Curtis had made other agreements in 1902—agreements that more fully explain the role that he and Mitscher had played in Kaw allotment.[49]

The alternatives for those allottees who were not able to secure competency papers from Washington were to cultivate their lands or to lease them to non-Indians or to those Kaws who were declared competent and thus able to borrow money for the pursuit of commercial agriculture. Lacking the capital that was needed to engage in the former, the majority of the allottees opted for leases. Difficulty was almost immediately encountered in the collection of lease fees. Bonds required of the lessors had to be certified by Mitscher, who soon was implicated in a skimming operation that involved the lessors and the bonding companies. In early 1904, Mitscher was fired by Secretary Hitchcock when it was announced that Mitscher was operating illegally in league with a Washington bond attorney, Walter S. Field. Mitscher later complained that he had been "the victim of a cattle and oil combination who had caught your [Hitchcock's] ear." In fact, Mitscher had come under fire as early as 1902, but he had weathered the storm because of a friendly letter from his friend Curtis. In 1904, however, the charges were too serious, and the agent was forced to leave the Indian service for the more lucrative business of dealing in bankrupt stocks and bonds in Oklahoma City.[50]

It was in June 1907, on the letterhead of "The Mitscher-Leach Co." that Addison Watson, superintendent of the Kaw school, learned about the arrangement that Curtis and Mitscher had worked out with Wah-shungah. Because it reveals in rich detail the roles Curtis and Mitscher played in the allotment for the Kaw people, it is worth including verbatim:

6/21/1907

My Dear Watson,
      Last week while at Pawhuska, I saw our old Friend Washun-gah. As usual he had some thing to tell me & among them one that I promised him that I would write you about. Not in a spirit of meddling. You should know that I wouldn't do that [sic]. But as you know I was all through the Kaw Allotment from the beginning to end, to accomplish it we had to get Washungah on our side, to do that we had to make him certain promises & it is in connection with these promises that I write you. Mr. Curtis & I told Washungah that if he would go into this allotment project that he should have his property to do with as he wished. That is there were to be no other than the implied restriction on him. We figured that he was already old and that he would have plenty to keep him from actual want. It seems that you have made a very Just rule to pay members of the $40 per month of their inherited money. This, it seems to me ordinarily is a very proper procedure, & results in keeping the indians in funds longer than otherwise, but this restriction on Washungah is directly opposed to the promise We made to him. He will, of course, use it up more speedily but he has sense enough to know that when it is gone he will have to depend on his regular and usual income for subsistence, but on the other hand, he will know that he is not hedged about his restriction, which is of far more consequence to him & in keeping with the promises Senator Curtis & I made him. Owing to Washungah's importance in the tribe, his treatment should not be that of the ordinary layman. He so views it & I so regard it.

Yours very Truly,
[signed] O. A. Mitscher[51]

      Whether Mitscher informed Curtis about this letter to Watson or if Watson informed Curtis is not known. What is known is that less than a year later, Wahshungah was dead. On 17 February 1908, wrote Watson to Curtis, the Kaw dignitary had driven into Kaw City to obtain some whiskey. He had started home in the evening, "got to the gate of Rufus Test—tried to open the gate, but failed—found the next morning—dead, laid out all night."[52]

11
Congressional Incompetent

Although he would remain in government for another twenty-six years, it is apparent that with the passage of the Kaw Allotment Act of 1 July 1902, Charles Curtis believed he had vindicated the mixed-blood as an instrument of Indian improvement and that his performance was a model for other mixed-bloods to emulate. The allotment agreement was mainly the product of his own pen, he had advised his tribe in the proper procedures for breaking up the reservation, he had calmed the fears of the full-bloods, he had cut through the Indian Office bureaucracy in record time, and all Kaws now enjoyed a legal claim to former reservation realty. When the Indian commissioner William Jones congratulated the Kaw allotment delegation in Washington on how fortunate they were to have a man of Curtis's caliber to look after their welfare, Jones's words were sweet sounds to Congressman Curtis of Kansas.[1]

If further proof was required, the skeptics needed only to consider the efficiency with which Kaw allotment was carried out in April 1903. In what surely was an all-time record for the distribution of more than one hundred thousand acres of reservation land, the actual selections were made in less than three days. Years later, in an interview with the historian Berlin B. Chapman, Curtis proudly recalled that the distributions had been accomplished with no additional clerical force at the agency level, at an expense of about $200, and "with remarkable harmony." Indeed, said Curtis, "there was not a single contest over the division of the lands."[2]

What made the distribution particulary astounding in 1903 was the difficulty that the Dawes Commission was then experiencing in its efforts to complete the allotment rolls of the Five Civilized Tribes. True, it was dealing with many more applicants—about 125,000—but quantity was not really the issue. Sound political leadership, insights that only a mixed-blood could have, and the ability to work with, not against, contending tribal factions made the difference. In fact, Curtis insisted, that if the Dawes people had not been cut down to size by the Curtis Act, the Five Tribes "would have been wiped off the face of the earth without their consent."[3]

No less satisfying to Curtis was an editorial which first appeared in the Purcell newspaper in early June 1903 and was widely reprinted in other newspapers in Oklahoma and Indian Territory soon thereafter. Entitled "He Ribs 'em up," the editorial extolled the accomplishments of Curtis's cohort Mitscher, while it ridiculed the incompetent Dawes Commission. Obviously unaware that by then Mitscher had been fired for fraud in the awarding of certain Kaw land leases, the Purcell editor praised Mitscher and the Kaw Allotment Commission:

> They were given thirty days to do the work. . . . The actual time of dividing the land did not practically exceed two days, says the Associated Press. It may be possible that Mr. Mitscher does not realize the enormity of his offense. It possibly may not have occurred to him that a body of men [the Dawes Commission] have been for ten years making "herculean efforts" to allot the land of the Five Tribes and that Mitscher's injection of real business methods into the work of the same nature has placed them [the Dawes Commission] in a bad light before the public. . . . Does Mr. Mitscher not bitterly regret his perverse action in rushing in the face of the great Dawes Commission, which has for ten years been giving such a beautiful example of how not to do the same class of work?[4]

In fact, by the time that Wahshungah, Hardy, Chouteau, and Pappan met with commissioner Jones and Curtis in Washington, many of the Kaws had selected their lands, and bickering over the most desirable locations was rampant. General Hardy, who had usually been able to weather the storms of factionalism, threatened to resign unless the squabbling subsided. The struggle between the mixed-bloods and the full-bloods was especially intense.[5]

An important example was the contest between the mixed-blood Rachel Cross and the full-blood Jesse Mehojah over a strategically located quarter section near the agency headquarters at the confluence of Beaver Creek and the Arkansas. First occupied by Wahamohki in the mid 1870s, the 160-acre plot was sold to Cross for $35 on 6 June 1894 in a transaction that the Kaw National Council endorsed. The council's action and the sale itself were not legally binding on the allotment proceedings of 1902, but they did provide the direction for land claims preceding the work of the Allotment Commission in 1903. On 26 May 1896, Cross transferred her "claim" to Hubert Pappan, but without any financial consideration. Then, on 12 December 1900, in an apparent effort to win full-blood support for the final allotment settlement, the Kaw Council awarded the land to Mehojah—who by then was one of the most powerful and respected members of the full-blood faction. Since Pappan had assumed ownership without making any payment to Cross, his heirs decided not to contest the Mehojah award. Cross, however, did contest it: she filed a complaint with the council, which, on 13 April 1901, sustained Mehojah's right to the property. Two years later, the Allotment Commission upheld the claim in the name of Mehojah's wife, Maggie. The transaction was certified by Wahshungah and by General Hardy's son William, over the objections of Cross and the mixed-bloods. This constituted clear evidence that Curtis's claim that "there was not a single contest over the selections" simply was not true.[6]

In fact, as in the allotment bill itself, Curtis exerted a heavy hand in the selection of individual plots. In the same letter (21 December 1901) in which he advised Secretary Hitchcock regarding his intent "to prepare the agreement," Curtis requested that the reservation be resurveyed at the government's expense. The reservation had been surveyed at the time of removal, but most of the stone markers had been vandalized or destroyed by livestock, so that it was impossible to locate or describe the individual tracts. The request, of course, was an admission that plots such as the one over which Cross and Mehojah were quarreling were imprecise and thus were impossible to identify in the legal sense. Dutifully, the Indian Office complied with Curtis's request. A month later, commissioner Jones advised Mitscher that $2,500 had been authorized for the project, thus "permitting the Indians to make selections with a view to future allotment." Walter M. Stumph of Washington was designated as the official surveyor and was authorized to hire assistants from the tribe, at two dollars per day.[7]

More, however, was involved than simple location of the original township, section, and quarter-section lines. "As soon as the surveys have progressed far enough," wrote Jones to Mitscher, "you should let the Indians begin to make their selections so that the surveys and selections may progress *simultaneously*." Individuals on the tribal roll as of 1 December 1901 and all those who had been born to persons on the roll between that date and the actual completion of the survey were to constitute the legal membership for the purpose of making the final selections. Moreover, "disputes between members as to *prior location* should be decided by you subject to confirmation by this office . . . and should any serious conflicts arise . . . , *the same shall be submitted to this*

office for consideration and determination.'' In short, the entire allotment process, including the authority of the Indian Office to determine
all final selections, had been worked out by Jones and Congressman
Curtis *prior to* the tribal agreement to send Wahshungah, Hardy, and
other members of the Allotment Commission to Washington and well
over a year *prior to* Mitscher's instructions to go ahead with the actual
selections.[8]

In 1873 the majority of the Kaws had established their homes near
the agency headquarters, located a mile north of the Beaver Creek
confluence with the Arkansas, on the southern boundary of the reservation. During the next three decades, the settlements had fanned out
mainly to the west, along the fertile Arkansas bottomlands, and then
north, to the area east of Newkirk. By the late 1890s a spur of the Santa
Fe Railway had been planned to connect Newkirk (the seat of present-
day Kay County) with Kaw City, directly across the river from the
agency. Because of Mitscher's unilateral approval of the Blackwell, Enid,
and Southwestern's rail right of way across the reservation toward the
Washungah town site, it was apparent to the inner circle of Kaw
leadership, certainly to Curtis, that here was the most desirable place to
select an allotment.[9]

On the model of the town-development article that he had written
into the Curtis Act four years earlier, Curtis made sure that the allotment
legislation reserved an 80-acre plot for the Washungah town site, with
proceeds from the sale of lots to be divided among the allottees. The site
was on the southern half of Wahshungah's allotment, directly west of
the agency buildings and the new Kaw Boarding School; its principal
streets were named for prominent mixed-bloods: Bellmard, Hardy, and
Curtis. Across the river at booming Kaw City, the firm of Fleming and
Hamman added to Curtis's popularity by announcing that its latest
investment would be in the Hotel Curtis. And not surprising, surely not
to agent Mitscher, directly north of Wahshungah's property was the
160-acre selection of Congressman Curtis. Eight miles north were the
allotments of his daughters Leona and Permelia, and due east of
Newkirk was the well-placed allotment of his son, Harry. In the
meantime, General Hardy was busy negotiating with the Taylor family
for its surplus lands in the northeastern quadrant of the former
reservation; he was also completing plans for a town site (to be named
Hardy) on the line of the Midland Valley Railway.[10]

Years later, when commenting on the circumstances that had led to
Curtis's selection as Hoover's running mate, a New York paper reported
that Curtis never forgot his own people. ''Year after year Curtis has
visited the tribe in September, when the annual festivities are held,''
and as in his childhood, ''he is always admitted into the Council

A detail (1905) of the township in the southern portion of the former Kaw Reservation in Indian Territory, located north of the Arkansas River, which is shown on the map. Note Charles Curtis's quarter-section homestead allotment immediately north of the Washunga town site. From Map of Kay County, Oklahoma (Newkirk, Okla.: Republican News Journal, 1905). Courtesy of the Kaw Tribe of Oklahoma.

Chamber." Surely, then, it was a great satisfaction for Curtis to learn that in the first national election in which adult Kaw males were qualified to vote, they—even the full-bloods—supported the Republican ticket overwhelmingly. The Kaw City newspaper reported: "This may be explained by saying that Congressman Curtis of Kansas is a member of the tribe and holds an allotment on the reservation. He truly is the idol of the tribe, having carefully looked after its interest in Washington and having advised his people to use their rights." Certainly, another factor was the guidance and hard work of W. E. Hardy. "General Hardy, who is a white man and a staunch Republican, but years ago was adopted into the tribe, is the political leader, and with him is closely associated the old chief of the tribe, Washungah."[11]

Curtis easily won reelection to his House seat in the election of 1904, and in that contest, he took pride in the businesslike manner in which his people had abandoned communal life. By comparison to the recalcitrant Osages and the ever-bickering Five Tribes, Kaw allotment was truly an astonishing success, even to Francis E. Leupp, the successor to William Jones in the Indian Office. Leupp, whose tenure as commissioner (1905–9) was known mainly for his failure to halt the assault on the Indians' land base and their natural resources after allotment and who admitted that miscegenation could be a "hazardous experiment," nevertheless identified Curtis as an invaluable instrument in the move toward assimilation:

> With his Indian blood he inherits keenness of observation, stoicism under suffering, love of freedom, a contempt for the petty things which lay so heavy a burden on our convention-bound civilization; with his white blood the competitive instinct, individual initiative; resourcefulness in the face of novel obstacles, and a constitution hardened to the drafts made upon its strength by the artificialities of modern life.[12]

What a happy union! What better tribute to the Kaw mixed-blood who in Leupp's time would take a seat in the United States Senate and would eventually occupy the second-highest office in the land. Other mixed-bloods, of course, were men of accomplishment: Alexander McGillivray, the "Talleyrand of Alabama"; Ohiyesa (Charles Alexander Eastman) of the Santee Sioux; and Senator Robert L. Owen, Jr., a Cherokee from the new state of Oklahoma. Yet, as a young man, McGillivray had been a student in one of the finest schools in Charleston; Ohiyesa had attended Beloit, had graduated from Knox, and then had taken a medical degree from the Boston School of Medicine. Owen had grown up in privileged surroundings in Virginia, had been the valedictorian of his class at Washington and Lee, and eventually had made a fortune as a claims attorney in Indian Territory. Curtis, by contrast, had been born in a log cabin, had been educated on a reservation and in the school of hard knocks, and had literally fought his way to the top by the very talents that Leupp so admired in the white component of the mixed-blood type. To those who knew him well, Curtis was *the* mixed-blood hero at the onset of the twentieth century.[13]

For Curtis, responsible allotment ownership was central to the new dispensation. Under the Kaw Allotment Act of 1902, homesteads were nonalienable and nontaxable for twenty-five years. Surplus lands were similarly restricted for ten years but not to exceed twenty-five. Yet, these restrictions could be rescinded if the allottee were declared competent by the secretary of the interior. The consequences of this proviso were not at all encouraging to Curtis. In fact, it was upsetting to learn that no fewer than seventy-five Kaw applications for competency were received by the Indian Office even before the formal deeds could be prepared. Curtis later recalled to the Kaw disbursement office: "I, like you, am exceedingly sorry the Kaws sold so much land so quickly. I tried to keep them from selling. I even agreed with Washungah that I would let my titles remain as they were during the twenty-five year period, so as to set an example and encourage the members to keep from taking certificates and selling their land."[14]

On the other hand, after *U.S.* v. *Richert* (1905), in which the Supreme Court held that county governments could not overturn the tax-exempt status of Indian landholders, Curtis saw a way of evading taxes on the appreciating value of his land just north of the Washungah town site. Even after it had become apparent that Washungah was no boom town, because it had failed to get a railroad, Curtis nevertheless held to his agreement, noting that he was "very sorry to hear about some of the tribal members being overly extravagant." In fact, he boasted that he was putting more money into his "Indian property" than he was receiving in return. And in 1909, when he learned that B. Olson and B. E. Reed had purchased 160 acres of his surplus lands at a Kay County sheriff's sale for nonpayment of taxes, Curtis fired a letter to Indian commissioner Robert G. Valentine, demanding that Valentine "take steps to stop it by injunction, if necessary." Valentine responded immediately, and four days later, the Kaw disbursement officer, Almond G. Miller, informed the Kay County Board of Commissioners that because Curtis was a bona-fide member of the Kaw tribe who "had not been granted a Certificate of Competency," the lands had been illegally assessed, and the property was therefore still his. Although the commissioners deferred action for more than a year, the sales were finally canceled when Curtis, through Valentine, threatened to turn the matter over to the United States attorney's office in Oklahoma City. Competency was indeed a very subjective matter.[15]

As chairman of the House Committee on Indian Affairs and as the only United States congressman to be considered legally incompetent to handle his own land, Curtis's action in retrospect may have been as much a protest against the government's indiscriminate granting of competency certificates as it was the pursuit of his own interests. In this manner, Curtis secured congressional approval for the right to serve as the guardian of Indian minors whose parents he considered to be incompetent to negotiate land leases with non-Indians, and on 27 February 1925, on the eve of his selection as Senate majority leader, he personally saw to it that an attempt to remove restrictions against the alienation of surplus land would fail. There simply were many Kaw Indians who would not or could not handle real property responsibly. He introduced another bill that extended until 3 March 1948 the restriction against Kaw minors' disposing of their remaining surplus land.[16]

Other legislation that was either introduced or supported by Curtis indicated his increasing frustration with the government's postallotment program. He succeeded in having Indians exempted from taking the civil-service examination as a prerequisite for employment on Indian reservations, on the grounds that "practical" experience in Indian matters was equal to formal education for simply passing the test. He took pride in recovering $250,000 for the Mexican Kickapoos, whose lands in Oklahoma were the object of vicious speculation. And he saw to it that an attempt to have the Papagos of Arizona pay $70,000 for an irrigation project that would mainly benefit the white citizens of Tucson was stricken from the tribe's accounts in the federal treasury. He led the fight against the funding of a major irrigation project on the Flathead reservation in Montana by reminding the Senate that it was difficult enough to teach the Indian to become a farmer, "and yet the attempt is being made here to transform the traditional Indian from an ordinary owner of ponies and cattle to an irrigation farmer." True, such actions were often viewed within the context of Curtis's well-known fiscal conservatism, but when he joined ranks with the Chippewa full-bloods to block tribal funding for a general Chippewa council at Bemidji, Minnesota, he justified his position from a different perspective: "I believe in standing by the full bloods whenever it is possible to do so, and I happen to believe the delegation of full bloods know what the full bloods want."[17]

On balance, however, it seems clear that by 1920, Curtis was agreeable to getting the government out of the Indian business, and apart from the mixed-bloods' responsibility to help as best they could, he had become more and more convinced that assimilation was misguided social science that had little to do with the political world in which he was obliged to toil. In 1919, from the chair of the Senate Indian Committee, he proudly recalled the efficiency with which an austere Indian bill under his guidance had run the congressional gauntlet:

> The record made on the Indian Appropriation bill was better than the District Bill. The Indian Bill was considered by the subcommittee one day, reported to the full committee the next, and considered and agreed to by the full committee and reported to the Senate the same day. The measure passed the Senate within forty-five minutes after it was called up . . . and it was claimed by old officers in the Senate that they were the first and only general appropriation bill that had ever passed the Senate carrying less than when they came to the Senate from the House.[18]

Such austerity, insisted Curtis, was encouraged by the excessive number of patents-in-fee that had been granted to Indians who had been declared competent during the Wilson administration. Goaded on by Secretary of the Interior Franklin K. Lane, who overreacted to charges of un-Americanism in the Indian Office during World War I, Indian commissioner Cato Sells issued more than twenty thousand land patents to Indians during the years 1913 to 1921, nearly twice the number that had been granted during the previous decade. Then came the pronouncement of Indian commissioner Charles Burke in late 1921 that the degree of blood was no guarantee of success for the Indian landowner. Indeed, said Burke, "There are numerous instances of full bloods who are clearly demonstrating their industrial ability by the actual use made of their land and who are shrewdly content with a restrictive title that exempts them from taxation." On the other hand, many mixed-bloods "put most of the proceeds in an automobile or some other extravagant investment, and in a few months are down and out as far as visible possessions are concerned." Fully two-thirds of *all* Indians, concluded Burke, simply were "unable or unwilling to cope."[19]

A flurry of oil and gas leasing on the Kaw allotments in the summer of 1911 prompted the acceleration of competency applications and, ultimately, the sale of much Kaw land to non-Indians. Nevertheless, Curtis refused to follow suit, and it was not until March 1930 that he finally leased some of his land for mineral exploration. The demonstrated productivity of the Shidler and Burbank fields nearby probably was the main consideration, although, as it turned out, Curtis's leases

A group of unidentified mixed-blood and full-blood Kaw Indians dressed in traditional and "progressive" attire, around 1905. Courtesy of the Kansas State Historical Society.

were beyond the perimeters of these fabulous oil pools. In the meantime, as he became more interested in prohibition, woman suffrage, domestic economic problems, and nonentanglement in world affairs, Indian matters lost their luster for Curtis. More important were higher political stations yet to be sought.[20]

12
A Different Path

The timing of Charles Curtis's public career is important to an understanding of his role as the most powerful mixed-blood in national
political life from the General Allotment Act of 1887 to the final
destruction of Indian Territory in 1907. From the early 1880s until about
1920, according to the traditional view, the government sought to
implement assimilation on the assumption that a truly homogeneous
society was possible. According to a recent study, however, the policy
had two distinct phases: the first, distinguished by the desire to
transform Indians into responsible citizens on the white model, while
taking much of their land and natural resources; and the second, which
intensified during the late nineteenth century and reached a high pitch
during the second decade of the twentieth, when the ideal of the
homogeneous society was abandoned and was replaced by the racist
strategy of partial membership, not just for Indians but for blacks,
Asians, and non-Anglo-Saxon immigrants as well.[1]

Curtis, who came to political maturity during the second phase,
presents an opportunity to refine certain aspects of the policy after 1900.
True, much of his attention was directed toward Indian Territory,
statehood for Oklahoma, and the future of his own tribe. But he did
sponsor and promote Indian legislation of national scope. When he
dismissed the Dawes Commission as incompetent lackeys, when he
unabashedly demonstrated his power in the swift allotment of his own
people, when he used his own Indianness to political advantage, and
especially when he insisted that the only practical solution to the Indian
question was intermarriage between Indians and whites, he was giving
notice that the homogeneous society was an impossible ideal. In 1860,
the year of Curtis's birth in North Topeka, Lewis Henry Morgan had
observed "that the white blood already taken up" was the main reason

the mixed-bloods were doing so well. A half-century later, at the time of Wahshungah's tragic death, Curtis agreed with Morgan and was convinced of a deficiency among full-bloods.[2]

In 1907, Congressman William J. Stone of Missouri sought to attach an amendment to the Indian appropriation bill that would have removed all restrictions on leasing and the alienation of allotments, regardless of the quantum of Indian blood. During the debate, there was much quibbling over property rights versus civil rights, which was occasioned by the *Matter of Heff* case of 1905, in which the Supreme Court had overturned the conviction of a non-Indian who had sold alcohol to some citizen allottees in northeastern Kansas. But in the end, the blood-quantum issue came to the fore, and in the deft hands of Curtis, it was used to kill the amendment.[3]

Speaking more bluntly than was his custom, Curtis emphasized the differences between mixed-bloods, who could be expected to handle property and their allotments responsibly, and full-bloods, who simply could not. For example, said Curtis, there was the case of Betsey Gallicatcher, a Cherokee full-blood, who, having been declared competent by the Interior Department, had sold 130 acres of her allotment, on which twenty-eight oil wells were producing an annual owner's royalty of $14,245, for the paltry sum of only $18 per acre. There was also the case of Senahooyusuttah, the full-blood owner of 50 acres with eight flowing wells, who had sold out completely for only $1,500. Curtis cited a dozen similar transactions, which prompted Senator John Spooner of Wisconsin to charge: ''You simply cannot by law change an Indian into a white man. These full bloods were no better qualified to manage, without improvidence, their own affairs the day after they became, under the operation of law, citizens of the United States, than the day before. Racial characteristics cannot be changed by an act of man. That is a matter of growth and it takes a long time.''[4]

Here, then, was a different path that Curtis would travel, as public policy abandoned the assimilationists' dream and substituted for it the strategies of having the Indians assume a marginal role in society and of devising new tactics ''for holding the race to its duties.'' No longer persuaded that allotment and individual landownership in themselves would usher in the good life for Indians, Curtis drew back and supported extended guardianship for full-bloods and more governmental paternalism, but he did not abandon his belief that responsible mixed-bloods such as himself could have a salutary effect on the full-bloods. This had been the charge assigned to his Grandmother Pappan more than a century earlier, and this was his responsibility now.[5]

Exemplary conduct was tantamount to political advancement—certain evidence that mixed-bloods *could* succeed. It was not enough simply to serve as a congressman or as a senator. It was not enough to expose governmental commissions for their inefficiency or to point to Indian policy that had gone awry. Nor was it enough to have profited from the dissolution of his own tribe. Moving up the political ladder by tenacity, whispering, and sheer hard work would finally exhibit the mixed-blood as the man of the hour.

An opportunity presented itself in the 1920 Republican National Convention in Chicago. After a deadlock had developed between the forerunners Frank O. Lowden and Leonard Wood, Curtis, George B. M. Harvey, and Senators Frank Brandegee of Connecticut and Henry Cabot Lodge of Massachusetts concluded that the deadlock was hopeless and that a compromise candidate was in order. The infamous "smoke-filled room" in the Blackstone Hotel was where the four Republican leaders had dined, and it was at this meeting that Curtis is reported to have recommended that they'd "best take [Warren G.] Harding." On the following morning, Senator Curtis prevailed upon the Kansas delegation to support the dark-horse candidate from Ohio, which action on the convention floor played an important role in the eventual ninth-ballot stampede for Harding. William A. White recalled that he "blew off" and told Curtis that his action would disgrace the Republican party. But "The Indian" had prevailed, and he was not worried that the selection of Harding may have been contrary to the will of the convention.[6]

Four years later, just before the 1924 Republican National Convention in Cleveland, Curtis's invalid wife, Anna, confided to her husband's half sister Dolly: "I think Charles should be President. You ought to go to Cleveland and see that he is nominated." Dolly replied: "But my dear, it's not possible this year. Mr. Coolidge has made good in the White House. . . . The party cannot name anybody else." Coolidge, of course, secured the nomination and, eventually, the presidency, but there was no doubt in Curtis's mind that one day he would make a bid for this highest office in the land.[7]

Only a few days after Coolidge's victory in November 1924, Senate Majority Leader Lodge died, and the mantle of this important position fell to Curtis. One commentator, in true journalistic oversimplification, described it as "high destiny," dating back to that fateful day when the young mixed-blood had been advised by his Grandmother Pappan to turn his back on reservation life. Another commentator wrote: "It has come to pass, in these democratic United States, than an Indian, who once wore the blanket and received government rations, is to guide the most august of Legislative bodies, the Senate of the United States." More to the point was an article that appeared ten months prior to Curtis's selection, which insisted that only a person like Curtis, who had "the endurance of the Kaws in his veins" and had risen to the extreme

Senate Majority Leader Charles Curtis of Kansas, riding with President-Elect Calvin Coolidge and Mrs. Coolidge in the inaugural parade on 4 March 1924. Courtesy of the Kansas State Historical Society.

heights of stoicism, could bear to listen, day after day, month after month, session after session, "to the leading ranters of the Senate." And for the "heredity and environment sharks" who craved to know how Curtis got that way, the author of "A Stoic in the Right Place" explained:

> He knows about every piece of legislation. . . . He knows how each member stands on each measure—each member, that is, who knows anything at all about it. . . . In the entire history of the Senate . . . there has never been a senator who held so many important jobs. In the last session . . . he was chairman of the Rules Committee, a member of the Appropriations Committee, the Finance Committee, the Indian Affairs Committee, the Committee on Committees and the Steering Committee, and on top of it all was Republican Whip and assistant Republican floor leader. Why the only way in which a senator can ever beat the Curtis record is to

hold, in addition to all of Curtis's appointments, the jobs of Senate page and doorkeeper. . . . Curtis has probably established a record that will be about as easy to break as the record for the hundred-yard-dash.[8]

As expected, Curtis cooperated with Coolidge-style conservatism and worked hard to promote economy in government. One study concluded that by reason of laws and/or amendments that he sponsored during his political career, the government had saved more than $83 million. Curtis was a strong advocate of dispatching all appropriations to one committee, so as to prevent duplication in appropriations, and according to Senator Arthur Capper of Kansas, Curtis's amendment to consolidate the customs districts saved $350,000 in less than a year. Curtis always displayed a surface concern with the problems of farmers, his principal constituents, and he insisted—in the face of much evidence to the contrary—that their welfare was closely tied to protective tariffs. Apparently for political reasons, he supported the McNary-Haugen bill, a measure that was designed to raise the price of farm commodities by creating a governmental agency that could buy and then dump surplus products on foreign markets. But then he voted to uphold President Coolidge's veto of the measure on the grounds that it involved the expenditure of too much money.[9]

Certainly, Curtis's interest in Indian affairs during the 1920s was minimal at best. He applauded Indian commissioner Charles Burke's success in securing legislation that canceled all Indian land patents that had been awarded since 1917 without owner consent. But he exercised no leadership in providing badly needed funds to operate Indian boarding schools or to increase the low salaries paid to physicians and nurses in the Indian service. He refused to help his former tribesmen obtain a separate agency that would be more responsive to their needs, and he refused to intervene when Burke turned down a proposal by the Kaws to lease their excess cemetery lands for oil exploration. The former Kaw allotment commissioner Forrest Chouteau stated in 1927 that Curtis "was not much help to the tribe," and recalling the senator's defection from the tribe during the early 1870s, Chouteau told a Wichita reporter that if Curtis had not "jumped from one of the wagons on the trail to Indian Territory, he would have been just like the rest of us Indians."[10]

The fact is that in 1927 Curtis was preoccupied with more important matters. When Coolidge announced in October that he would not seek another term, the whispering Indian was bitten by the presidential bug, and few Republicans were surprised when shortly thereafter he threw his hat into the ring. Always confident, he was convinced that his fellow Republicans owed him the nomination as a reward for his extensive

Senator Charles Curtis, a Kansa mixed-blood, on the steps of the Capitol about 1925. Courtesy of the Kansas State Historical Society.

experience and party regularity. There was also the possibility that a deadlock between the front runners Herbert C. Hoover of California and Governor Frank Lowden of Illinois might result in the selection of Curtis as the compromise candidate. Most outsiders, however, believed that Curtis was seeking the top nomination as a means of solidifying his claim to the vice-presidency.[11]

With the selection of Hoover on the first ballot in Kansas City, Curtis quickly emerged as the favorite candidate for the second office. On the first vice-presidential ballot, he won easily, with 1,052 votes—215 more than Hoover had received for the presidency. Significantly, as had been the case when J. N. Tichner of Hutchinson, Kansas, had nominated Curtis for the presidency, the speech of Senator William E. Borah, when he nominated Curtis for vice-president, did not include a single reference to Curtis as an Indian. Nor did the words of Curtis's daughter, Leona Curtis Knight, of Providence, Rhode Island, who was called upon to deliver an extemporaneous second to the nomination. Incompetent Indians were no longer in vogue. Curtis's acceptance speech was short and to the point: he was pleased to accept the vice-presidential nomination and to represent Kansas and the West, and he was determined "to settle all our party disagreements." But there was no reference to his Indian past or to his Indianness in the present or in the future. There may have been informal, unreported talk about "Indian Charley" on the convention floor, but it did not extend to the platform for pen and press to exploit.[12]

On the stump, Curtis was obliged to engage in the very activity that he so intensely despised, and as in the past, he relied mainly on platitudinous and repetitious speeches and handshaking, rather than on addressing the complex economic and social issues of the times. As early as October 1927, it was reported that Curtis would receive "lots of electoral votes" in Oklahoma and other states that had large Indian populations, because "Charley has always stood for the rights of the Indians." On the campaign trail, however, he made no promises whatsoever regarding modification or change in federal Indian policy. In 1926, Secretary of the Interior Hubert Work had authorized the Brookings Institution to conduct a comprehensive study of the deplorable condition of Indian people, and a year later, John Collier, soon to be Indian commissioner, had persuaded the Senate's Indian Committee to undertake a similar study. The Brookings report prompted the Democratic presidential candidate, Alfred E. Smith, to issue statements of concern regarding the shocking social and economic status of American Indians and to demand reform for these "first Americans." But Curtis was not willing to involve himself in the debate that these studies prompted.[13]

Hamilton Fish, Jr., described Curtis as "that regular of regulars, that American of Americans," while others less generously characterized Curtis as a plodding reactionary, an aged anachronism out of tune with the present. On one occasion, Curtis played into the hands of an angry farm heckler by charging him with being "too damned dumb to understand" the economic crisis facing the nation. Curtis was ridiculed as a Hardy crony, "one-eighth Kaw Indian and seven-eighths incompetent," and Curtis's use of a dancing Indian "princess," who recited *The Song of Hiawatha* from the rear platform of his campaign train, appeared singularly inappropriate as a response to the poverty and the high mortality rates that were then being reported in the Indian community. On a campaign junket through the West in the late summer and early fall of 1928, Curtis accepted official membership in the Crow Tribe in Billings, Montana, after Chief Plenty Coups had "waved the scalp stick over my [Curtis's] dear boy and placed a feathered headdress on him." To a few Cheyennes in attendance at the same ceremony, Curtis reminisced about the good old days on the Kansas frontier, noting that in 1868 they had "scared the life out of the Kaws at Council Grove." And speaking in Okmulgee, Oklahoma, shortly thereafter, Curtis broke out in a broad smile when a former Creek chief proudly introduced Curtis as a truly great man, "The Father of Oklahoma."[14]

Republican campaign officials counted on Curtis to organize the Indian vote, which in fact was statistically insignificant; but on the platform, about all that Curtis could muster for his kinsmen was to repeat conservative Republican homilies and encourage them "to avoid the firewater and vote." For Indians in general, surely one of the most mindless aspects of the Hoover-Curtis victory in 1928 was to have a large delegation of Indians, dressed in traditional garb, parade on the Washington streets on Inauguration Day, 1929, to celebrate the installation of the first Indian vice-president of the United States.[15]

Just before taking the oath of office, Curtis was showered with the traditional tribute of the Senate, delivered by his good friend Senator Reed Smoot of Utah. As expected, Senator Smoot dwelled at length on Curtis's long and dedicated career in both houses of Congress, as well as on his zeal in serving both the country and the Republican party. Beyond that, two themes stood out in Smoot's remarks. The first applauded Curtis for his unflagging industry and self-reliance and emphasized how Curtis had reached his zenith "without riches and without powerful influences." The second grasped for the very essence of his greatness:

Senator, now Vice President Curtis, began life amid primitive and humble surroundings. In his veins runs the blood of a Puritan

Senator Charles Curtis on the vice-presidential campaign trail, with an unidentified Potawatomi Indian in Kansas in 1928. Courtesy of the Kansas State Historical Society.

Englishman, a French-Canadian, and an Indian maiden. That remarkable fusion brought forth the real American, whose career demonstrates the boundless possibilities in the land we love. . . . We will feel more tolerant, more considerate, and more wise, as we look into his kindly eyes. We will profit by the example you have set for us.[16]

These were sweet words to Curtis, because they articulated what he surely wanted to hear. But after a few months of seemingly endless receptions and dinner parties and of "shattering the gavels as fast as they could make them" in his dull role of presiding over the Senate, remembrances of high achievement gave way to disillusionment and frustration. On the eve of the stock-market crash of 1929, evidence on all sides indicated that conditions among Indians were worsening, that fully two-thirds of all Indians were earning less than one hundred dollars a year, and that the dispossession of the Indians' allotment domain had reached scandalous proportions.[17]

Insulating himself in the massive vice-presidential suite that he personally had decorated with Indian artifacts, a huge "throne chair" with the gilded words "The Chief" carved on the top, and innumerable memorabilia of the past, Curtis immodestly admitted his "deep pride in the layout" to a Washington columnist. But the sumptuous surroundings could not disguise the changes in the Indian from Kansas:

> Once smitten by ambition and racked by suppressed desires Charley lost his equilibrium. With the robes of purple dangling teasingly before him, he has trimmed his straggling hairs and craggy lip-furze, keeps a pretty regular crease in his pants, and ties his neckties with considerably more than his wonted care. He has taken up a permanent relation with a stiff topper and the old black sombrero that he wore for so long is gone. His goodnatured and friendly growls have given way to an affected pronunciation, and if he whispers it is only in his sleep. Dignity oozes from his every pore, for he has set himself to the heroic task of making the Vice-Presidency a potent estate.[18]

Curtis busied himself wielding the gavel over the Senate, moving from a modest residential section of Washington to a ten-room suite in the Mayflower Hotel, and hosting hundreds of official dinner parties; but he exerted no significant influence in the Hoover administration. President Hoover did invite him to attend cabinet meetings, but Curtis's advice was seldom sought, perhaps, as one study has noted, because he had little to offer. On occasion, he attempted to influence farm policy, but without success. He continued to support prohibition and the venerable protective tariffs. He criticized the Federal Reserve System on the grounds that it drained money from rural to urban areas that were "too speculative"; he called for the deportation of alien criminals; he viewed the depression as a natural occurrence that would run its course and eventually give way to even greater prosperity; he also supported Hoover's dispersal of the "Bonus Marchers" and, in general, called on all Americans to support the courts, the country, and the Constitution. "It is not pleasing," he stated in July 1930, "to note the wave that is sweeping over the country which disregards law and order and the Constitution, and substitutes man's desire, and weakens opinion of the law." Since his complaint was directed to the American citizenry in general, it presumably applied to Indians as well.[19]

Toward the end of the Hoover administration, it was evident that Curtis had become disillusioned with the vice-presidency, particularly when he dropped hints that he might be interested in regaining his old seat in the Senate. How serious they were was questionable, but there is no doubt that the worsening of the depression and his association with the infamous Doctor John R. Brinkley had done Curtis's cause no good.

Brinkley—an enterprising political opportunist who, at his Milford, Kansas, clinic, used his goat-gland-transplant nostrum to allegedly rejuvenate the failing virility of males of middle and advanced age—very nearly won the 1930 Kansas gubernatorial election in a spectacular write-in campaign that saw the leadership of both parties work hard to throw out write-in votes on technicalities and thus keep the "gland-man" from the state's highest office. In 1922, Brinkley had established Kansas' first radio station, KFKB—Kansas First Kansas Best—and in 1928 the American Medical Association and the *Kansas City Star* had pursued investigations that were designed to disbar Brinkley from practicing medicine in the state. In this, they succeeded: in 1930, the Kansas State Board of Medical Examination and Registration revoked his medical license. Brinkley feared that he might soon lose his radio license as well. His abortive 1930 gubernatorial race, then, was a rash effort to refurbish his tarnished reputation and to save his business.[20]

Fearing that his radio license would be permanently revoked, Brinkley sold KFKB to a Wichita insurance company in early 1931 and then announced that he was going to move his station to Mexico, with the 50,000-watt transmitter of XER to be located at Villa Acuna, across the Rio Grande from El Paso and beyond the jurisdiction of the United States Federal Radio Commission. Brinkley's detractors responded by encouraging the United States State Department to pressure the Mexican government into denying Brinkley's application for a radio permit.[21]

At this point, Vice-President Curtis, who had used KFKB in Milford "to say nice things" about himself and the Republican party, took Brinkley with him to the State Department, where officials were advised not to make an international affair out of the good doctor from Kansas. In January, in a Wichita hotel room, the columnist Walter Davenport learned more details about the whispering Indian's role in the unfolding drama. A "scout," who was interested in Curtis's return to the Senate, said: "When this Doc Brinkley . . . got thrown off the air here for doing goat-gland operations without a license . . . , the government tried to get him barred out of Mexico. . . . [So] what did Charley Curtis do? Well, he went to the State Department down in Washington with the Doc and told one of the big shots down there . . . to quit bearing down on the Doc."[22] Why? Another reporter explained: "Charley Curtis, who is always taking sides with the under dog on account of him being part Indian, fixed it so's the Doc ain't thrown out of Mexico." And still another in the Wichita hotel said: "If it hadn't been for Charley there wouldn't be any Station XER and Doc Brinkley would be as dead as the goats he used up in his Milford hospital."[23]

Brinkley received his permit from the Mexican government, and XER's power soon extended north to Kansas and beyond. But his second bid for the Kansas governorship in 1932 fell victim to the deepening depression, his unrealistic promises for economic recovery, and the misguided efforts on his behalf by Curtis. Surely, the sour publicity that accompanied the affair loomed large in Curtis's decision not to run for the Senate, and Curtis's subsequent support for the Republican gubernatorial victor, Alfred M. Landon, indicated that Curtis realized that his association with Brinkley had been a serious mistake.[24]

In the face of considerable opposition, Curtis was nevertheless retained on the GOP ticket in 1932. During the campaign, he spoke out against Hoover's support of prohibition repeal, which prompted one wag to conclude that the Republican ticket was "half-dry head and dried-out tail." Curtis continued to oppose international cooperation, in a manner that was reminiscent of his fight against Woodrow Wilson and the League of Nations; and in regard to the farm crisis, Curtis reaffirmed his support of high tariffs, adding simply that cooperative marketing agencies and the extension of farm mortgages through the Federal Land Banks might encourage the return of prosperity to rural America. His dull and plodding speeches were punctuated with calls for nonpartisanship and "a restoration of confidence," and he insisted that the depression was nearly over, that prosperity was within grasp if only Hoover and Curtis were retained in office. In fact, as one recent study has suggested, Curtis in 1932 "was a sandbag around the neck of a drowning Hoover."[25]

In 1928, Curtis said he supported legislation "to improve the status of the American Indian," but without stating what kind of legislation he had in mind. In subsequent years, he was equally detached from Indian Affairs. Rather than respond to John Collier's call for reform in Indian policy, Curtis cast his lot with voluntary organizations such as the Exposition of Indian Tribal Arts, over which he served as honorary chairman, or an association of New Mexico artists who attacked Collier's proposal for a national Indian Arts and Crafts Board on the grounds that it would undermine the value and the integrity of Indian products. And unlike Hoover, who at least went on record in support of reforms for the Indian service as proposed by a Brookings Institution study compiled by Lewis Merriam and his associates in 1928, Curtis issued no public statement for or against the report. Indeed, with Curtis on the campaign trail in 1932, it was as if an Indian problem no longer existed. Certainly his status as a roll model for Indians in general, which had diminished dramatically since the mid 1920s, reached its nadir with the Hoover-Curtis defeat in 1932.[26]

The victory of Franklin D. Roosevelt in November 1932 ended the public career of Charles Curtis. When early election returns indicated a Democratic triumph, Curtis nevertheless predicted that the Republicans would prevail in the end, and according to most reports, he was genuinely surprised with the Hoover-Curtis defeat. Even his home state of Kansas went for Roosevelt, and this rejection may have contributed to his remaining in Washington and establishing his legal residence in the District of Columbia. He retained a nominal association with a law firm in Topeka, and he made occasional trips to Kansas. But after 1932, his main interest was his law office in the nation's capital, which became widely known as a rendezvous for Republican regulars to discuss "the fine art of politics" and the future of the GOP. Kansans, who "gave him almost everything he asked for or even intimated he would like to have," were disappointed that Curtis did not return to his native state. Yet, he remained interested in Kansas politics, and in August 1935 he was one of the first politicians of national stature to call for the nomination of Alf M. Landon of Kansas as the Republican presidential candidate.[27]

On 8 February 1936, Curtis was found dead in bed, apparently of a heart attack, in the Washington home of his half sister, where he had been residing since relinquishing the vice-presidency. Hundreds paid their last respects to Curtis in the Gann house where he had died, after which his body was taken from Washington to Topeka for a memorial service that was attended by thousands in the rotunda of the state capitol and then to Representative Hall, where Dr. Harold Case of the First Methodist Church presided over the final rites. Only one bow and two arrows, gifts from Chief Deerfoot of the Apache tribe, adorned the coffin. "May the great spirit speed you on your way to the happy hunting ground, is the grateful prayer of the [Kaw] council members, which fellowship Charles shared," was the most widely quoted portion of Dr. Case's memorial. In a similar vein a Wichita paper printed a large photograph of Curtis alongside one of Chief Wahshungah, with the caption, "Who can say but what they are together in the happy hunting grounds." Final interment, with the Apache bow and arrows, was in a Topeka cemetery that is not far from the site where Curtis had been born three-quarters of a century earlier.[28]

Having exerted enormous power in the Republican party for more than a quarter of a century and having been elected to the second-highest office in the nation, Charles Curtis was, of course, a towering figure in the increasing mixed-blood community throughout the country. Yet he was not alone in achieving prominence and recognition that often transcended the derogatory societal labeling that was the result of the happenstance of mixed-blood birth. There was, for example, Henry

Chee Dodge (1857–1947), a mixed-blood Navajo leader who was the first of his people to become fluent in the English language and who played a large role in Navajo business affairs after he was elected as tribal chairman in 1923. And Dr. Susan LaFleche Picotte (1865–1915)—the Omaha daughter of Joseph ("Iron Eyes") LaFleche and Mary Gale—who achieved well-deserved recognition as the first Indian woman doctor of medicine and who worked hard to cut through the Indian-service bureaucracy as it affected the welfare of her own people. There was Quanah Parker (1852–1911) of the Comanches, a mixed-blood who rose to a position of reservation leadership by closely cooperating with federal agents and who secured considerable material rewards for his efforts. Charles Eastman, or Ohiyesa (1858–1939), a mixed-blood Santee Sioux, earned a prestigious medical degree, worked as a government physician at the Pine Ridge Agency, and retained an interest in his roots while exhibiting a strong commitment to assimilation as a desirable goal. There was the distinguished mixed-blood Osage Oxonian John Joseph Mathews (1894–1979), who earned an international reputation as the author of books on Osage history and culture, who served on the Osage Council, and who was a supporter of John Collier and the Indian Reorganization Act of 1934. And there was the Cherokee mixed-blood Robert Latham Owen, Jr. (1856–1947), who became one of Oklahoma's first senators and an unsuccessful candidate for the Democratic nomination for president in 1920.[29]

These mixed-bloods evinced disparate degrees of support for assimilation, ranging from Parker's vacillation and ultimately bitter capitulation to allotment, on the one hand, to Owen's undisguised belief in the malleability of the full-bloods, on the other hand. In 1904, Owen informed a congressional committee that "without inbreeding" it was possible to change the full-bloods by means of white versions of education and economic development. He pointed to three full-blood girls in a picture of the graduating class of an Indian Territory school who absolutely could not be differentiated from their mixed-blood classmates. "There is nothing in the form of the face to indicate the degree of blood," said Owen; "indeed, one of the full blood girls is the prettiest of the party. It shows what education will do with the human face."[30]

During Curtis's early years, after he had abandoned reservation life and returned to Topeka "to make something of himself," as his Indian grandmother had advised, he might have applauded Owen's exhortations for full-blood improvement. But by the 1890s, after Curtis had entered the national political arena and had begun to play a practical role in fine tuning the government's allotment policy, he was no longer certain that assimilationist legislation was the answer. Proper laws, including the requirement of tribal dissolution, were desirable; but the key was the mixed-blood himself—*the* solution to the Indian problem. In his own tribe, however, mixed-blood leadership proved inconsequential and seemed not to have the desired effect on those whom it should have benefited the most. By the mid 1920s, then, Curtis had become disillusioned to the degree that he opted for what Hazel W. Hertzberg has called a policy of accommodation—that is, acceptance of the dominant society while still searching for values that are peculiar to the world of the Indian.[31]

For Curtis, the most important of these were a sense of self-worth and an unwavering belief that one's *individual* performance was what really mattered. The Indian commissioner John Collier caught the essence of this at the time of Curtis's death in 1936. Admitting that the whispering Indian may have kept his name on the tribal roll simply for "sentimental reasons," Collier nevertheless emphasized, with not a little irony, that Curtis's land was still being administered by the government, as an example for other Indians to follow."[32]

Epilogue
The White Man's Law and the Curtis Indian Estate

True to his promise, Charles Curtis did not during his lifetime alienate his 160-acre homestead allotment near the Washungah town site. This did not mean, however, that he was averse to disposing of other real property that had been awarded to him as an official member of the Kaw Tribe. According to the Kaw Allotment Act of 1902, all Kaws who were listed on the final allotment roll received, in addition to their restricted homesteads, approximately 245 additional "surplus" acres of the former reservation. In many instances these tracts were sold to non-Indian ranchers and farmers in the decade after allotment, with the proceeds going to the allottee without restriction. This was a quick way to turn land into cash.[1]

Less than three years after the allotment act went into effect, Curtis had disposed of all but twenty acres of his surplus land. The small tract was retained in the hope of profits from what, in fact, turned out to be the unprofitable Hardy town site that General W. E. Hardy promoted in the northeastern part of the former reservation, some ten miles north of Washungah. Although Curtis had had good fortune with his land in North Topeka, he was unsuccessful as an urban developer in Indian Territory.[2]

After Wahshungah's death in 1909, the Interior Department approved Curtis's request that his homestead be placed in trust, to be divided into equal shares upon his death for his three children—who themselves were allottees under the 1902 act. Curtis's wife, Anna, died in 1924, and when he died twelve years later, the trust agreement was carried out. By then Permelia had married C. P. George, a career army officer whose base was in Virginia. Harry had graduated from Harvard and was practicing law in Chicago, and Leona had married Webster Knight II, a prominent industrialist of Providence, Rhode Island. As assimilated sixteenth-bloods with virtually no cultural ties with their distant Indian relatives in Oklahoma, their interest in post-allotment Kaw affairs seldom transcended the practical realm of absentee landlords on the former reservation.[3]

Curtis's land in North Topeka presents a more complex picture. During the Civil War years, Curtis's Indian grandmother had engaged in several land transactions involving her 1825 grant, including the land that eventually went to Curtis. After she moved to the Indian Territory reservation in 1873, Julie Gonville Pappan had not taken any further interest in her grandson's land ventures in Kansas. Apparently the situation was reciprocal, for in contrast to the admiring references in the later part of his autobiography to his paternal grandmother, Permelia Hubbard Curtis, there is a notable absence of commentary by Curtis regarding his Indian grandmother, who had advised him to stay in Kansas and "try to make something of himself."[4]

After he had secured the right to manage his own affairs, Curtis proceeded to dispose of his North Topeka estate. First he sold half a city block to a distillery and a similar plot to a brewery. Other sales followed in the early 1880s, mainly smaller plots for shops and for individual family housing. The more valuable property, which abutted the north bank of the Kansas River, eventually came into the hands of railroad-related industry and sand-dredging operations. The income from these sales was substantial.[5]

During his early adult years, Curtis established his residence in the twelve-room mansion that his Grandfather Curtis had erected in 1864 at 905 North Van Buren Street in North Topeka, and in 1896, Curtis acquired title to the property from his aging grandmother. The disastrous flood of 1903 damaged the property, and in 1907, Curtis sold it and purchased a new home across the river at 1107 Topeka Avenue, just southwest of the Kansas capitol building. Eventually the house on Van Buren Street was subdivided as an apartment building and then was demolished as a deteriorating private property. During the congressional and vice-presidential years, of course, Curtis maintained a residence in the nation's capital as well. The home at 1107 Topeka Avenue was sold by Curtis's heirs in 1937; it is currently owned by Gordon Toedman.[6]

The Kaw Agency at Washungah was abolished in 1928, the year that Charles Curtis was elected vice-president of the United States. Records dating back to allotment were poorly maintained. Some had been transferred to the Ponca and Osage agencies in the early 1920s. In 1928, the remainder were transferred to the Pawnee Agency, and noncurrent files dating back to the late nineteenth century were placed in the custody of the Oklahoma Historical Society according to federal law in

The home of Charles Curtis at 1107 Topeka Avenue in Topeka. Courtesy of the Kansas State Historical Society.

1934. A 1940 census taken by the Pawnee agent Lem A. Towers revealed that the number of Kaw full-bloods had declined to less than 11 percent of the tribal total of 531. Factionalism had given away to disillusionment and disinterest at the very time when many other tribes were developing a new sense of identity by using funds provided by the Oklahoma Indian Welfare Act of 1936. Even the tribal cemetery at Washungah, where Curtis's Indian grandmother was buried, was badly neglected.[7]

In one of the major ironies of Kaw history, the silence of the dead accomplished more than the living in calling attention to legal problems associated with the half-blood reserves of which Curtis's former North Topeka land had been a part. In 1951 the federal government authorized a modest maintenance fund for the tribal cemetery at Washungah, with the stipulation that the fifteen acres reserved for future burials be rented as a means of sustaining the fund and keeping the cemetery in repair. The Kaw Cemetery Association was established, with the understanding that two Kaw Indians would be elected as officers of the association each Memorial Day, to administer the maintenance of the cemetery.[8]

The association became the impetus for a meeting, held on 8 October 1958 at the old council house in Washungah, that resulted in the creation of the Kaw Business Committee and the drafting of the Constitution and Bylaws of the Kaw Tribe of Oklahoma. Elected chairman was Tom J. Dennison, a sixteenth-blood relative of Charles Curtis's and a descendant of Clement Lessert, the recipient of half-blood tract number 2 under the 1825 Kansa treaty.[9]

Until a federal court order ousted Dennison sixteen years later on the grounds that he did not meet the 1958 requirement that all committee members have minimum of one-fourth quantum of Kaw blood, he was the driving force in tribal revival and in the clarification of the property rights of heirs to the 640-acre half-blood tracts established in 1825. On the theory that federal legislation of the early 1860s had not abrogated restrictions against alienation as provided in article 11 of the 1825 treaty, Dennison insisted that all real-estate transactions since that date were invalid—including those of Curtis and his family—and that the living heirs to the tracts still held legal title to the land.[10]

But attorneys for the Interior and Justice departments turned Dennison down, arguing that the 1862 legislation stood firm as a deterrent to the quiet-title suit that Dennison was seeking. He then sought redress with an appeal to Congress for a private relief bill. In this he succeeded, aided by Congressman Page Belcher of Oklahoma and Senator Sam Irwin of North Carolina. As worded in the final version, dated 8 August 1968, the bill provided payment "in full and final satisfaction of all claims of the named individuals or their heirs against the United States based upon the loss of Indian lands included in the twenty-three halfbreed Kaw allotments . . . and in full satisfaction of any claims of the original allottee or his heirs for the consequent loss of land."[11]

Financially, the relief bill was a hollow victory. It judged the value of the lands at only five dollars an acre in 1862 and made no provision for the payment of interest since that date. Yet as early as 1857 the Kansa agent had reported the lands were worth "twenty-five . . . to forty dollars per acre," and in 1862, the federal investigator William H. Coombs had reported: "I made frequent inquiries of those living in the neighborhood and well acquainted with these lands as to their present value, but their estimates were so widely variant that but little reliance could be placed on them." The variance, of course, was the result of the speculative mania then being directed at the half-blood lands. In fact, according to the land files kept for Shawnee County, Kansas, Curtis's grandmother had sold nearly a quarter section in 1863 for ten dollars an acre. Moreover, the relief bill made no provision for the large amount of timber taken by intruders, which Coombs himself reported in 1862 to have constituted "almost all the lumber used in the [Kansas River] valley, including the towns of Lecompton, Tecumseh, and Topeka."[12]

When Dennison failed to obtain interest on the land award, which the Interior Department vigorously opposed on the ground that it would open "a Pandora's box" of claims that had previously been adjudicated with other tribes without interest, he turned back to the courts in a manner that would have been the envy of Charles Curtis himself. Like Curtis, who during more than four decades of official involvement in Indian affairs at the national level had stood as a champion of the judicial protection of individual Indian property rights, Dennison was firm in his belief that individual Indians were entitled to the protection of individual realty that had been established by treaty, regardless of subsequent congressional interference.[13]

On 11 December 1979, Dennison and his brother, Leonard Franklin Dennison, "for certain heirs of 23 Kaw Half-Breed Indians," filed a complaint in the United States District Court in Wichita, stating that the "reservees and the plaintiffs through them were and are now vested with all right, title and interest in said land, including the right of possession." Named as defendants were the Topeka Chambers Industrial Development Corporation and the Security Benefit Life Insurance Company, "for all persons claiming an interest in Kaw Half-Breed Reserves 1-23, Shawnee and Jefferson County, Kansas." Article 11 of the Kansa treaty of 1825 had placed restrictions on the individual alienation of the twenty-three reserves, and no alienation was possible without the prior permission of the United States government. The plaintiffs asked further that because they had been "denied the possession, use and enjoyment of the land," the court should declare "their in praesenti right and title to the land, in fee simple, subject to the treaty restriction." The defendants responded by arguing that the original treaty had placed no restrictions on the half-blood reserves, that the congressional acts of 1860 and 1862 had vested title in the half-blood allottees without restriction in regard to alienation, that the complaint was barred by the statute of limitations, and that in any case, the 1968 private-relief bill had extinguished any claims that Dennison and the mixed-blood heirs might previously have had.[14]

Judge Frank J. Theis handed down his ruling on 2 November 1981, with the almost apologetic observation that it provided "an opportunity to journey back in American history and to close the book on another unsalutary volume in the history of the treatment of the Indian people by the white immigrants to this land." Theis added: "Plaintiffs ask the Court to add a final chapter to this saga that . . . would constitute a happy ending. Defendants state that the Court is bound to follow what has already been written and cannot rewrite history at this later date." Because no genuine issue of material fact was discovered, the defendants' request for a summary judgment was granted on the grounds that the decision turned exclusively on the meaning and interpretation of the 1825 treaty, the congressional acts of 1860 and 1862, and the private act of 1968. ''The Court believes,'' emphasized Theis, ''that in light of the large amount of uncontroverted historical background material supplied . . . , it would be a waste of both Judicial and legal resources to hold a trial merely to decide the legal questions in this case.''[15]

Legally, the court's opinion in favor of the defendants offered no surprises. Agreeing that the 1825 treaty had restricted the right of the half-bloods to alienate their lands and affirming the well-established power of Congress to amend or completely abrogate Indian treaties, Theis ruled that under the 1860 legislation the restriction had remained intact. But this legislation was not the final ''pronouncement by Congress on the subject.'' While the 1862 act did not wholly supercede the 1860 act, it did provide that the land could ''pass by traditional laws of alienation and inheritance.'' In fact it constituted a major change of attitude by the United States in terms of what was best for the twenty-three half-bloods (or their heirs) by giving them ''the right of free will alienation possessed by American citizens.'' It was, emphasized Theis, a deliberate and forceful expression of national sovereignty by Congress.[16]

Theis admitted that the legislative history of the 1862 act was ''so scanty as to be of little help in determining what intent should be imputed to Congress.'' As a result, the court was obliged to consider ''contemporaneous'' interpretations. Attention was called to two court cases heard after 1862—*Swope* v. *Purdy*, 23 F.Cas. 576 (C.C.D.Kan., 1870), and *Smith* v. *Stevens*, 77 U.S. (10. Wall.) 321, 19 L.Ed. 933 (1870), both of which upheld the 1862 removal of restriction. Greater weight, however, was given to federal administrative interpretations that had been submitted soon after the act had gone into effect, as well as those of a much later date. Included in the latter were letters written by Secretary of the Interior Stewart L. Udall in 1966 and by Congressman Emmanuel Celler in 1965, both of which sustained the 1870 court findings. In a comparable vein were two letters written by the Indian commissioner William P. Dole more than a century earlier, in 1863. But the one letter that seemed to have the greatest relevance to the question of alienation was one that bore directly on the family and Indian estate of Charles Curtis.[17]

Less than a month after the 1862 act had become law, Curtis's father, Orren, had written to the Indian Office in Washington, requesting clarification of the recently announced legislative reversal in regard to alienation. For Orren there was a sense of urgency, for at that very time his mother-in-law, Julie Gonville Pappan, was in the process of deeding a valuable part of her 1825 allotment to her daughter Ellen and to her two infant grandchildren, Charles and Elizabeth Curtis. Orren was being left out, and he apparently was seeking assistance in his effort to block the deed. In this he was disappointed, for on 26 July 1862, the acting commissioner of Indian Affairs, Charles E. Mix, wrote to Orren:

> The Act of Congress of July 17, 1862 . . . has deprived this Department of all jurisdiction. . . . All questions as to the rights of grantees, heirships, titles, liability to taxation, in short the whole subject matter, belong exclusively to the courts of Kansas by virtue of said act of Congress and to those courts you must therefore necessarily apply for their adjudication.

Attached to Theis's decision were two appendices. One was the treaty of 1825, which impressed the court with its "fascinating names and descriptive titles of the Indian signatories." The other was an 1857 letter by the Kansa agent John Montgomery to the superintendent of Indian Affairs in St. Louis, in which "the filthy speculation" of white squatters on the half-blood reserves was clearly documented. It was true, Judge Theis conceded, that "a great injustice" had probably been inflicted on some of the half-bloods, and it was true that the late 1850s had constituted "a shameful period of Kansas territorial history." But to require retribution of the current landowners in North Topeka "for the sins of their great-grandfathers would merely add to injustice, not right it."[18]

Had the Whispering Indian survived to observe the legal proceeding, there is little doubt that he would have applauded the ruling. Well within the tradition of Curtis's advocacy of the mixed-blood cause, *Dennison* v. *Topeka Chambers* confirmed the positive impact that private property had had on the achievement of mixed-bloods, as well as its importance to the well-being of Indians in general. Congress had not erred when it had altered the 1825 treaty in favor of mixed-bloods, not even in the face of admitted injustices and shameful events before and after that change. After all, the noble performance of mixed-bloods such as Curtis—whose accomplishments Judge Theis somehow saw fit to mention in his opinion—had been a vital factor in Indian adjustment to the white man's world.[19]

Appendix

Tommy Joe Dennison and Leonard Franklin Dennison, for certain heirs of 23 Kay Half-Breed Indians, Plaintiffs, v. Topeka Chambers Industrial Development Corporation, a Kansas corporation, and Security Benefit Life Insurance Company, a Kansas corporation, for all persons claiming an interest in Kaw Half-Breed Reserves 1–23, Shawnee and Jefferson Counties, Kansas, Defendants. Civ. A. No. 79-1668. United States District Court, D. Kansas. Nov. 2, 1981.

OPINION OF THE COURT

THEIS, District Judge.

Defendants' motion for summary judgment in this case affords the Court an opportunity to journey back in American history and to close the book on another unsalutary volume in the history of the treatment of the Indian people by the white immigrants to this land. Plaintiffs ask the Court to add a final chapter to this saga that, to the plaintiffs at least, would constitute a happy ending. Defendants state that the Court is bound to follow what has already been written and cannot rewrite history at this late date. They ask the Court to add only a postscript affirming the finality of what has already transpired. The Court will offer a condensed version of the established facts to date and then will apply the law to produce the ending that law and policy deem appropriate.

This action is brought by the named plaintiffs on behalf of themselves and others claiming to be the heirs of 23 Kaw (also known as Kansa or Kansas) Indian half-breeds. Half-breed is a term used to denote the offspring of white and Indian parents. The Treaty of 1825 between the United States and the Kaw Indians reserved to each of 23 named half-breed Kaws a one-mile square tract of land. The 23 tracts were along the north bank of the Kansas (Kaw) River. Plaintiffs ask the court to declare that the heirs of the 23 half-breeds are the owners of "all right, title, interest in and to" the land, which comprises

179

approximately 14,500 acres stretching along the north bank of the Kaw River from North Topeka, Kansas, to east of Perry, Kansas, the classic verbiage of what is known as a quiet title suit, ordinarily a state court cause of action. Plaintiffs argue that the land received by the half-breeds was restricted so that it could not be sold without the permission of the United States. The plaintiffs argue that the tracts granted to the half-breeds were transferred in numerous transactions over the years, were made without the approval of the United States, that such transfers were void, were made under fraud and duress, and that the heirs of the half-breeds are the present true owners of the land.

Defendants made several arguments in support of their motion for summary judgment: (1) The Treaty of 1825 did not place restrictions on alienation on the lands received by the half-breeds; (2) Congress, by legislation in 1860 and 1862, superseded or voided the treaty provision, thus vesting title in the half-breed reserves without restriction, at least as of passage of the 1862 Act; (3) plaintiffs' claims, based on prior transfers of the land, are barred by the statute of limitations; and (4) any claims plaintiffs may have had were extinguished by a 1968 Private Act in which Congress gave money to the heirs of the reservees.

[1] The threshold issue is whether the case is suitable for summary judgment. A summary judgment motion cannot be granted if there is a genuine issue of material fact. Summary judgment is a drastic remedy and should be applied with caution. *Redhouse v. Quality Food Sales, Inc.*, 511 F.2d 230, 234 (10th Cir. 1975). The movant must demonstrate his right to prevail beyond a reasonable doubt. *Madison v. Deseret Livestock Co.*, 574 F.2d 1027, 1037 (10th Cir. 1978). Defendants state that there are no issues of material fact, only issues of law as to interpretation of the 1825 Treaty and the subsequent congressional legislation. Plaintiffs argue that the interpretation of the Treaty and statutes are issues of material fact and assert that there are issues of material fact as to the evidence of ownership of the current landholders, such as whether the transfers from the half-breeds were marked with fraud, duress, or other factual indicia of invalidity.

[2, 3] The Court believes that the facts as to evidence of ownership are wholly immaterial unless the Court decides to accept plaintiffs' proposed interpretation of the Treaty and statutes. Despite plaintiffs' assertions to the contrary, the interpretation of the Treaty and statutes are questions of law for the Court to resolve. Summary judgment is appropriate when a decision turns on the meaning of words in a statute. *Standard Oil Co. v. Dept. of Energy*, 596 F.2d 1029, 1060 (Em.App.1978); *Mobil Oil Co. v. FEA*, 566 F.2d 87, 92 (Em.App.1978); *Intn'l. Society for Krishna Consciousness v. Rocheford*, 425 F.Supp. 734, 738 (N.D.Ill. 1977). Likewise, "the interpretation of a treaty presents a question of law which is appropriately considered upon a motion for summary judgment." *Upton v. Iran Nat. Airlines Corp.*, 450 F.Supp. 176 (S.D.N.Y. 1976), aff'd., 603 F.2d 215 (2d Cir. 1979). If the Court believed that it required more exposure to the background of this controversy, a trial might be worthwhile. The Court believes, however, that in light of the large amount of uncontroverted historical background material supplied to the Court by the parties, it would be a waste of both judicial and legal resources to hold a trial merely to decide the legal questions in this case.

In sum, then, the Court's opinion and judgment in this case will be based on interpretation of four historical official documents of our government, viz., the 1825 Treaty, the Congressional Acts of 1860 and 1862, and the Congressional Private Act of 1968. The evidence in the case besides these documents will consist of other documentary evidence from governmental archives, which includes official activities of both Congress and the Executive Departments, and Indian archival records, all of which may illuminate the facts and circumstances surrounding the enactment and/or administration of the four principal documents so as to further clarify their intent. The able counsel for all of the parties agree on the authenticity of this evidence.

THE TREATY OF 1825

The foundation of plaintiffs' claim is the Treaty of 1825 (Appendix A) between the United States and the Kansas Nation, 7 Stat. 244. In Article 1 of the Treaty, the Kaws ceded all of their lands in Missouri and Kansas to the United States. From the cession a tract of land was reserved for the use of the Kansas Nation, in Article 2. The United States agreed to pay the Kansas Nation an annuity and to help provide for the tribes in other respects. Article 6 of the Treaty provided in pertinent part:

"From the lands above ceded to the United States, there shall be made the following reservations, of one mile square, for each of the half breeds of the Kanzas nation, viz: [the half breeds are named] . . . to be located on the North side of the Kanzas river, in the order above named, commencing at the line of the Kanzas reservation, and extending down the Kanzas river for quantity."

Article 11 of the Treaty provided:

"It is further agreed on, by and between the parties to these presents, that the United States shall forever enjoy the right to navigate freely all water courses or navigable streams within the limits of the tract of country herein reserved to the Kanzas Nation; and that the said Kanzas Nation shall never sell, relinquish, or in any manner dispose of the lands herein reserved, to any other nation, person or persons whatever, without the permission of the United States for that purpose first had and obtained. And shall ever remain under the protection of the United States, and in friendship with them."

One question of initial interpretation before the Court is whether the restrictions on land disposition in Article 11 apply to the reservations made in Article 6 for the half-breeds. Defendants contend that the restriction in Article 11 does not apply to the Article 6 lands because the language in Article 11 refers to "the Kanzas Nation" disposing of the land. Since the lands in Article 6 were given not to the Kansas Nation but to the half-breeds, defendants contend, it would be the half-breeds, not the Kansas Nation, who would dispose of the lands. Thus, they contend, any restriction on the Kansas Nation would not apply.

[4–6] While defendants' analysis is initially appealing, the Court must exercise caution in deciding the meaning of an Indian treaty on the basis of fine distinctions in language, although as in the law of contracts and interpretation of legislative acts, clarity of language is a paramount factor in determining the intent of the parties. Historical facts in the growth of our country as a sovereign nation, and its related historical principles of law known as stare decisis, have resulted in some fixed axioms of law in this area of legal determination. Indian cessions are not ordinary conveyances, due to the dependent status of the Indians and the often nonconsensual nature of the cessions. Cession treaties must be interpreted as the Indians intended them, and doubtful expressions must be resolved in favor of the Indians. E.g., *Choctaw Nation v. Oklahoma*, 397 U.S. 620, 630-31, 90 S.Ct. 1328, 1334-35, 25 L.Ed.2d 615 (1976). See Cohen, *Handbook of Federal Indian Law* (1942 ed.), at 37. It must be understood that the best interests of the Indians are not necessarily best served by giving them the broadest power over their lands. Cohen, at 37. See *Starr v. Long Jim*, 227 U.S. 613, 33 S.Ct. 358, 57 L.Ed. 670 (1913).

[7] To determine the understanding of the Indians as a party to an accord, the Court must analyze the prior history, the surrounding circumstances and the subsequent construction of the treaty. See, e.g., *Choctaw Nation v. United States*, 318 U.S. 423, 431, 63 S.Ct. 672, 678, 87 L.Ed.2d 877 (1943). The Court agrees with Felix Cohen's statement that:

"Although an interpretation of a treaty should be made in the light of conditions existing when the treaty was executed, as often indicated by its history before and after the making, the exact situation which caused the inclusion of the provision is often difficult to ascertain. New conditions may arise which could not be anticipated by the signatories to a treaty. A practical administrative construction of a treaty which has long been acquiesced in by congressional inaction is usually followed by the courts." Cohen, supra, at 37.

The court notes that while the historical circumstances surrounding the drafting of the 1825 Treaty do not conclusively settle the issue of whether the Article 11 restrictions apply to the Article 6 lands, they do give the Court some guidance. It is known that four of the 23 half-breeds who received lands under Article 6 were grandchildren of White Plume, the leading Kaw chief at the time and the principal Kaw signatory to the treaty. Unrau, *The Kansas Indians*, 34, 118-19 (1971); Miner & Unrau, *The End of Indian Kansas*, 101-102 (1978). It is also known that the Kaws were plagued with tribal factionalism before and after the signing of the Treaty and that White Plume's influence within the tribe tended to ebb and flow. It is known that the granting of land to the half-breeds caused jealousy among many of the Kaws and helped to undermine White Plume's influence and raise the influence of those chiefs who had nothing to do with the half-breeds. H. Miner & W. Unrau, supra, at 101-102; W. Unrau, supra, at 30, 34, 118-119.

[8] With these historical facts before the Court, plaintiffs' argument that the restrictions were intended to help protect the half-breeds as well as the Kansas Nation appears to be sound. The half-breeds apparently needed protection from both the whites and the full blood tribal Kaw Indians, and White Plume appeared interested in doing all he could for the half-breeds. Standing alone, these historical circumstances would not be enough to convince the Court that the Article 11 restrictions apply to the half-breed lands. In conjunction with the clear purpose of the treaty language and the later administrative and judicial interpretations of the Treaty, however, the Court is convinced that the half-breed lands were so restricted.

A comment about the Court's own view of the historical perspective purpose of Article 11 of the Treaty may be in order to explain why it was never repealed nor alluded to in the subsequent legislation relevant to this case.

As to Article 11 of the 1825 Treaty, upon which plaintiffs place great reliance, it appears to this Court that such provision was a generic one designed mainly for the benefit of the United States as a contracting party under which the Kansas Nation agreed twofold: first, to the principle of free navigation by anyone on all waters within the reservations of land to both the Kaw nation and the named half-breeds; and second, ''never to sell, relinquish, or in any manner dispose of the lands herein reserved, to any other nation, person or persons whatever, without the permission of the United States for the purpose first had and obtained, and shall forever remain under the protection of the United States, and in friendship with them.''

Such a provision would appear to be most appropriate for a new and growing nation like the United States living in an era where the nations of England, France and Spain were still retaining parts of the New World, where unbridled conquest or acquisition of foreign lands was a fixed principle in international law, and where each Indian tribe or group of related tribes considered themselves, and were so considered by the United States as well as other foreign nations, as independent nations. The second announced generic purpose of Article 11 was thus to guarantee perpetual national sovereignty and control over the reserved lands, and not as a traditional legal restriction on alienation by individual titleholders except as to anyone asserting sovereignty against the United States.

Such a generic viewpoint of Article 11 in the light of historical circumstances might well seem in accord with the defendants' base contention that the 1825 Treaty never contained a reference to a restriction upon alienation by the half-breed allottees, but only plainly in its words as to ''Kansas nation.'' However, reference to the descriptive words of Article 6, ''for each of the half breeds of the Kansas nation,'' indicates they were a part of the whole Kansas Nation. Likewise, apparently the full blood reservations and 23 half-breed reserves were contiguous to each other, that is, one total reservation area. As stated above, the principle of free navigation applied to all the Kansas Indian reserved land, including that of the half-breeds. The same Article 11 as to the restrictions on disposal must be read as plainly intending to restrict the whole reserved lands. Therefore, using the principle of liberal interpretation of Indian treaties later discussed herein, this Court has no difficulty in reaching the legal conclusion that *all* of the lands reserved in the Treaty required the permission of the United States for disposal or alienation of title. The Court's viewpoint is based also on the scanty administrative and judicial interpretation available. Again, however, in view of the Court's holding as to the effect of the legislative acts of 1860, 1862, and 1968, the Court can agree with defendants' contention that whether or not the 1825 Treaty restrained the right of alienation of the half-breed lands is of little consequence.

Controversy over the type of title held by the half-breeds raged in the 1840's and 1850's as land speculators, squatters, and timber cutters swarmed over the lands in question. W. Unrau, supra, at 138–139, 155–156, 171–178; Plaintiffs' Ex. 1; Defendants' Ex. 5, 7, 9. The efforts by the white settlers to drive the Indian half-breeds off their lands were strenuously resisted by some government officials, notably the Indian agents in the area. W. Unrau, supra, at 171–178. The government officials also resisted efforts by white settlers to have the government state that the half-breed titles had lapsed or that the half-breeds could alienate their land. Plaintiffs' Ex. 1; W. Unrau, supra, at 171–178. Appendix B, referred to in the "Foreword to Appendices" of this opinion and attached hereto, illustrates the mistreatment of the Kansas half-breeds during this pre–Civil War era.

On January 19, 1858, a resolution of the House of Representatives (Defendants' Ex. 8), titled "Kansas Half-Breed Indians," was passed, in which the House requested the opinion of the Secretary of Interior:

"[a]s to the policy or propriety of taking the necessary steps to extinguish the Indian title to all reservations under any treaty with the said Indians in the Territory of Kansas, protecting the rights of the Indians, and of giving said Indians the fee in said land."

In response, the Secretary of Interior wrote:

"In my opinion, it would be proper to authorize the original reservees or their heirs to sell their land, under such restrictions as may be necessary to protect them against fraud, and to secure them a fair price for the land, should they desire to sell. This would be equivalent to granting the fee of the land, and is a measure of relief to which the half-breeds are equitably entitled.

"From all these circumstances it may be fairly inferred that the right of occupancy granted was not designed to be personal merely, but was to exist as a perpetuity in the half-breeds and their descendants. They had all the rights incident to an estate in fee simple, except the right to sell, and this, I think should now be given them." Defendants' Ex. 9.

The administrative construction of the Treaty thus supports the position that the restrictions of Article 11 apply to the Article 6 reservations. The Supreme Court appeared to favor the same position, stating in dicta in *Stephens v. Smith*, 77 U.S. (10 Wall.) 321, 19 L.Ed. 933 (1870), that:

"By the 6th article of the Treaty, there was reserved for the benefit of each of the half breeds named in it (Victoria Smith being one of them), a certain specified allotment of land out of the quantity ceded by the Nation to the United States. The 11th Article contains a stipulation that the Nation shall not sell these lands without permission of the government, and it would seem that the contracting parties intended this prohibition to apply to the individual members of the tribe; for, if it were not so, the policy which dictated the restriction would be in danger of being defeated altogether."

In light of the historical circumstances surrounding the Treaty and the administrative and judicial interpretations of the Treaty, the Court concludes that the Treaty of 1825 did restrict the right of the half-breeds to alienate their lands.

The 1860 and 1862 Congressional Acts

In 1860, Congress, in an apparent attempt to solve the confusion surrounding the Kansas half-breed lands, passed the following Act, entitled "An Act to settle the Titles to certain Lands set apart for the Use of Certain Half-Breed Kansas Indians, in Kansas Territory."

"Whereas by the sixth article of a treaty made and concluded at the City of St. Louis in the State of Missouri, on the third day of June, eighteen hundred and twenty-five, between the United States of America and the Kansas nation of Indians, there was reserved from the lands ceded by said treaty to the United States by said Kansas nation of Indians, one mile square of land for each of the half-breeds of the Kansas nation named in the said sixth article, which land has been surveyed and allotted to each of the said half-breeds in the order in which they are named in, and in accordance with, the provisions of the said sixth article of said treaty: therefore,

Be it enacted by the Senate and House of Representatives of the United States of America in Congress assembled, That all the title, interest and estate of the United States is hereby vested in the said reservees who are now living, to the land reserved, set apart and allotted to them respectively by the said sixth article of said treaty; and in case any of the said reservees named in the said sixth article are deceased and leaving heirs, then all the title, interest or estate of the United States to the land allotted to such deceased reservees, is hereby vested and confirmed in such persons as shall by the Secretary of the Interior be decided to be the heirs of such deceased reservees; but, nothing herein shall be construed to give any force, efficacy or binding effect to any contract, in writing or otherwise, for the sale or disposition of any lands named in this act, heretofore made by any of said reservees or their heirs.

Sec. 2 And be it further enacted, That in case of any of the reservees now living, or the heirs of any deceased reservees, shall not desire to reside upon, or occupy the lands to which such reservees or such heirs are entitled by the provisions of this act, the Secretary of the Interior, when requested by them or by either of them to do so, is hereby authorized to sell such lands belonging to those so requesting him, for the benefit of such reservees, or such heirs; and the Secretary of the Interior is also authorized to sell, with the assent of the Kansas nation of Indians the lands allotted to the reservees who are deceased leaving no heirs for the benefit of the living reservees, their heirs and the heirs of those deceased, equally; said lands to be sold in accordance with such rules and regulations as may be prescribed by the Commissioner of Indian Affairs, and approved by [the] Secretary of the Interior; and patents in the usual form shall be issued to the purchasers of said lands, in accordance with the provisions of this act.

Sec. 3 And be it further enacted, That the proceeds of the land, the sale of which is provided for by this act, shall be paid to the parties entitled thereto, or applied by the Secretary of the Interior for their benefit, in such manner as he may think most advantageous to their interest."

This Act clearly restricted the right of the half-breeds to alienate their land, as the land could only be sold by the Secretary of the Interior. Congress also emphasized that the Act gave no force or legal sanction to any prior disposition of the land. If the 1860 Act had been the last pronouncement by Congress on the subject, it is clear that any transfers by the half-breeds after 1860 not undertaken by the Secretary of the Interior under the scheme in the 1860 Act would be void and the land would legally belong to the heirs of the half-breeds. This was the interpretation of the 1860 Act given by the Supreme court in *Stephens v. Smith,* wherein the court declared that a land deed dated August 14, 1860, which purported to convey a tract from a half-breed was void. The Court said:

> "There is no ambiguity in the Act, nor is it requisite to extend the words of it beyond their plain meaning in order to arrive at the intention of the Legislature. It was considered by Congress to be necessary, in case the reservees should be desirous of relinquishing the occupation of their lands, that some method of disposing of them should be adopted which would be a safeguard against their own improvidence. . . . It was, manifestly, the purpose of Congress, in conferring the authority to sell (on the Secretary of the Interior), to save the lands of the reservees from the cupidity of the white race."

Stephens v. Smith, 77 U.S. (10 Wall.) 321, 19 L.Ed. 933 (1870).

After the passage of the Act of 1860, the Secretary of the Interior appointed two men, W. H. Walsh and William H. Coombs, to carry out the mandate of Congress to determine the status of the reservees and their heirs. On May 20, 1862, after the reports of the two men were submitted to the Secretary of the Interior, the Senate passed a resolution directing the Secretary to send it copies of the reports. The Secretary did so on June 3, 1862, and also sent to the Senate a letter in which he stated:

> "[T]here is a large number of settlers upon portions of the land, some of whom have made improvements. These settlers claim that they have a right to purchase the lands. This department cannot recognize such a claim under the existing law, and unless Congress shall interpose by some new legislation, it only remains to execute the act of Congress above referred to, by deciding who are the heirs of the deceased reservees, and perfecting their titles."

Defendants' Ex. 13.

Congress responded by considering a joint resolution (S.98), reported out by the Senate Committee on Indian Affairs on July 20, 1862, to repeal sections two and three of the Act of 1860, and as much of section one as authorized the Secretary to determine the heirs of the reservees. The sponsor of S.98, Senator Doolittle, said:

> "I am directed by the committee on Indian Affairs, to whom the subject was referred, to report a joint resolution in relation to a certain act concerning title to lands set apart for the use of the half-breed Kansas Indians in Kansas Territory, and it is necessary that there should be immediate action upon it; for there may result such a decision on the part of the Secretary of the Interior, based upon *ex parte* testimony, as may affect the titles of a great many persons. . . . The committee were unanimous in supporting this resolution."

Cong. Globe, 37th Cong., 2nd Sess. 3324 (1862). S.98 passed the Senate on July 14, 1862, and was passed with an amended title in the House on July 15, 1862. The Senate concurred in the House amendment on July 16 and the joint resolution was enrolled and signed July 17, 1862. It reads as follows:

> *"Resolved by the Senate and House of Representatives of the United States of America in Congress assembled,* That sections two and three of an act entitled 'An act to settle the titles to certain lands set apart for the use of certain Half-breed Kansas Indians in Kansas Territory,' approved May twenty-six, one thousand eight hundred and sixty, and so much of the first section as authorizes the Secretary of the Interior to decide what persons are heirs to deceased reservees as mentioned therein be and the same are hereby, repealed."

Defendants contend that the effect of the 1860 Act and the 1862 Joint Resolution, when read together, was to grant the half-breeds full title to the lands reserved to them by the 1825 Treaty, with no restrictions on alienation. They point to administrative and judicial interpretations which support their view. Plaintiffs contend that the legislation fails to change the provisions of the 1825 Treaty restricting alienation, especially since no reference was made in either legislative act to Article 11 of the Treaty which had imposed the restriction on disposition of any of the Treaty land. Plaintiffs rely on a large body of case law setting high standards to be met before it can be said that Congress has abrogated Indian treaty rights. Both arguments have merit in legal foundation.

[9] It is unquestioned that Congress has the power to amend or completely abrogate Indian treaties. E.g., *DeCoteau v. District County Court for Tenth Jud. Dist.*, 420 U.S. 425, 95 S.Ct. 1082, 43 L.Ed.2d 300 (1975). While Congress has the power to abrogate Indian treaties, the courts are frequently called upon to determine whether or not Congress has in fact abrogated part or all of a particular treaty. In so determining, the courts have been disposed to protect Indian treaty rights from what the Supreme Court has termed abrogation in "a backhanded way." *Menominee Tribe v. United States*, 391 U.S. 404, 412, 88 S.Ct. 1705, 1711, 20 L.Ed.2d 697 (1968). There is an element of truth in the statement that:

> "[T]he body of law protecting basic Indian treaty rights is in evident disarray. There are so many tests for determining whether an abrogation has been effected, and most of them are so vague, that a court has little recourse but to arrive at an ad hoc, almost arbitrary decision when faced with the question of whether a particular treaty guarantee has been abrogated by Congress."

Wilkenson & Volkman, *Judicial Review of Indian Treaty Abrogation*, 63 Cal.L.Rev. 601 (1975).

While there are a number of formulations extant as to how the Court should determine if an abrogation has been effected, the Court does not share the despair of Wilkenson & Volkman as to the Court's ability to reach a principled decision. While the language varies, all the formulations offer a good deal of protection to the Indians.

[10,11] The Supreme Court has said that "the intention to abrogate or modify a treaty is not to be lightly imputed to Congress." *Menominee Tribe of*

Indians v. United States, supra. A treaty will not be deemed to have been abrogated or modified by a later statute unless such purpose on the part of Congress has been clearly expressed. *Cook v. United States,* 288 U.S. 102, 120, 53 S.Ct. 305, 311, 77 L.Ed. 641 (1933); *United States v. Winnebago Tribe of Nebraska,* 542 F.2d 1002 (8th Cir. 1976). A later Act of Congress should be harmonized with the letter and spirit of the treaty so far as can reasonably be done. *United States v. White,* 508 F.2d 453 (8th Cir. 1974).

At times, courts have required a "definite expression of intention" (to abrogate), *United States v. Shoshone Tribe of Indians,* 304 U.S. 111, 118, 58 S.Ct. 794, 798, 82 L.Ed. 1213 (1938), or have said that the intention to abrogate must be "clearly and unequivocally stated." *Bennett County v. United States,* 394 F.2d 8, 11-12 (8th Cir. 1968). It has also been said that the statute in question should be liberally construed in favor of the Indian treaty rights. *Choate v. Trapp,* 224 U.S. 665, 32 S.Ct. 565, 56 L.Ed. 941 (1912).

There may well be "a growing judicial tendency to require clarity and specificity in legislative abrogation." Wilkenson & Volkman, supra, at 630. In *United States v. White,* supra, the Court stated that to affect Indian treaty rights, "it was incumbent upon Congress to expressly abrogate or modify the spirit of the relationship between the United States and Red Lake Chippewa Indians."

Thus, the tests employed by the courts range from liberally construing the statute in favor of Indian treaty rights to requiring Congress to expressly abrogate the treaty rights. All of the tests require the Court to make a careful study of the statutory language.

It must first be noted that nowhere in either the 1860 Act or the 1862 Resolution is Article 11 of the 1825 Treaty mentioned. There is no language in either piece of legislation flatly abrogating Article 11 of the Treaty. However, the Court has previously suggested the real reason for no attempt to repeal Article 11 in his discussion of its generic purpose to preserve United States sovereignty over the reserved lands (pp. 615-616). Noting in the 1860 Act talks of abrogating any portion of the Treaty. The Act mentions the provisions of Article 6 of the Treaty and then states that "all of the title, interest and estate of the United States is hereby vested in the said reservees." While this language would, standing alone, appear to be fee simple title with no restriction on alienation, such a meaning would be inconsistent both with the terms of the Treaty and with the rest of the Act which sets forth restrictions on alienation of the tracts. Nothing in the 1862 Resolution addresses abrogation of the 1825 Treaty. In fact, the Treaty is not even mentioned.

[12] Thus, if the Court were to be bound solely by the language in *United States v. White,* requiring *express* abrogation, the Court would have to hold that the legislation did not modify the Article 11 restrictions of the Treaty. The Court is convinced, however, that an express abrogation is not always required. The Supreme Court's statement in *Menominee Tribe* that the intent to abrogate is not to be lightly imputed to Congress would, to the Court, mean that the intent to abrogate can, under some circumstances, be imputed to Congress in the absence of express language of abrogation. If the intent of Congress is sufficiently clear, then abrogation, or partial abrogation, can be imputed.

In order to determine whether to impute to Congress the intent to abrogate the 1825 Treaty restrictions on alienation, the Court will first examine the statutory language. Defendants contend that the 1860 and 1862 Acts, when read together, cleary vest fee simple title in the half-breeds. This Court agrees that such is the effective result of the two enactments. They must, however, be read singly and in time sequence as to enactment in light of the historical circumstances of the times. The Court should liberally construe the statutory language in favor of the Indian treaty rights. *Choate v. Trapp,* supra. Such liberal construction yields a plausible interpretation. The 1860 Act upheld the general restriction on alienation embodied in the 1825 Treaty, but provided that the lands could be passed through inheritance and set forth a particular system for alienating the land and protecting the Indian beneficiaries. Under this system, the Secretary was given the power to either give the proceeds directly to the parties or apply them for their benefit in the way he saw as most advantageous to them.

[13] Thus, the 1860 Act carried out or was in accord with the treaty provisions of Article 11, which provided there could be no disposition of the treaty land reserved without the permission of the United States, and the further provision that henceforth from the treaty date the Kansas Indians "shall ever remain under the protection of the United States" by providing, first, the requisite permission of the United States, and second, for a method of land transfer to best protect the interests of the half-breeds or their heirs. Indeed, what clearer way could exist to give the permission of the United States than by an official act of Congress signed by the President. This 1860 Act is clear and unambiguous in its language, carried out the 1825 Treaty provisions, and effectively terminated and superseded it as a governing instrument over the half-breed lands. The 1862 Resolution in clear language repealed the authority of the Secretary of the Interior to sell the land for the Indians, but left intact that portion of the 1860 Act which carried out the consent provision of the Treaty while expressing the intent that the lands could pass by traditional laws of alienation and inheritance.

Thus, while retaining the provision of the 1860 Act, giving the sovereign permission of the United States to disposition of the half-breed lands, it also reflected an official change of attitude by the United States as a sovereignty that the best protection of the interest of the 23 individual half-breeds or their heirs was to give them the right of free will alienation possessed by American citizens.

There was allusion in the plaintiffs' argument, with considerable historical foundation, to the effect that the Civil War began between 1860 and 1862, which caused a change in moral attitude towards the Indians as the vicissitudes of war may have dictated, and more particularly, as the best interests of the Union were seen in pleasing the profiteers in the potential free state of Kansas. Nevertheless, the 1862 Resolution was and remained a deliberate expression of national sovereignty by the Congress. Defendants' Ex. 31, 32, 33, by Department of Interior.

This interpretation is in harmony with the terms of the Treaty through the enactment of the 1860 Act, and effectively and plainly abrogated Article 11 of the 1825 Treaty as it applied to the Kansas half-breeds.

If the Court were to rely solely on the statutory language, which does carry a clear expression of congressional intent, some case law dealing with treaty abrogation would appear to compel the Court to look further to other indicia of congressional intent. The legislative history, as previously discussed, is so scanty as to be of little help in determining what intent should be imputed to Congress.

The Court is aware of prior judicial interpretation of these acts. In *Swope v. Purdy,* 23 F.Cas. 576 (C.C.D.Kan.1870) (No. 13,704), the federal court held that the joint Resolution of 1862 removed the restrictions on alienation imposed by the Act of 1860, and that a deed made in 1864 conveyed legal title. In *Smith v.*

Stevens, 77 U.S. (10 Wall.) 321, 19 L.Ed. 933 (1870), the Court, in dicta, assumed that the joint Resolution of 1862 removed all restrictions on alienation. These decisions, while substantially on point with this case, predate the evolution of legal protection of Indian treaty rights embodied in more recent case law. In light of the subsequent great changes in the principles of stare decisis law regarding the Indians, the Court views these two cases as less authoritative than being res judicata on the issue here, but must view them as contemporaneous judicial holdings of congressional intent.

[14, 15] Much more important, however, is the administrative interpretation of the 1860 and 1862 legislation. It is clear that this Court, as a matter of law, must consider the history of administrative interpretation of the 1860 and 1862 legislation. Interpretation of a statute by those charged with administering and enforcing it, and their practices which reflect their understanding of the statute, have been given deference by the courts when faced with a problem of statutory construction. *Red Lion Broadcasting v. FCC,* 395 U.S. 367, 381, 89 S.Ct. 1794, 1801, 23 L.Ed.2d 371 (1969). Even greater weight must be given to ''contemporaneous'' interpretations, those made soon after enactment of the statute. *Udall v. Tallman,* 380 U.S. 1, 16, 85 S.Ct. 792, 801, 13 L.Ed.2d 616 (1964). The uniform and contemporaneous interpretations of those charged with administering Indian affairs are entitled to special weight, as these persons are presumed to be familiar with the backgrounds and purpose of Indian legislation. *Assinbone & Sioux Tribe v. Nordwick,* 378 F.2d 426 (9th Cir. 1967). Archival documents revealing the contemporaneous views of those charged with administering Indian legislation have been given great weight. *Russ v. Wilkins,* 624 F.2d 914 (9th Cir. 1980).

In this case, there are numerous uniform and contemporaneous interpretations of the meaning of the 1860 and 1862 legislation which support both this Court's and defendants' interpretation of the statutes.

On July 28, 1862, Acting Commissioner of Indian Affairs, Mix, wrote to United States Senator O. H. Browning. In his letter he commented on the effect of the 1862 Resolution:

''The effect of this resolution as construed by this Office is that the title of the parties interested is vested in them absolutely by virtue of the Act of May 26th, 1860, and consequently their conveyances are not subject in any manner to the control of this Department. In other words the owners of these lands are by said Resolution empowered to sell and convey said lands as fully and freely as purchasers of public lands may do when holding by patent from the United States.''
Defendants' Ex. 15.

A copy of the above letter was sent on July 30, 1862, to the Bellmards, a family of reservees and heirs who had made inquiries as to their ability to convey.

On August 26, 1862, Acting Commissioner Mix, said in a letter to Oren Curtis, the father of Vice-President Charles Curtis, of Kansas, a representative of some reservees:

''The Act of Congress of July 17th, 1862, to which allusion is made in the communication last mentioned has deprived this Department of all jurisdiction as to the subject of the various inquiries submitted. . . . All questions as to the rights of grantees, heirships, titles liability to taxation, in short the

whole subject matter, belong exclusively to the courts of Kansas by virtue of said act of Congress and to those courts you must therefore necessarily apply for their adjudication.''
Defendants' Ex. 18.

In a letter dated February 19, 1863, Secretary of the Interior, Usher, wrote to United States Senator S. Pomeroy:

''[The reservee] is not under any disability requiring this Department to ratify his act of conveyance. . . . There is no law making it necessary to its validity, or proper that it shall be approved by the Secretary of the Interior.''
Defendants' Ex. 21.

Commissioner of Indian Affairs, William Dole, said in a letter dated February 27, 1863:

''The effect of this legislation as construed by this office is to vest the absolute title to said lands in the original grantees their heirs or assigns and to transfer to the courts of Kansas exclusive jurisdiction as to all questions relating to said titles. Consequently the copies of evidence you request will be of no value in the adjudication of the questions in which you are interested.''
Defendants' Ex. 22.

On May 20, 1863, Commissioner of Indian Affairs, Dole, stated in a letter to D. M. Jones:

''As this Resolution is construed by this Department the entire jurisdiction of all questions of identity of person or right to said lands is thereby vested in the local courts of Kansas. . . . The effect of the resolution already mentioned was to vest an absolute title in the original grantees their heirs or assigns. . . .''
Defendants' Ex. 23.

Recent administrative interpretations have been consistent with those made near the time of the legislation. In a letter to Congressman Emmanuel Celler, December 17, 1965, Secretary of the Interior, Stewart Udall, stated:

''The effect of the 1862 Act was to remove completely the Federal interest in the lands and to terminate any trust responsibility that may have existed under the earlier legislation.''
Defendants' Ex. 28.

In a letter of October 31, 1966, to Congressman Page Belcher, Secretary Udall stated:

''By the 1860 and 1862 Acts Congress gave the allottees full and unrestricted title to their lands. . . . From that time on, the allottees had full authority to sell their lands.''
Defendants' Ex. 29.

In light of the uniform, contemporaneous and longstanding administrative interpretation of the 1860 and 1862 legislation, the Court experiences no hesitation in imputing to Congress the intent to abrogate the restriction on alienation embodied in the Treaty of 1825 as it applied to Kansas half-breed lands allotted therein. The statutory language is certainly more than capable of being construed as giving the reservees title in fee simple with no restrictions on alienation. As noted previously, while this is the most reasonable construction, it is not the only possible construction, as borne out by plaintiffs' contentions. The evidence of contemporaneous administrative interpretation, however, adds such strong weight to the construction favoring abrogation that the Court believes it is not "lightly" imputing to Congress the intent to abrogate, but rather the Court finds a clear intent to abrogate. While the case law requires the Court to take a sympathetic view of the position of the Indians, the law does not permit the Court to disregard the intent of Congress. E.g., *Rosebud Sioux v. Kneip*, 430 U.S. 584, 97 S.Ct. 1361, 51 L.Ed.2d 660 (1977); *DeCoteau v. District County Court*, 420 U.S. 425, 95 S.Ct. 1082, 43 L.Ed.2d 300 (1975).

[16] The effect of the abrogation in 1860 of the treaty restriction on alienation and the 1862 Resolution, was to free the owners of the tracts to convey the land without federal approval. No transfer subsequent to the July 17, 1862 Resolution can be invalid for lack of federal approval. As to any pre-1862 conveyances which may have violated the restriction on alienation contained in the 1825 Treaty and reaffirmed in the superseding 1860 Act, the statute of limitations began to run against the grantees and their heirs as of the date of the 1862 Resolution removing the restriction. *Schrimpscher v. Stockton*, 183 U.S. 290, 22 S.Ct. 107, 46 L.Ed. 203 (1902); *Cohen*, supra, at 163. Such claims are clearly time-barred, as are the other nineteenth century claims advanced by plaintiffs based on fraud and duress. All possibly applicable statutes of limitation have run. These include K.S.A. § 60–503 (15 year limit for adverse possession); K.S.A. § 60–504 (5 year limit for execution sales); K.S.A. § 60–505 (5 year limit for sales by guardians, administrators and executors); K.S.A. § 60–506 (2 year limit on forcible detention of real property); K.S.A. § 60–507 (15 year limit for unspecified real property transactions). K.S.A. § 58–2249, first enacted in 1874, also sets up a three year limit applicable to former Indian lands.

THE 1968 PRIVATE ACT

While the Court has held that plaintiffs' claim to quiet title against the class of defendant landowners is definitely barred on the basis of the effect of the 1860 and 1862 Acts of Congress, the Court is equally convinced that another sound legal basis also bars the plaintiffs' claim.

In 1968, after several previous years' activity in Congress motivated by the zeal of these same two individual plaintiffs on behalf of their Kaw brethren, the 90th Congress enacted Private Law 90–318, 82 Stat. 1420, on August 8, 1968, for the financial relief of the 23 named half-breed individuals mentioned in Article 6 of the 1825 Treaty previously discussed, or their heirs. In this Act, Congress directed the sum of $73,600 to be paid to heirs of the 23 named allottees in amounts of $3,200 to each set of heirs.

The most significant language in Private Law 90–318 reads as follows:

"The amounts paid under the authority of this Act shall be paid in full and final satisfaction of all claims of the named individuals or their heirs against the United States based upon the loss of Indian lands included in the twenty-three halfbreed Kaw allotments granted the above named individuals under article 6 of the treaty of June 3, 1825 (7 Stat. 244) in the Territory of Kansas, and in full satisfaction of any claims of the original allottees or his heirs for the consequent loss of use of the land."

Defendants rely on the above-quoted language of the Act and its legislative history as a complete bar in itself to plaintiffs' claim, as well as a ratification of previous governmental conduct as to the handling of the treaty lands of the 23 allottees. Plaintiffs would explain away the language of the Act and its history as a moral and sentimental gesture of conscience by the Congress for past oversights and omission of duty by the United States to these Indian wards, and state that the appropriated compensation was for "loss of use" by the Indians for pre–Civil War exploitive and predatory actions of white Americans, and not as compensation for the loss of title and ownership.

Again, following time honored legal precepts of statutory interpretation, the Court will first look to the language of the legislation to determine whether its words and meaning are clear. Next, the Court will examine the legislative intent as expressed by the congressional authors of, the congressional supporters or opponents of, and the witnesses for, such legislation.

A reading of the above-quoted principal paragraph of Private Law 90–318 indicates a twofold purpose, viz.:

"The amounts paid under authority of the Act shall be paid

(1) in full satisfaction of all claims of the named individuals or their heirs against the United States based upon the loss of Indian lands included in the twenty-three half breed Kaw allotments granted under article 6 of the treaty of June 3, 1925 . . . and,
(2) in full satisfaction of any claims of the original allottees or his heirs for the consequent use of the land." (Underlining and numerical emphasis supplied.)

It appears to the court that the clear meaning of the first purpose was under use of the word "all" and the phrase "loss of Indian lands," to express loss of title and ownership. It appears abundantly clear also that the meaning and intent of the second stated purpose was to forever bar *"any"* claims for *"the consequent loss of use"* of the land. It has always been a hornbook tenet of property law that there exists two types of compensatory damages, viz., the fair market value of the land for loss of title and ownership (loss of Indian lands), and damages for loss of use because of or (consequent) to a titled owner being deprived of the temporary use and profits of such land by a wrongful taking.

[17] Both the language, standing alone, and the dual stated purposes, indicate that the clear intention of the lawmakers was to "cover the waterfront" or blanket out any lingering possible future legal claims. It is true that the language of the Act reads "claims . . . against the United States." Seemingly and arguably, as the plaintiffs urge, the statutory wording did not release any claims against present landowners. However, there appear to be very valid and cogent legal reasons precluding such a judicial conclusion.

The legislative history of Private Law 90–318 serves to confirm that it was indeed the intent of Congress to discharge any possible claims against the present private landowners, as well as the United States. The legislation was first introduced in the House as H.R. 10590, and in the Senate as S.2203, in the First Session of the 89th Congress by Congressman Page Belcher and Senator Fred Harris, both from Oklahoma, and presumably in close touch with individually named plaintiffs and prominent tribal leaders in carrying out their desires and intentions. Failing to pass the 89th Congress, the Act was reintroduced in the 90th Congress by the same authors, as H.R. 8391 in the House. Hearings were held and extensive congressional reports were made, shown as Defendants' Ex. 31, 32 and 33.

These reports, all containing nearly the same language, adopted by the various committees and by the Congress on final passage, disclose in an expression of views by the Bureau of the Budget for the Executive Office of the President, the following verbiage:

"Finally, the bill provides that when the payments are accepted, they shall be in full settlement of any and all claims of the allottees or their heirs of any nature whatsoever concerning the allotments involved. We assume that this last provision is intended not only to settle any claims against the United States for failure to fulfill any trust responsibilities it may have had toward the 23 allottees but also to settle any title claims which the heirs of the allottees now might have to the lands comprising the original allotments. These lands are now and have been for many years, privately owned and used and have been bought and sold by various owners."

Most strongly convincing, however, is the expression by Congressman Page Belcher, the primary sponsor of the Private Law, who made it crystal clear in the 1967 hearing held on the matter that the legislation was intended to extinguish all further claims to the 23 reserves by alleged heirs of the reservees. By written statement, Belcher told his fellow congressmen that the proposed act would benefit the present owners by removing any uncertainty regarding their titles due to the previous Indian ownership. He declared:

"Not only does this situation demand equity for the Indians. The land is today in a state of confusion; and, titles for the present occupants, who have no personal responsibility in this matter whatsoever, are not clear. *This legislation would serve to quiet the titles to the disputed lands for the benefit of the present occupants."* (Emphasis supplied.)

Purportedly also, the hearing records before the Congressional Committees contained a similar statement of one of the individual plaintiffs which the Court need not consider to determine congressional intent as such. The Court does note that it is improbable that Congressman Belcher was making such a statement of intent contrary to the desires of his constituency.

One other matter must be noted as disclosed in the various committee reports. That is the basis or standard upon which ultimate recipients of the payments were awarded damages or compensation in the 1968 Act. Each contains the identical following paragraph or its substance:

"In recommending this legislation, the committee has fixed the land value of the allotment on the basis of a valuation of $5.00 an acre. The valuation of this land is based upon the fact that an appraisal was made of the property in 1862, and that each allotment was given a valuation on the basis of its value per acre. Averaging the values made at that time approximates $5.00 an acre, so that is the value adopted by the committee in fixing the amounts set forth in the amended bill.''

In another part of the reports appears the following statement:

''According to the report of the Department of Interior, some of the allottees or their heirs were in possession of their property for many years after 1862. In another instance, there is evidence that the alleged loss of land was in fact a sale by the allottee for a total consideration of $3,450. In still other instances, as Interior points out, there were successful actions in ejectment maintained by the allottees or heirs.''
Defendants' Ex. 31 and 33.

While these plaintiffs and the interested heirs of the allottees as a class may privately complain—as all unsuccessful litigants usually do—about inadequacies of valuation, as to fee title ownership of the lands and the stolen resources thereof, and the fact that they were unsuccessful in their Court of Claims action for interest on the awards of Private Act 90–318, this Court, who has had considerable exposure to eminent domain litigation, views these facts originating in archival records, shown in the Congressional Committee reports, and undoubtedly relied on by Congress, as buttressing a congressional intent to preclude possible claimants by paying the 1862 fair value for the fee simple ownership value at that time for all allottees and their heirs, even though not all were shown to have been bilked, cheated or imposed upon by some avaricious white Americans.

Thus, both the language and the legislative history of Private Law 90–318 demonstrate that the law was designed to extinguish all claims of the 23 individual reserves against *anyone* arising out of the events related to the 1825 Treaty.

For the above reasons, defendants' motion for summary judgment must be granted. The Court believes that this decision is mandated not only by law on two sound legal grounds, but also by public policy. The words of the Supreme Court in *Logan v. Davis*, 233 U.S. 613, 627, 34 S.Ct. 685, 690, 58 L.Ed. 1121 (1914), are as meaningful today as the day they were written:

''Many thousands of acres have been patented to individuals under that interpretation, and to disturb it now would be productive of serious and harmful results. The situation, therefore, calls for the application of the settled rule that the practical interpretation of an ambiguous or uncertain statute by the executive department charged with its administration is entitled to the highest respect, and, if acted upon for a number of years, will not be disturbed except for very cogent reasons.''

Nothing in this opinion should be read to indicate that the Court is unsympathetic toward the plaintiffs and their position. The Court believes that a great injustice was probably done to some of the Kansas half-breeds in allowing forcible entries and inequitable or fraudulent conveyances to stand, an injustice all too typical of the general treatment of those American natives upon whom the white man chose to impose a conqueror's terms. Justice would not be served, however, by wresting those lands away, more than a century later, from equally innocent landowners. To exact retribution on the current landowners for the sins of their great-grandfathers would merely add to injustice, not right it.

To conclude, this Court is most strongly convinced that our legal jurisprudence correctly closes the door to any further relief or remedy for these particular Kaw Indian claimants, regardless of their subjective feelings that an injustice still persists. The appellate processes to review the legal correctness of this opinion is the last legal recourse available to these plaintiffs, and this Court trusts such a step to legal finality will be invoked.

IT IS THEREFORE ORDERED that the defendants' motion for summary judgment is hereby sustained.

IT IS FURTHER ORDERED that the costs in this case are to be assessed against the plaintiffs. If counsel for defendants believe that this judgment may affect any present real estate titles originating from these so-called Kansas half-breed lands, they may submit an appropriate journal entry in the nature of the traditional quiet title journal entry of state courts, incorporating this opinion by reference.

FOREWORD TO APPENDICES

Both because of the historical aspect of this interesting case and the necessity for interpretation and discussion of the Treaty as a complete legal instrument, the whole text, including the fascinating names and descriptive titles of the Indian signatories, is set forth in Appendix A hereto.

Additionally, since frequent reference is made in this opinion to our national unfairness to Indians generally and to the Kansas half-breeds in particular, the Court felt it proper to attach as Appendix B, the Department of Interior report of John Montgomery, Indian Agent, dated October 1, 1856, received in evidence as Plaintiffs' Exhibit 8, which graphically reflects a shameful period of Kansas territorial history.

APPENDIX A

ARTICLES OF A TREATY

June 3, 1825.
———————
Proclamation,
Dec. 30, 1825.

Made and concluded at the City of Saint Louis, in the State of Missouri, between William Clark, Superintendent of Indian affairs, Commissioner on the part of the United States of America, and the undersigned Chiefs, Head Men, and Warriors of the Kansas Nation of Indians, duly authorized and empowered by said Nation.

ARTICLE 1.

Cesion by the
Kansas.

The Kansas do hereby cede to the United States all the lands lying within the State of Missouri, to which the said nation have title or claim; and do further cede and relinquish, to the said United States, all other lands which they now occupy, or to which they have title or claim, lying West of the said State of Missouri, and within the following boundaries: beginning at the entrance of the Kansas river into the Missouri river; from thence North to the North-West corner of the State of Missouri; from thence Westwardly to the Nodewa river, thirty miles from its entrance into the Missouri; from thence to the entrance of the big Nemahaw river into the Missouri, and with that river to its source; from thence to the source of the Kansas river, leaving the old village of the Pania Republic to the West; from thence, on the ridge dividing the waters of the Kansas river from those of the Arkansas, to the Western boundary of the State line of Missouri, and with that line, thirty miles, to the place of beginning.

ARTICLE 2.

Reservation for the use of the Kansas.

From the cession aforesaid, the following reservation for the use of the Kansas nation of Indians shall be made, of a tract of land, to begin twenty leagues up the Kansas river, and to include their village on that river; extending West thirty miles in width, through the lands ceded in the first Article, to be surveyed and marked under the direction of the President, and to such extent as he may deem necessary, and at the expense of the United States. The agents for the Kansas, and the persons attached to the agency, and such teachers and instructors as the President shall authorize to reside near the Kansas, shall occupy, during his pleasure, such lands as may be necessary for them within this reservation.

ARTICLE 3.

Payment to them for their cession.

In consideration of the cession of land and relinquishments of claims, made in the first Articles, the United States agree to pay to the Kansas nation of Indians, three thousand five hundred dollars per annum, for twenty successive years, at their villages, or at the entrance of the Kansas river, either in money, merchandize, provisions, or domestic animals, at the option of the aforesaid Nation; and when the said annuities, or any part thereof, is paid in merchandize, it shall be delivered to them at the first cost of the goods in Saint Louis, free of transportation.

ARTICLE 4.

Cattle, hogs, &c. to be furnished by U.S.

The United States, immediately upon the ratification of this convention, or as soon thereafter as may be, shall cause to be furnished to the Kansas Nation, three hundred head of cattle, three hundred hogs, five hundred domestic fowls, three yoke of oxen, and two carts, with such implements of agriculture as the Superintendant of Indian Affairs may think necessary; and shall employ such persons to aid and instruct them in their agriculture, as the President of the United States may deem expedient; and shall provide and support a blacksmith for them.

ARTICLE 5.

Land to be sold
for support of
schools.

Out of the lands herein ceded by the Kanzas Nation to the United States, the Commissioner aforesaid, in behalf of the said United States, doth further covenant and agree, that thirty-six sections of good lands, on the Big Blue river, shall be laid out under the direction of the President of the United States, and sold for the purpose of raising a fund, to be applied, under the direction of the President, to the support of schools for the education of the Kanzas children, within their Nation.

ARTICLE 6.

Reservations for
the use of half-
breeds.

From the lands above ceded to the United States, there shall be made the following reservations, of one mile square, for each of the half breeds of the Kanzas nation, viz: For Adel and Clement, the two children of Clement; for Josette, Julie, Pelagie, and Victoire, the four children of Louis Gonvil; for Marie and Lafleche, the two children of Baptiste of Gonvil; for Laventure, the son of Francis Laventure; for Elizabeth and Pierre Carbonau, the children of Pierre Brisa; for Louis Joncas; for Basil Joncas; for James Joncas; for Elizabeth Datcherute, daughter of Baptiste Datcherute; for Joseph Butler; for William Rodgers; for Joseph Coté; for the four children of Cicili Compáre, each one mile square; and one for Joseph James, to be located on the North side of the Kanzas river, in the order above named, commencing at the line of the Kanzas reservation, and extending down the Kanzas river for quantity.

ARTICLE 7.

Agreement en-
tered into by the
U.S. for certain
purposes.

Proviso.

With the view of quieting all animosities which may at present exist between a part of the white citizens of Missouri and the Kanzas nation, in consequence of the lawless depredations of the latter, the United States do further agree to pay to their own citizens, the full value of such property as they can legally prove to have been stolen or destroyed since the year 1815: *Provided,* The sum so to be paid by the United States shall not exceed the sum of three thousand dollars.

ARTICLE 8.

Payment to
F. G. Choteau.

And whereas the Kanzas are indebted to Francis G. Choteau, for credits given them in trade, which they are unable to pay, and which they have particularly requested to have included and settled in the present Treaty; it is, therefore, agreed on, by and between the parties to these presents, that the sum of five hundred dollars, toward the liquidation of said debt, shall be paid by the United States to the said Francois G. Choteau.

ARTICLE 9.

Merchandise to
amount of $2000
to be delivered at
the Kanzas river.

There shall be selected at this place such merchandize as may be desired, amounting to two thousand dollars, to be delivered at the Kanzas river, with as little delay as possible; and there shall be paid to the deputation now here, two thousand dollars in merchandize and horses, the receipt of which is hereby acknowledged; which, together with the amount agreed on in the 3d and 4th articles, and the provisions made in the other articles of this Treaty, shall be considered as a full compensation for the cession herein made.

ARTICLE 10.

Punishment of offences.

Lest the friendship which is now established between the United States and the said Indian Nation should be interrupted by the misconduct of Individuals, it is hereby agreed, that for injuries done by individuals, no private revenge or retaliation shall take place, but instead thereof, complaints shall be made by the party injured, to the other by the said nation, to the Superintendent, or other person appointed by the President to the Chiefs of said nation. And it shall be the duty of the said Chiefs, upon complaints being made as aforesaid, to deliver up the person or persons against whom the complaint is made, to the end that he or they may be punished, agreeably to the laws of the State or Territory where the offence may have been committed; and in like manner, if any robbery, violence, or murder, shall be committed on any Indian or Indians belonging to said nation, the person or persons so offending shall be tried, and, if found guilty, shall be punished in like manner as if the injury had been done to a white man. And it is agreed, that the Chiefs of the Kanzas shall, to the

Chiefs to exert themselves to recover stolen property, &c.

utmost of their power, exert themselves to recover horses or other property which may be stolen from any citizen or citizens of the United States, by any individual or individuals of the Nation; and the property so recovered shall be forthwith delivered to the Superintendent, or other person authorized to receive it, that it may be restored to its proper owner; and in cases where the exertions of the Chiefs shall be ineffectual in recovering the property stolen as aforesaid, if sufficient proof can be adduced that such property was actually stolen, by any Indian or Indians belonging to the said nation, the Superintendent or other officer may deduct from the annuity of the said nation a sum equal to the value of the property which has been stolen. And the United States hereby guarantee, to any Indian or Indians, a full indemnification for any horses or other property which may be

Proviso.

stolen from them by any of their citizens: *Provided,* That the property so stolen cannot be recovered, and that sufficient proof is produced that it was actually stolen by a citizen of the United States. And the said Nation of Kanzas engage, on the requisition or demand of the President of the United States, or of the Superintendent, to deliver up any white man resident amongst them.

ARTICLE 11.

U.S. to enjoy the right of navigating the water courses, &c.

It is further agreed on, by and between the parties to these presents, that the United States shall forever enjoy the right to navigate freely all water courses or navigable streams within the limits of the tract of country herein reserved to the Kanzas Nation; and that the said Kanzas Nation shall never sell, relinquish, or in any manner dispose of the lands herein reserved, to any other nation, person or persons whatever, without the permission of the United States for that purpose first had and obtained. And shall ever remain under the protection of the United States, and in friendship with them.

ARTICLE 12.

Treaty binding
when ratified.

This Treaty shall take effect, and be obligatory on the contracting parties, as soon as the same shall be ratified by the President, by and with the consent and advice of the Senate of the United States.

In testimony whereof, the said William Clark, Commissioner as aforesaid, and the Deputation, Chiefs, Head-men and Warriors of the Kanzas Nation of Indians, as aforesaid, have hereunto set their hands and seals, this third day of June, in the year of our Lord eighteen hundred and twenty-five, and of the Independence of the United States of America the forty-ninth year.

WILLIAM CLARK

Nom-pa-wa-rah, or the white plume.
Ky-he-ga-wa-ti-nin-ka, or the full chief.
Ky-he-ga-wa-che-he, or the chief of great valour.
Ky-he-ga-shin-ga, or the little chief.
Ke-bah-ra-hu.
Me-chu-chin-ga, or the little white bear.

Hu-ru-ah-te, or the Real Eagle.
Ca-she-se-gra, or the track that sees far.
Wa-can-da-ga-tun-ga, or the great doctor.
O-pa-she-ga, or the cooper.
Cha-ho-nush.
Ma-be-ton-ga, or the American.

WITNESSES PRESENT:—R. Wash, Secretary. W. B. Alexander, Sub-Indian Agent. John F. A. Sandford. G. C. Sibley, United States' Commissioner. Baronet Vasquez, United States S. Agent. Russell Farnham. Jno. K. Walker. Jno. Simonds, jr. Sanderson Robert. L. T. Honore, U. S. Intptr. William Milburn. Baptis Ducherut, Interpreter for Kansas. Paul Louise, Osage Interpreter. Noel Dashnay, Interpreter. Ant. Le Claire, Interpreter.

APPENDIX B

No. 42.

KANSAS AGENCY,
Kansas Territory, October 1, 1856

SIR: It seems that the affairs and present condition of this agency should attract more than the usual attention of those whose duty and whose business it is to exercise a supervision for the present interest and future welfare of those people, whose rights, established by treaty and by law, have been encroached, but who have remained remarkably quiet and unobstrusive, refraining from any infringement or violation of their sacred treaties with the government, relying upon those in whom they never fail to repose the greatest confidence for that protection of their rights, their land and property, which is justly due them.

While the Kansas have been almost entirely surrounded by those white people who have for the last twelve months incessantly engaged in a sanguinary warfare among themselves, they have witnessed, with amazement and disgust, the horrid scene of political contention in the Territory; astonished and affrighted by the proceedings of their friends, the whites, for a period they abandoned their homes for the safety of themselves and property. Although everything has occurred on the part of the people of Kansas

Territory that would tend to excite the passionate feelings of the totally uncivilized red man, and to prompt him to actions not peculiar to him while in a state of uncivilization and almost barbarism, and although the Kansas have seen their country taken from them, and their property maliciously destroyed by unprincipled and lawless white men, they have remained quiet and peaceable, for which they deserve credit; only wishing to live in the enjoyment of their rights and in obedience to the laws of the land, and not seeking private revenge, as might reasonably be expected of the Kansas from their past history.

The tract of country on the north side of the Kansas river, known as the half-breed Kansas reservation, has for the last two years been the object of filthy speculation. It will be remembered that several of the government functionaries for the Territory of Kansas engaged in purchasing a portion of this land of the grantees yet living on the upper part of the reservation, in which undertaking the purchasers failed; from that time to this, the lower portion of the reservation, on which there are no Indians residing, has been, and is at this time, subject to the intrusion of lawless men; stripping the land of its timber, opening farms, cultivating the soil, and appropriating the fruits to their own use.

The general instructions, issued October 8, 1855, for the removal of intruders on Indian lands, were on the 23d and 24th of June last being complied with on my part in regard to the half-breed Kansas lands, when the whole weight and influence of those whose duty it was to co-operate with me in the removal of those people who were found in the Indian country in open transgression of the law were thrown in favor of the intruders; and they receiving the advice and counsel of official men, and of men of more intelligence and prudence than themselves, declared the land was not Indian land, that it was public land, and that they would occupy it at all hazards. Thus they having presumptuously set up a title to the land, and simply because I had somewhat transcended my instructions by destroying some cabins in order to facilitate the removal of the intruders, Captain Walker, of the United States army, who had been ordered to aid me in the removal, at the very time that he should have been vigoron and prompt in his duty, refused to give me any further assistance.

Thus the matter ended, after every exertion on my part to carry out the views and instructions of the Department of Indian Affairs. The larger portion of the half-breed Kansas reserve now quietly rests in the possession of the intruders, after actually driving by force and violence from one or two of the tracts the identical Indians for whom the land was reserved. Those who have unhesitatingly, and in defiance of all law and authority, settled upon and occupied this land, may for some time live in the enjoyment of their illegal proceedings; but I do sincerely hope there will be some action taken on the part of Congress during its next session that will result in the benefit of those poor, inoffensive, unsuspecting Indians, who have been wronged and outraged by lawless and crafty white men. The half-breed Kansas, or the greater number of them, are industrious and intelligent, well-versed in the English, French and Kaw languages, profess the Catholic religion, and have almost a thorough knowledge of the arts of husbandry, in which some of the Indians are considerably engaged. Owing to the remoteness of this part of my agency from the main tribe with whom I am stationed, and owing to the great inconvenience of travelling, I have not been able to visit the half-breeds as often as necessary. I do not know what may have been the policy adopted by the government in the civilization of the Kansas at the time they were separated from the half-breeds, but I am forced to believe that the separation of the main tribe and the half-breeds has only retarded the progress of the civilization and christianizing of the former; from the fact, that there has been no change in the Indian customs and manners to those of the white man; and from the fact that there has been no white people or half-breeds among the full-blooded Indians since they were removed from the Kansas river to this place. The native Indians having no white people affiliated with their tribe have strictly adhered to their natural customs and pursuits of life. The Canadian French, in my opinion, have done more to civilize the Kansas than all the schools and moral institutions that have ever been established for their benefit. In consequence of the boundaries of the Kansas reservation not having been surveyed and marked at the time the Territory of Kansas was thrown open to settlement, many persons ignorant of the designated bounds of the Kansas reserve, and guided only by a map of the geographical position of the Indian reservations respectively, unhesitatingly settled upon a stream called Rock creek, which stream, since the bounds of the reserve have recently been surveyed, is found to be entirely within the country of the Kansas Indians. Those settlers, and also those on the Neosho, above this place, who thought at the time they settled there, that they were on government lands, and also those settlers on the Neosho, below the junction of Rock creek with the Neosho river, and within the bounds of the Kansas reserve, have been of great annoyance and trouble to this agency. Measures are soon to be taken for their removal; but judging from former experience in removing people from Indian lands, I fear that I will not be able to succeed. Where a certain class of people assume to themselves the right to judge of matters pertaining to the Indian country, it is very difficult for an Indian agent to perform with promptness the duties of his office. I much regret to say that the worst evil that ever befel the Indian race has been for the last year or two greatly indulged in by the Kansas Indians. Whiskey is obtained by quantities in the Territory, and when not immediately made use of, is secretly brought into the Indian country where it is freely and excessively used; while the Indians are enabled to procure a full supply of this filthy, adulterated stuff, it seems that I cannot, by ordinary means, suppress this detestable practice which will inevitably result in a great injury to the Indians. There are some of the Kansas who are becoming tired of the roving life, and wish to adopt the modes and customs of the white people; and if they only had twice the annuity that is paid to them, with a liberal agricultural fund, it is now my belief that several of the Indians could easily be induced to throw off the blanket and breech-cloth, and adopt the apparel of the white man, dwell in houses instead of the skin or bark lodge, and to cultivate the soil. I have done all in my power to stimulate their desire to acquire a knowledge of the principle arts of civilized life. That these Indians can be *civilized*, there is no doubt; but they must first be free from all annoyance and embarrassment, confined to a smaller scope of country, and sufficient means furnished them to begin with; and also a school, conducted on a liberal scale, would be greatly to the advantage of this nation; as it is, their present condition is anything but good or promising. The Kansas have done unusually well throughout the past year—only one or two cases of the small-pox having occurred; and notwithstanding the extreme drought the last season, they have raised corn, beans and pumpkins sufficient for their subsistance during the coming winter. Although there has been from the last December, 1855, up to this time, no blacksmith for these Indians, it cannot be inferred that the absence of that mechanic would be of material injury to them, as the labor in this shop consisted chiefly in the repairing of fire-arms. I have recently employed another smith, who is by me instructed to abstain from any work on fire-arms, as it is my opinion the *gun* is in nowise advantageous to the cause of civilization.

Respectfully submitted by your obedient servant.

JOHN MONTGOMERY,
Indian Agent.

Col. A. CUMMING,
Superintendent Indian Affairs, St. Louis, Mo.

Notes

Acronyms used in the notes:

FRC	Federal Records Center, Fort Worth, Texas, and Kansas City, Missouri
IAD, OHS	Indian Archives Division, Oklahoma Historical Society, Oklahoma City
KSHS	Kansas State Historical Society, Topeka
LC	Library of Congress
LD, KSHS	Library Division, Kansas State Historical Society
LROIA	Letters Received, Office of Indian Affairs
M	Microfilm
MD, KSHS	Manuscript Division, Kansas State Historical Society
MD, MHS	Manuscript Division, Missouri Historical Society, St. Louis
NA	National Archives
R	Roll
RCIA	Report of the Commissioner of Indian Affairs
RAGO	Records of the Adjutant General's Office
RG	Record Group
T	Target
WHC, UO	Western History Collections, University of Oklahoma, Norman

CHAPTER 1. "WHAT IS AN INDIAN?"

1. *Congressional Record*, 54th Cong., 1st sess., 24 Feb. 1896, 28:2079.

2. Ibid. According to the law of 24 February 1891, Congress provided 80-acre allotments to married Indian women who had been denied land under the General Allotment Act of 1887. While section 5 of the 1891 law legitimized the children "of any male and female Indian" who had lived together as husband and wife according to "traditional tribal custom," it restricted the descent of land to heirs through the male line only; see *U.S. Stat.*, 26:794–95.

3. Commissioner of Indian Affairs, *Annual Report*, 1892, NCR microcard ed. (Washington, D.C.: Government Printing Office, 1892), 30–37 (hereafter cited as

203

COIA, *Annual Report*); see also William T. Hagan, "Full Blood, Mixed Blood, Generic, and Ersatz: The Problem of Indian Identity," *Arizona and the West* 27 (Winter 1985): 309-26.

4. William H. Crawford to John Gaillard, 13 Mar. 1816, *American State Papers: Indian Affairs*, 2:28; and [Thomas Cooper], *Strictures Addressed to James Madison on the Celebrated Report of William H. Crawford, Recommending the Intermarriage of Americans with the Indian Tribes, Ascribed to Judge Cooper, and Originally Published by John Binns, in the Democratic Press* (Philadelphia: Jesper Harding, 1824), 1-22.

5. William J. Scheick, *The Half-Blood: A Cultural Symbol in Nineteenth Century Fiction* (Lexington: University of Kentucky Press, 1979), 16-18. For the problems associated with the fear of mongrels and hybridity and for the arguments in regard to the American School of ethnology see Robert E. Bieder, *Science Encounters the Indian, 1820-1880* (Norman: University of Oklahoma Press, 1986); Reginald Horsman, "Scientific Racism and the American Indian," *American Quarterly* 27 (May 1975): 152-68; and Francis Paul Prucha, *American Indian Policy in the Formative Years: The Indian Trade and Intercourse Acts, 1790-1834* (Cambridge: Harvard University Press, 1963), 180-97.

6. Robert E. Bieder, "Scientific Attitudes toward Indian Mixed-Bloods in Early Nineteenth Century America," *Journal of Ethnic Studies* 8 (Summer 1980): 24; and *Congressional Record*, 54th Cong., 1st sess., 24 Feb. 1896, 28:2078.

7. Hagan, "Full Blood," 310-15. As a staunch Republican, Curtis was elected to the United States House of Representatives from the Fourth Kansas Congressional District in 1892, in a race against the Populist candidate, John G. Otis. According to one study of Curtis's political career, his opponents in this election "made the mistake of stressing his Indian blood in ignominy"; see Marvin Ewy, "Charles Curtis of Kansas: Vice President of the United States, 1929-1933," *Emporia State Research Studies* 10 (Dec. 1961): 20-21.

8. In 1673, Father Jacques Marquette used the name Kansa, which became the federal government's preferred spelling until about 1870. The Reverend Isaac McCoy reported that during the nineteenth century, "we have chosen to adhere to the pronunciation of the natives themselves, which is "Kau-zau." A government interpreter advised that "the people" called themselves Konzas, with the second syllable scarcely audible; hence, the spelling was changed to Kaw. Kaw became the official spelling used by the Office of Indian Affairs during the late 1860s, and in this study, I use it for references to the tribe after 1870. For a discussion of the problem see William E. Unrau, *The Kaw People* (Phoenix, Ariz.: Indian Tribal Series, 1975), 3-4.

9. Testimony of Laban Miles, 1910, in *Osage Enrollment: Hearings before a Subcommittee of the House Committee on Indian Affairs on H.R. 17819 and H. 21199*, 61st Cong., 2d sess., 1910, 91-92.

10. William Barrows, "The Half-Breed Indians of North America," *Andover Review* 12 (July 1899): 15-36.

11. Ibid., 29, 36.

12. William T. Hagan, "Squaw Men on the Kiowa, Comanche, and Apache Reservation: Advance Agents of Civilization or Disturbers of the Peace?" in *The Frontier Challenge: Responses to the Trans-Mississippi West*, ed. John G. Clark (Lawrence: University Press of Kansas, 1971), 197-98; and *Congressional Record*, 54th Cong., 1st sess., 24 Feb. 1896, 28:1079.

13. Cited by Robert W. McCluggage, "The Senate and Indian Land Titles, 1800-1825," *Western Historical Quarterly* 1 (Oct. 1970): 415-16.

14. Crawford to John Gaillard, 13 Mar. 1916, *American State Papers*, 2:28; George A. Schultz, *An Indian Canaan: Isaac McCoy and the Vision of an Indian State* (Norman: University of Oklahoma Press, 1972), 192; and Prucha, *American Indian Policy in the Formative Years*, 192.

15. Horsman, "Scientific Racism," 165–66; Alexander Ross, *The Red River Settlement: Its Rise, Progress, and Present State, with Some Accounts of the Native Races and Its General History to the Present Day* (London: Smith, Elder, 1856), 305–6; and Francis A. Walker, *The Indian Question* (Boston, Mass.: James R. Osgood, 1874), 94.

16. Beider, *Science Encounters the Indian*, 219, 226–27; Theodora R. Jenness, "The Indian Territory," *Atlantic Monthly* 43 (Apr. 1879): 449; and Thomas J. May, "The Future of the American Indian," *Popular Science Monthly* 33 (May 1888): 104–8.

17. *Eighteenth Annual Report of the Board of Indian Commissioners*, 1886, app. D, 52–53, cited by Barrows, "Half-Breed Indians," 32; and Hagan, "Full Blood," 315.

18. In January 1907 the Kansas legislature selected Curtis to fill the senatorial seat of Joseph R. Burton, who resigned on 7 June 1906, following his conviction for having violated a federal statute; see Ewy, "Charles Curtis," 26–27; David L. Beaulieu, "Curly Hair and Big Feet: Physical Anthropology and the Implementation of Land Allotment on the White Earth Chippewa Reservation," *American Indian Quarterly* 7 (Fall 1984): 282.

19. Charles Curtis, "Qualities That Lead to Success," address before the Pierce School of Business Administration, Philadelphia, 22 Jan. 1930, LD, KSHS; and Eric Kiel, "Curtis's Indian Blood," *Nation*, 1 Aug. 1928, 109.

20. Don C. Seitz, *From Kaw Teepee to Capitol: The Life Story of Charles Curtis, Indian, Who Has Risen to High Estate* (New York: Frederick A. Stokes, 1928), 214.

21. Ibid., 215–17.

CHAPTER 2. KINSHIP BEGINNINGS

1. *Dictionary of American Biography*, 1958 ed., suppl. 2, s.v. "Curtis, Charles," by James C. Malin, 136; and Ewy, "Charles Curtis," 6.

2. *Dictionary of American Biography*, 136.

3. The various spellings of this surname are Papin, Papan, and Pappan. Papin was the most common spelling in the eighteenth and the first half of the nineteenth centuries. By the early 1860s, due mainly to the governmental reports of W. H. Walsh and William H. Coombs, Pappan became the most common spelling; it will be used throughout this study. There is some evidence that Papin may have been a variation of Pepin, which appears in the St. Charles, Missouri, marriage records in 1788 and 1789; see Paul Chrisler Philips, *The Fur Trade*, 2 vols. (Norman: University of Oklahoma Press, 1961), 2:243; Louise Barry, *The Beginning of the West: Annals of the Kansas Gateway to the American West, 1540–1854* (Topeka: Kansas State Historical Society, 1972), 38–39, 258, 335, 409, 454–99; and U.S., Congress, Senate, *Letter of the Secretary of the Interior, in Answer to a Resolution of the Senate of the 29th ultimo, transmitting copies of the Reports of W. H. Walsh and William H. Coombs, in relation to the "Half-Breed Kaw Lands" on the Kansas river, in the state of Kansas*, 37th Cong., 1st sess., 5 June 1862, Senate Executive Document 58 (ser. 1122), 3.

4. Ewy, "Charles Curtis," 6–7; "Mackinac Register of Baptisms and Interments, 1695–1821," *Collections of the State Historical Society of Wisconsin* 19 (1910):

32; and Charles Curtis, "Autobiography," typed copy in the possession of Tom Dennison, Ponca City, Oklahoma. This copy, which is more complete than the copy in the Manuscript Division of the Kansas State Historical Society, was given to Dennison by the late William P. Colvin, Charles Curtis's nephew and the son of Curtis's sister Elizabeth and her second husband, Jerome A. Colvin. William P. Colvin was Kaw allottee no. 117 on the 1902 Kaw Allotment Roll; see Allotment Roll of Kaw Indians, 1 July 1902, RG 72, Pawnee Miscellaneous Files, FRC, Fort Worth, Texas; see also Barry, *Beginning of the West*, 74, 85, 357. In 1880, Frederick Chouteau informed officials of the Kansas State Historical Society that Wyhesee was White Plume's niece (Frederick Chouteau to W. W. Cone, 15 Nov. 1880, Chouteau Papers, MD, MHS), but more precise governmental records indicate that Wyhesee was in fact White Plume's daughter; see U.S., Congress, Senate, *Joint Resolution for the Enrollment of Certain Persons as Members of the Osage Tribe of Indians, and for Other Purposes*, 60th Cong., 1st sess., 29 Apr. 1908, Senate Document 482 (ser. 5269), exhibit D-1, following p. 133.

5. Curtis, "Autobiography," Colvin's copy, art. 1, p. 5.

6. Ewy, "Charles Curtis," 9.

7. William E. Unrau, *The Kansa Indians: A History of the Wind People, 1673–1873* (Norman: University of Oklahoma Press, 1971), 55. The fortification was established in 1744 and was named Fort de Cavagnial. It was located on Salt Creek, opposite Kickapoo Island in present-day Leavenworth County, Kansas, just north of present Fort Leavenworth; it was abandoned in 1764; see Charles E. Hoffhaus, "Fort de Cavagnial: Imperial France in Kansas, 1744-1764," *Kansas Historical Quarterly* 30 (Winter 1964): 425-54.

8. Unrau, *Kansa Indians*, 55-79; and William E. Unrau, "The Depopulation of the Dhegiha-Siouan Kansas Prior to Removal," *New Mexico Historical Review* 48 (Oct. 1973): 315. For the power and diplomatic prowess of the Osages in the eighteenth century see Gilbert C. Din and Abraham P. Nasatir, *The Imperial Osages: Spanish-Indian Diplomacy in the Mississippi Valley* (Norman: University of Oklahoma Press, 1983).

9. *American State Papers: Indian Affairs*, 2:708; Richard Edward Oglesby, *Manuel Lisa and the Opening of the Missouri Fur Trade* (Norman; University of Oklahoma Press, 1963), 17-19; and Unrau, *Kansa Indians*, 85.

10. Sylvia Van Kirk, *Many Tender Ties: Women in Fur Trade Society, 1670-1870* (Norman: University of Oklahoma Press, 1980), 4.

11. Din and Nasatir, *Imperial Osages*, 224, 253-54, 362; William E. Foley and C. David Rice, *The First Chouteaus: River Barons of Early St. Louis* (Urbana: University of Illinois Press, 1983), 53, 94; Philips, *Fur Trade*, 2:249; and John Joseph Mathews, *The Osages: Children of the Middle Waters* (Norman: University of Oklahoma Press, 1961), 283-85.

12. Foley and Rice, *First Chouteaus*, 45.

13. Ibid., 181; John C. Ewers, "'Chiefs of the Missouri and Mississippi' and Peale's Silhouettes of 1806," *Smithsonian Journal of History* 1 (Spring 1966): 7; and Charles J. Kappler, comp., *Indian Affairs: Laws and Treaties*, vol. 2: *Treaties* (Washington, D.C.: Government Printing Office, 1904), 225.

14. Unrau, *Kansa Indians*, 33; and Charles Curtis Papers, Chambo Collection, no. 22, MD, KSHS.

15. "Extracts from the Diary of Major Sibley," *Chronicles of Oklahoma* 5 (June 1927): 199; and Senate Document 482 (ser. 5269), 31.

16. Abraham P. Nasatir, ed., *Before Lewis and Clark: Documents Illustrating the History of Missouri, 1785-1804*, vol. 2 (St. Louis, Mo.: St. Louis Historical

Documents Foundation, 1952), 708; and the Rev. John Rothenstiner, "Early Missionary Efforts among the Indians in the Diocese of St. Louis," *St. Louis Catholic Historical Review* 2 (Apr.–July 1920): 79.

17. "Mackinac Register," 32.

18. Washington Irving, *Astoria: Or, Anecdotes of an Enterprise beyond the Mountains*, rev. ed. (New York: G. P. Putnam, 1859), 134.

19. Frederick Chouteau to W. W. Cone, 10 May 1880, Chouteau Papers.

20. Barry, *Beginning of the West*, 59; and *Missouri Gazette and Louisiana Advertiser* (St. Louis), 20 May 1815.

21. Foley and Rice, *First Chouteaus*, 153; Kappler, *Treaties*, 124; and speech by White Plume to William Clark, 17 May 1827, RG 75, LROIA, St. Louis Superintendency, M 234, R 748, NA.

22. Frederick Chouteau to W. W. Cone, 10 May 1880, Chouteau Papers; Unrau, *Kansa Indians*, 32; and Barry, *Beginning of the West*, 77.

23. Barry, *Beginning of the West*, 76, 87–88.

24. George R. Brooks, ed., "George C. Sibley's Journal of a Trip to the Salines in 1811," *Missouri Historical Society Bulletin* 21 (Apr. 1965): 174–75.

25. Barry, *Beginning of the West*, 84, 94–95.

26. *National Intelligencer*, 16 Feb. 1822, 9, 12; Katherine C. Turner, *Red Man Calling on the Great White Father* (Norman: University of Oklahoma Press, 1951), 56; and Herman J. Viola, *Diplomats in Buckskins: A History of Indian Delegations in Washington City* (Washington, D.C.: Smithsonian Institution Press, 1981), 25, 72, 96–97, 175.

27. Paul Wilhelm, duke of Wuerttenberg, *First Journey to North America in the Years 1822 to 1824*, trans. William G. Beck, *South Dakota Historical Collections* 19 (1938): 313; and Barry, *Beginning of the West*, 52, 181.

28. *National Intelligencer*, 12 Feb. 1822.

29. Speech by White Plume to William Clark, 17 May 1827.

30. Letter of Secretary of the Interior, 13; and Kappler, *Treaties*, 223.

31. Wilhelm, *First Journey to North America*, 301–2.

Chapter 3. The Estate

1. "Lo, the Poor Senator," *Saturday Evening Post*, 9 Feb. 1907, 15; and *New York Times*, 14 Apr. 1929.

2. "Charles Curtis, Indian," 17 Jan. 1925, Interior Department pamphlet, Haskell-1-17-1925-10M, Kaw Indian Agency Collection, box 34, no. 138, WHC, UO.

3. Ibid.

4. Kappler, *Treaties*, 223.

5. Prucha, *American Indian Policy in the Formative Years*, 226; and Kappler, *Treaties*, 74, 96.

6. Edwin C. McReynolds, *Missouri: A History of the Crossroads State* (Norman: University of Oklahoma Press, 1962), 72.

7. Unrau, *Kansa Indians*, 103; Sibley to Clark, 5 Nov. 1818, Indian Papers, MD, MHS; and "Memorandum of a preliminary arrangement made on the 30th day of September 1818 at Fort Osage between G. C. Sibley . . . and chiefs and headmen of the Kansas nation," George C. Sibley Papers, MD, MHS.

8. Barry, *Beginning of the West*, 52.

9. Sibley to Clark, 15 Nov. 1818, Indian Papers, MD, MHS; and William A. Schroeder, "Spread of Settlement in Howard County, Missouri, 1810–1859," *Missouri Historical Review* 43 (Oct. 1968): 9–12.

10. William E. Unrau, "George C. Sibley's Plea for the 'Garden of Missouri' in 1824," *Missouri Historical Society Bulletin* 17 (Oct. 1790): 8.

11. Henry Nash Smith, *Virgin Land: The American West as Symbol and Myth* (New York: Vintage Books, 1957), 142-46.

12. Prucha, *American Indian Policy in the Formative Years*, 227-30; Kappler, *Treaties*, 214-17; and Herman J. Viola, *Thomas L. McKenny: Architect of America's Early Indian Policy* (Chicago: Swallow, 1974), 117.

13. Kappler, *Treaties*, 222-23.

14. Clark to Barbour, 11 June 1825, Documents Relating to the Negotiations of Ratified and Unratified Treaties with Various Tribes of Indians, 1801-1869, Introduction and Ratified Treaties, 1801-26, RG 75, T 494, R 1, NA.

15. Kappler, *Treaties*, 225.

16. Wilhelm, *First Journey to North America*, 313; and Barry, *Beginning of the West*, 166-67.

17. *U.S. Stat.*, 4:100-101; and Kappler, *Treaties*, 248-50.

18. Kappler, *Treaties*, 249-50.

19. Ibid., 222.

20. Brooks, "George C. Sibley's Journal," 174-77.

21. Ibid.

22. Ibid.

23. Unrau, "George C. Sibley's Plea," 8; and Kappler, *Treaties*, 218-19, 223.

24. Clark to Barbour, 11 June 1825, Ratified Treaties, 1801-26; and Kappler, *Treaties*, 223.

25. Clark to Barbour, 11 June 1825, Ratified Treaties, 1801-26; Kappler, *Treaties*, 225; and Barry, *Beginning of the West*, 166.

26. Louise Barry, "The Kansa Indians and the Census of 1843," *Kansas Historical Quarterly* 39 (Winter 1973): 482; and Kappler, *Treaties*, 225.

27. Lewis Henry Morgan, ed., *The Indian Journals, 1859-1862* (Ann Arbor: University of Michigan Press, 1957), 34; and Senate Document 482 (ser. 5269), exhibits D-1, D-2, D-3, 133ff.

28. Senate Document 482 (ser. 5269), exhibits D-1, D-2, D-3, 133-H.; Senate Executive Document 58 (ser. 1122), 6; and Barry, *Beginning of the West*, 317.

29. Speeches by White Plume, Chingacahega, and Wasabase to Clark, 17 May 1827, RG 75, LROIA, St. Louis Superintendency, M 234, R 748, NA.

30. Clark to Barbour, 11 June 1825, Ratified Treaties, 1801-26.

31. Ibid.

32. Barry, *Beginning of the West*, 357; and *Boston Missionary Magazine* 20 (Feb. 1840): 42. By 1838, the main villages of the Kansa full-bloods were those of Fool Chief, located on the north side of the Kansas River immediately west of Half-Breed Reserve No. 1, in present-day Silver Lake Township, Shawnee County, and of American Chief and Hard Chief, located on the south side of the Kansas River, near the mouth of Mission Creek, Dover Township, Shawnee County; see map, p. 167, in Barry, *Beginning of the West*.

33. Barry, *Beginning of the West*, 134-35; and Robert Joseph Keckeisen, "The Kansa 'Half-Breed' Lands: Contravention and Transformation of United States Indian Policy in Kansas" (Master's thesis, Wichita State University, 1982), 25-30.

34. Richard Cummins to William Clark, 16 June 1837, RG 75, LROIA, Fort Leavenworth Agency, M 234, R 301, NA.

35. Keckeisen, "Kansa 'Half-Breed' Lands," 29-30; and Isaac McCoy to John C. Spencer, 21 Dec. 1841, Isaac McCoy Papers (microfilm), MD, KSHS.

36. Keckeisen, "Kansa 'Half-Breed' Lands," 33.

37. Timothy Flint, *Recollections of the Last Ten Years*, Introduction by James D. Norris (New York: Da Capo, 1968), 163; and John Francis McDermott, ed., *Tixier's Travels on the Osage Prairies* (Norman: University of Oklahoma Press, 1940), 203–4.

38. Kate L. Gregg and John Francis McDermott, *Prairie and Mountain Sketches by Matthew C. Field* (Norman: University of Oklahoma Press, 1957), 210.

39. Keckeisen, "Kansa 'Half-Breed' Lands," 31.

40. White Plume's speech to William Clark, 17 May 1827, RG 75, LROIA, St. Louis Superintendency, M 234, R 748, NA.

41. Fred Chouteau to W. W. Cone, 10 May 1880, Chouteau Papers; and Barry, *Beginning of the West*, 258, 291–92, 335, 419.

42. Barry, *Beginning of the West*, 419.

43. Ibid., 160, 166–67, 257, 312. Marriage customs among the Kansa traditionalists, which Julie Gonville appears to have followed, were not complicated; the same is true about the customs for divorce. According to the testimony of several Kansas in 1871, "When the parties agree with each other to live together as man and wife according to the Indian custom they do so so long as they live together. When a man and wife get tired of living together, and wish to part, then all they have to do to cease to be man and wife under the Indian custom is to separate and throw off or abandon each other, and quit living together and go apart. Then they are no longer husband and wife according to the Indian custom. And then after such separation there is no Indian custom that prevents either or both of the parties from marrying again who they please"; see *Jacob Smith et al.* v. *James H. Brown et al.*, 8 Kan. 610–11.

44. William R. Swagerty, "Marriage and Settlement Patterns of Rocky Mountain Trappers and Traders," *Western Historical Quarterly* 11 (Apr. 1980): 180.

45. Barry, *Beginning of the West*, 335; and Barry, "Kansa Indians," 487.

46. *William W. Cone's Historical Sketch of Shawnee County, Kansas* (Topeka: Kansas Farmer Printing Office, 1877), 6.

47. Barry, *Beginning of the West*, 409; and Gregg and McDermott, *Prairie and Mountain Sketches*, 211.

48. Gregg and McDermott, *Prairie and Mountain Sketches*, 210–11.

49. Ibid., 212.

50. Charles Curtis, "History of North Topeka," typed copy, LD, KSHS; and *North Topeka Times*, 27 Dec. 1878.

CHAPTER 4. BORN IN A LOG HOUSE

1. Colin G. Calloway, "Neither White nor Red: White Renegades on the American Indian Frontier," *Western Historical Quarterly* 14 (Jan. 1986): 53, 66; and Jacqueline Peterson, "Ethnogenesis: The Settlement and Growth of a 'New People' in the Great Lakes Region, 1702–1815," *American Indian Culture and Research Journal* 6 (1982): 54–55.

2. Francis Paul Prucha, *The Indian in American Society* (Berkeley: University of California Press, 1985), 15–16.

3. Ibid., 16–17; Clark to Barbour, 11 June 1825, Introduction and Ratified Treaties, 1801–26, RG 75, T 494, R 1, NA; and Kappler, *Treaties*, 185–86, 199–200, 205–6, 210–11, 128–29.

4. John D. Unruh, *The Plains Across: The Overland Emigrants and the Trans-Mississippi West, 1840–1860,* paperback ed. (Urbana: University of Illinois Press, 1982), 198.

5. Barry, *Beginning of the West,* 428.

6. Ibid., 452.

7. George A. Root, "Ferries in Kansas: Part II: Kansas River," *Kansas Historical Quarterly* 4 (Nov. 1933): 363–66.

8. Unruh, *Plains Across,* 224, 242; and Barry, *Beginning of the West,* 516, 584–85, 795, 842.

9. Barry, *Beginning of the West,* 1094; and *New York Daily Tribune,* 18 Nov. 1852.

10. Unrau, *Kansa Indians,* 133, 135–36, 150–51, 159.

11. Ibid., 14, 154, 166; Root, "Ferries in Kansas," 367; and Kappler, *Treaties,* 552–54.

12. *Missouri Republican* (St. Louis), 12 July 1854, cited by Barry, *Beginning of the West,* 1232.

13. William Phillips, *The Conquest of Kansas, by Missouri and Her Allies* (Boston, Mass.: Phillips, Sampson, 1856), 18; Phillips was a correspondent for the *New York Daily Tribune.* See also H. Craig Miner and William E. Unrau, *The End of Indian Kansas: A Study of Cultural Revolution, 1854–1871* (Lawrence: Regents Press of Kansas, 1978), 4–5.

14. Paul Wallace Gates, *Fifty Million Acres: Conflicts over Kansas Land Policy, 1854–1890* (Ithaca, N.Y.: Cornell University Press, 1954), 44–45; Homer E. Socolofsky, "Wyandot Floats," *Kansas Historical Quarterly* 36 (Autumn 1970): 243–57; and Kappler, *Treaties,* 534–37, 681.

15. Gates, *Fifty Million Acres,* 39–40.

16. Kappler, *Treaties,* 224; and Keckeisen, "Kansa 'Half-Breed' Lands," 37–38.

17. For a discussion of commissioner Manypenny's futile attempts to prevent speculation on the Indian reserves west of Missouri see Miner and Unrau, *End of Indian Kansas,* 8–24.

18. "Governor Reeder's Administration," *Transactions of the Kansas State Historical Society* 5 (1891–96): 225–27. Reeder's letter was printed in the *Missouri Republican,* 5 May 1855.

19. John Montgomery to James W. Denver, 30 June 1857, RG 75, LROIA, Kansas Agency, M 234, R 365, NA.

20. Chloe Berry Howe, "Our Peerless Pawhuskan," n.d., Edgar Watson Howe Papers, 298, MD, KSHS; and Dolly Gann, *Dolly Gann's Book* (Garden City, N.Y.: Doubleday, Doran, 1933), 3.

21. Barry, *Beginning of the West,* 1060; George M. Martin, "Some of the Lost Towns of Kansas," *Collections of the Kansas State Historical Society* 22 (1911–12): 427–29.

22. *Leavenworth* (Kans.) *Daily Times,* 26 Mar. 1861, cited by Albert Castel, *A Frontier State at War: Kansas, 1861–1865* (Ithaca, N.Y.: Cornell University Press, 1958), 4.

23. Keckeisen, "Kansa 'Half-Breed' Lands," 57–66; Unrau, *Kansa Indians,* 174–75; George W. Clarke to George Manypenny, 26 Dec. 1856, RG 75, LROIA, Central Superintendency, M 234, R 55, NA; and John H. Gihon, *Geary and Kansas* (1857; reprint, Freeport, N.Y.: Books for Libraries, 1971), 21.

24. Ewy, "Charles Curtis," 7–9; and "Founder of North Topeka, William Curtis, Who in His Day was the Boss Town Boomer of the West," n.d., typed copy, Charles Curtis Family Articles, LD, KSHS.

25. Charles Curtis Papers, Chambo Collection, no. 22, MD, KSHS; Curtis, ''Autobiography,'' Colvin copy; and Ewy, ''Charles Curtis,'' 7.

26. ''Vermillion [Ind.] Circuit Court Transcript, February, 1858 Term,'' copy in Chambo Collection, no. 22; Miscellaneous Material Relating to Charles Curtis and His Ancestors, vol. 1-A, LD, KSHS; entries for 1859, box S, folder 2, ms. 3626, Michael Shine Papers, Nebraska Historical Society; and Curtis, ''Autobiography,'' Colvin copy, art. 2, p. 1.

27. Curtis, ''Autobiography,'' Colvin copy, art. 2, p. 1; and Charles Curtis to George A. Root, 16 Sept. 1933, cited by Root, ''Ferries in Kansas,'' 368.

28. Curtis, ''History of North Topeka,'' 2; and Root, ''Ferries in Kansas,'' 368.

29. *Topeka Tribune*, 14 Jan. 1860.

30. Root, ''Ferries in Kansas,'' 370–73; *Kansas State Record* (Topeka), 4 Feb. 1860; and *Private Laws of Kansas Territory*, 31 Jan. 1860, 273.

31. *New York Daily Tribune*, 9 June 1859; and John Farwell to Board of Indian Commissioners, cited by Miner and Unrau, *End of Indian Kansas*, 141.

CHAPTER 5. THE ESTATE ENDANGERED

1. William H. Carruth, ''The New England Emigrant Aid Company as an Investment Society,'' *Kansas Historical Collections* 6 (1897–1900): 93.

2. Robert W. Richmond, *Kansas: A Land of Contrasts* (St. Louis, Mo.: Forum, 1974), 88; and Curtis, ''Autobiography,'' Colvin copy, art. 2, p. 1.

3. Curtis, ''Autobiography,'' Colvin copy, art. 2, p. 1; W. G. Cutler, *History of the State of Kansas* (Chicago: A. T. Andreas, 1883), 559; and Charles Curtis Papers, Chambo Collection, no. 22, MD, KSHS.

4. Curtis, ''History of North Topeka,'' 2; *Topeka Mail and Breeze* (Illustrated Historical Edition), 22 May 1896; Fannie E. Cole, ''Pioneer Life in Kansas,'' *Kansas Historical Collections* 12 (1911–12): 355; and Edward King, ''The Great South: The New Route to the Gulf,'' *Scribner's Monthly* 6 (July 1873): 257.

5. Curtis, ''Autobiography,'' Colvin copy, art. 2, pp. 1–2.

6. Ibid.

7. Kappler, *Treaties*, 804–6; and Gates, *Fifty Million Acres*, 117.

8. Kappler, *Treaties*, 614–18, 806; Richard Cummins to William Clark, 16 June 1827, RG 75, LROIA, Fort Leavenworth Agency, M 234, R 301, NA; Keckeisen, ''Kansa 'Half-Breed' Lands,'' 29–30; and Petition to Congress of Adel Clement, Joseph James, Louis Pepin [Pappan], Julie Gonville, Vickie [Victoria] Gonville, 2 Oct. 1855, RG 75, LROIA, Kansas Agency, M 234, R 364, NA.

9. Kappler, *Treaties*, 223.

10. Eight Half-Breeds to Commissioner of Indian Affairs, 8 Apr. 1857, Appeal of Hard Hart and others to Commissioner of Indian Affairs, 12 June 1857, RG 75, LROIA, Kansas Agency, M 234, R 365, NA; Kappler, *Treaties*, 802.

11. Alexander Bayne and J. E. Waddin to James Buchanan, 20 June 1860, and R. S. Stevens to Charles Mix, 24 Aug. 1860, RG 75, LROIA, Kansas Agency, M 234, R 365, NA; Senate Executive Document 58 (ser. 1122), 12–14; and Keckeisen, ''Kansa 'Half-Breed' Lands,'' 71–73.

12. Jeremiah Black to Jacob Thompson, 9 Sept. 1857, RG 75, LROIA, Kansas Agency, M 234, R 365, NA.

13. *U.S. Stat.*, 12:21–22.

14. *George W. Ewing* v. *John McManamy,* Kansas Territorial District Court, 1st Judicial District, Jefferson County, K. T. (10 Dec. 1858), cited by Keckeisen, "Kansa 'Half-Breed' Lands," 103-7.

15. Senate Executive Document 58 (ser. 1122), 2.

16. Ibid., 8.

17. Ibid., 10.

18. *U.S. Stat.,* 12:628; Keckeisen, "Kansa 'Half-Breed' Lands," 114-18; and *John Brown and Jane Brown* v. *Adel (Clement) Belmarde,* 3 Kan. 35.

19. Gates, *Fifty Million Acres,* 116-21; and Miner and Unrau, *End of Indian Kansas,* 36-37.

20. Deed Transfer Ledger (copy), Louis and Julie Pappan, Miscellaneous Curtis Material.

21. Senate Executive Document 58 (ser. 1122), 11-15; and Clark to James Barbour, 11 June 1825, Ratified Treaties, 1801-26.

22. Deed Transfer Ledger, Abstract of Titles—Charles Curtis, Topeka Title and Bond Company (copy), Abstract of Title Transfers (copy), Julie Gonville, Miscellaneous Curtis Material; and "Founder of North Topeka," Curtis Family Articles.

23. Margaret Holman, "The History of North Topeka," *Bulletin of the Shawnee County Historical Society* 24 (Dec. 1955): 7-8; and Deed Transfer Ledger (copy), Miscellaneous Curtis Material.

24. Curtis, "History of North Topeka," 2; Curtis, "Autobiography," Colvin copy, art. 2, pp. 3-4; *Topeka Mail and Breeze,* 22 May 1896; and John D. Cruise, "Early Days on the Union Pacific," *Kansas Historical Collections* 2 (1909-10): 540.

25. Holman, "History of North Topeka," 7-8.

26. "Founder of North Topeka," Curtis Family Articles; and Curtis, "Autobiography," Colvin copy, art. 2, pp. 3, 13.

27. "Founder of North Topeka," Curtis Family Articles.

28. Curtis, "Autobiography," Colvin copy, art. 2, p. 7; and *Kansas State Record,* 25 June 1868.

CHAPTER 6. A MIXED-BLOOD
ON THE RESERVATION

1. Hagan, "Full Blood," 309.

2. Seitz, *From Kaw Teepee,* 33-34; and *Topeka State Journal,* 29 Mar. 1898.

3. Martin, "Some of the Lost Towns of Kansas," 427.

4. Cutler, *History of the State of Kansas,* 559; and Stephen Z. Starr, *Jennison's Jayhawkers: A Civil War Cavalry Regiment and Its Commander* (Baton Rouge: Louisiana State University Press, 1973), 366-67, 378.

5. Starr, *Jennison's Jayhawkers,* 368; and Charles Curtis Papers, Chambo Collection, no. 22, MD, KSHS.

6. Ewy, "Charles Curtis," 9; and Charles Curtis Papers, Chambo Collection, no. 22, MD, KSHS.

7. Root, "Ferries in Kansas," 373; Cutler, *History of the State of Kansas,* 559; and Pension File, Capt. Orren A. Curtis, Records of the Adjutant General's Office, RG 94, NA.

8. Curtis, "Autobiography," Colvin copy, art. 2, p.13.

9. Miner and Unrau, *End of Indian Kansas,* 77-78.

10. Kappler, *Treaties*, 552–54; Cummins to Thomas Harvey, 6 Mar. 1844, RG 75, LROIA, Fort Leavenworth Agency, M 234, R 302, NA; and Barry, "Kansa Indians," 481.

11. Register of Kansa Indians Vaccinated by Dr. [J. Andrew] Chute, May–June 1838, RG 75, LROIA, Fort Leavenworth Agency, M 234, R 364, NA; *The Kansas Press* (Council Grove), 10 Oct. 1859; and *Council Grove* (Kans.) *Press*, 30 Mar. 1861.

12. Barry, "Kansa Indians," 487; and Kappler, *Treaties*, 801–3.

13. Kappler, *Treaties*, 802.

14. Unrau, *Kansa Indians*, 197; and *Council Grove Press*, 13 Apr. 1863.

15. Istalashe to My Great Father (trans. Joseph James), 17 July 1863, RG 75, LROIA, Kansas Agency, M 234, R 366, NA; Unrau, *Kansa Indians*, 200, 203.

16. Curtis, "Autobiography," Colvin copy, art. 2, p. 7.

17. Ibid., 4–6.

18. Seitz, *From Kaw Teepee*, 34–35; Curtis, "Autobiography," Colvin copy, art. 2, p. 10.

19. Curtis, "Autobiography," Colvin copy, art. 2, pp. 7–8.

20. Unrau, *Kansa Indians*, 204, 206–7.

21. Ibid., 208–9.

22. Ibid., 209.

23. Ibid., 210.

24. Ibid.

25. *New York Times*, 14 Apr. 1929; *Wichita* (Kans.) *Eagle*, 25 Oct. 1930; and Seitz, *From Kaw Teepee*, 122–24.

26. Curtis, "Autobiography," Colvin copy, art. 2, pp. 11–12.

27. Ibid.

28. Samuel J. Crawford, *Kansas in the Sixties* (Chicago: A. C. McClurg, 1911), 188–89.

CHAPTER 7. THE MIXED-BLOOD MOUNTED

1. "Dolly" was the nickname given to Permelia Curtis by her father; see Gann, *Dolly Gann's Book*, 3–4.

2. Kappler, *Treaties*, 977–89.

3. Mark A. Plummer, *Frontier Governor: Samuel J. Crawford of Kansas* (Lawrence: University Press of Kansas, 1971), 113–33; and Samuel J. Crawford to Edmund G. Ross, 29 June 1867, Governor's Correspondence, Samuel J. Crawford, 1865–68, Subject File, MS, KSHS.

4. Plummer, *Frontier Governor*, 129–32.

5. Curtis, "Autobiography," Colvin copy, art. 2, p. 13.

6. For the role of the mixed-bloods in tribal dissolution in Kansas and their role in removal to Indian Territory see Miner and Unrau, *End of Indian Kansas*, 71–72, 84–95; and William E. Unrau and H. Craig Miner, *Tribal Dispossession and the Ottawa Indian University Fraud* (Norman: University of Oklahoma Press, 1985), 78–92, 112–13, 122–24.

7. Gann, *Dolly Gann's Book*, 4; and Cutler, *History of the State of Kansas*, 559.

8. Deed Transfer Ledger, Miscellaneous Curtis Material.

9. Cutler, *History of the State of Kansas*, 559; and Ewy, "Charles Curtis," 9.

10. *William Curtis* v. *Orren A. Curtis, Guardian of Elizabeth Curtis and Charles Curtis, Minors, O. O. Kelsa, Louis and Julie Pappan*, District Court of Shawnee

County, Kansas, 21 May 1871 (copy), Abstract of Titles, Charles Curtis, Miscellaneous Curtis Materials.

11. "Founder of North Topeka," Curtis Family Articles; and Castel, *Frontier State at War*, 4.

12. *Topeka Mail and Breeze*, 22 May 1896.

13. Ibid.; and "Founder of North Topeka," Curtis Family Articles.

14. Ibid.; and Seitz, *From Kaw Teepee*, 18–19.

15. Curtis, "Autobiography," Colvin copy, art. 2, pp. 14–15.

16. Ibid., 15.

17. James A. Clifton, *The Prairie People: Continuity and Change in Potawatomi Indian Culture, 1665–1965* (Lawrence: Regents Press of Kansas, 1977), 351; and Kappler, *Treaties*, 824–28, 970–74.

18. Cato Sells to Charles Curtis, 15 June 1917, RG 75, LROIA, Education-Indians, NA; and Curtis, "Autobiography," Colvin copy, art. 3, pp. 4–5.

19. Henry G. Waltmann, "Ely Samuel Parker," in *The Commissioners of Indian Affairs, 1824–1977*, ed. Robert M. Kvasnicka and Herman J. Viola (Lincoln: University of Nebraska Press, 1979), 124.

20. Paul W. Gates, "Indian Allotments Preceding the Dawes Act," in *The Frontier Challenge: Responses to the Trans-Mississippi West*, ed. John G. Clark (Lawrence: University Press of Kansas, 1971), 161–62.

21. Keckeisen, "Kansa 'Half-Breed' Lands," 121–23.

22. Platting Deed, 29 Mar. 1867 (copy), Abstract of Titles, Miscellaneous Curtis Materials; and *John Brown and Jane Brown* v. *Adel [Clement] Belmarde*, 3 Kan. 35.

23. "Aderial Hebard Case," in *The United States Biographical Dictionary, Kansas Volume* (Chicago: S. Lewis & Co., 1879), 640–42; and *Curtis* v. *Curtis* (copy).

24. Abstract of titles, Curtis Miscellaneous Materials.

25. Curtis, "Autobiography," Colvin copy, art. 3, pp. 5–7.

26. Ibid., 9.

27. Ibid., 9–19, and art. 4, pp. 1–9.

28. H. Craig Miner, *The Corporation and the Indian: Tribal Sovereignty and Industrial Civilization in Indian Territory, 1865–1907* (Columbia: University of Missouri Press, 1976), 46, 61.

29. Curtis, "Autobiography," Colvin copy, art. 4, p. 9.

30. Ibid., 8; and Miner, *Corporation and the Indian*, 30–31.

31. Curtis, "Autobiography," Colvin copy, art. 4, p. 9; "Founder of North Topeka," Curtis Family Articles; and Mortgage Deeds, William and Permelia Curtis, 8 Dec. 1866, 1 May 1867, 15 May 1868 (copies), Quit-Claim Deed, 4 May 1874 (copy), Tax Deed, 7 May 1874 (copy), In the Matter of the Guardianship of Charles Curtis and Elizabeth Curtis, Minor Heirs of Ellen Curtis, Deceased, Shawnee County, Kansas (copy), *Curtis* v. *Curtis* (copy), Abstract of Titles, Miscellaneous Curtis Materials.

32. Unrau, *Kaw People*, 69.

CHAPTER 8. "OUR CHARLEY"

1. Curtis, "Autobiography," Colvin copy, art. 4, p. 9.

2. V. V. Masterson, *The Katy Railroad and the Last Frontier* (Norman: University of Oklahoma Press, 1952), 12; and "Articles of Agreement Made and Concluded at the City of Washington on the Thirteenth Day of February, One

Thousand Eight Hundred and Sixty-Seven, between Lewis Bogy, Commissioner of Indian Affairs, and Chiefs of the Kansas," Unratified Treaties, 1866–67, T 494, R 9, NA.

3. Unrau, *Kansa Indians*, 212–14; and Mahlon Stubbs to Enoch Hoag, 7 Jan. 1871, RG 75, LROIA, Kansas Agency, M 234, R 368, NA.

4. Unrau, *Kansa Indians*, 214–15; and Geo. T. Nicholson to Cyrus Beede, 24 Apr. 1876, RG 75, LROIA, Osage Agency, box 2, FRC, Fort Worth.

5. Curtis, "Autobiography," Colvin copy, art. 4, pp. 10–14, and art. 5, p. 3.

6. Ibid., art. 5, pp. 7–8.

7. Kappler, *Treaties*, 533.

8. *Topeka Mail and Breeze*, n.d., in Curtis Family Articles; and Gann, *Dolly Gann's Book*, 1.

9. Edgar Watson Howe, "Our Peerless Pawhuskan," 289, in Edgar Watson Howe Papers, MD, KSHS.

10. Miner and Unrau, *End of Indian Kansas*, 134.

11. Curtis, "Autobiography," Colvin copy, art. 5, pp. 14–15.

12. Ibid., art. 6, pp. 2–5.

13. Ibid., pp. 4–10; and William E. Unrau, "The Mixed-Blood Connection: Charles Curtis and Kaw Detribalization," in *Kansas and the West: Bicentennial Essays in Honor of Nyle H. Miller*, ed. Forrest R. Blackburn (Topeka: Kansas State Historical Society, 1976), 155.

14. Horatio Alger, Jr., *Risen from the Ranks; Or, Harry Walton's Success* (Philadelphia: John C. Winston, 1874); and Curtis, "Autobiography," Colvin copy, art. 6, p. 5.

15. "Founder of North Topeka," Curtis Family Articles.

16. Statement of Laban Miles, 1910, in *Osage Enrollment*, 91–92.

17. Curtis, "Autobiography," Colvin copy, art. 6, pp. 5–7; Elizabeth Layton, Power of Attorney to Charles Curtis, 27 Aug. 1879, J. B. Evans, Notary Public, Shawnee County, Kans. (copy), Miscellaneous Curtis Material; and *Commonwealth* (Topeka), 19 and 20 June 1879. For a general account of the refugee experience in Topeka in 1879/80 see Robert G. Athearn, *In Search of Canaan: Black Migration to Kansas, 1879–80* (Lawrence: Regents Press of Kansas, 1978), chap. 4.

18. Ewy, "Charles Curtis," 14–15.

19. *Topeka Daily Capitol*, 7 Feb. 1886; and Curtis, "Autobiography," Colvin copy, art. 10, pp. 1–2.

20. An important recent analysis of the shift to the total assimilationist program is Frederick E. Hoxie's *A Final Promise: The Campaign to Assimilate the Indians, 1880–1920* (Lincoln: University of Nebraska Press, 1984); see also Francis Paul Prucha, *American Indian Policy in Crisis: Christian Reformers and the Indian, 1865–1900* (Norman: University of Oklahoma Press, 1976); and Robert W. Mardock, *The Reformers and the American Indian* (Columbia: University of Missouri Press, 1971).

21. Curtis, "Autobiography," Colvin copy, art. 7, pp. 1–4; and William Allen White, *Calvin Coolidge: The Man Who Is President* (New York: Macmillan, 1925), 176–77, 178.

22. Robert Smith Bader, *Prohibition in Kansas: A History* (Lawrence: University Press of Kansas, 1986), 22.

23. Hiram Farnsworth to William P. Dole, 17 July 1863, RG 75, LROIA, Kansas Agency, M 234, R 366. For additional accounts of whiskey smuggling on the Kansa reservation see *Emporia* (Kans.) *News*, 16 Feb. 1860, 10 and 17 May 1862; *Topeka Mail and Breeze*, 26 May 1896; and *North Topeka Times*, 27 Dec. 1878.

24. Bader, *Prohibition in Kansas*, 60; *Topeka Daily Capitol*, 15 and 16 May 1885; and *Dearborn* (Mich.) *Independent*, 22 July 1922, cited in *Western Spirit* (Paola, Kans.), 4 Aug. 1922.

25. *Western Spirit*, 4 Aug. 1922; and Ewy, "Charles Curtis," 16.

26. Ewy, "Charles Curtis," 17–18; *Topeka Mail and Breeze*, 20 Feb. 1885; and *Topeka Daily Capitol*, 4 Feb. 1885.

27. White, *Calvin Coolidge*, 177; and Ewy, "Charles Curtis," 19.

28. Ewy, "Charles Curtis," 19–20; and William Allen White, *The Autobiography of William Allen White* (New York: Macmillan, 1946), 196.

29. White, *Calvin Coolidge*, 179–80; and White to Curtis, 19 May 1925, ser. C, box 66, William Allen White Papers, LC.

30. *U.S. Stat.*, 26:388–91; and Hoxie, *Final Promise*, 36–37.

31. Brian W. Dippie, *The Vanishing American: White Attitudes and U.S. Indian Policy* (Middletown, Conn.: Wesleyan University Press, 1982), 137.

32. Ibid., 248

33. T. D. Isaacs to Jas. I. David, 1 Sept. 1886, RG 75, LROIA, box 9, FRC, Fort Worth.

34. *U.S. Stat.*, 26:391.

35. Acting Commissioner of Indian Affairs to C. H. Potter, 1 June 1888, RG 75, LROIA, Osage Agency, box 11, FRC, Fort Worth.

36. Gregory C. Thompson, "John D. C. Atkins," in *The Commissioners of Indian Affairs, 1824–1977*, ed. Robert M. Kvasnicka and Herman J. Viola (Lincoln: University of Nebraska Press, 1979), 185; and *Congressional Record*, 50th Cong., 1st sess., 26–27 July and 10 Aug. 1888, 20:6885–86, 6903, 7429.

37. *Congressional Record*, 50th Cong., 1st sess., 26–27 July 1888, 20:6886.

38. Ibid.

CHAPTER 9. WHISPERING IN WASHINGTON

1. Robert Sherman La Forte, *Leaders of Reform: Progressive Republicans in Kansas, 1900–1916* (Lawrence: University Press of Kansas, 1974), 39; and Ewy, "Charles Curtis," 21–22.

2. Ewy, "Charles Curtis," 21.

3. La Forte, *Leaders of Reform*, 17–18.

4. Ewy, "Charles Curtis," 25–26; and *Topeka State Journal*, 17 Jan. 1903.

5. Ewy, "Charles Curtis," 22–23; Gann, *Dolly Gann's Book*, 8–9; Oswald Garrison Villard, "Charles Curtis," *Nation*, 129 (7 Apr. 1928): 400; and White, *Calvin Coolidge*, 180–81.

6. La Forte, *Leaders of Reform*, 83; and *Washington Merry-Go-Round* (New York: Blue Ribbon, 1931), 96–97.

7. Ewy, "Charles Curtis," 36; *Topeka Daily Capitol*, 1 May 1896, 28 Mar, 21 Apr., and 25 May 1897; and *Western Spirit* (Paola, Kans.), 4 Aug. 1922.

8. Joe Mitchell Chappell to Curtis, 20 Nov. 1930, and Lillian M. Mitchner to Curtis, 10 Aug. 1927, Curtis Papers.

9. *Topeka Daily Capitol*, 28 May 1986; and *New York Times*, 16 June 1928.

10. *Muskogee* (Indian Terr.) *Phoenix*, 9 Aug. 1900; Curtis, "Qualities That Lead to Success," LD, KSHS; and *Topeka Daily Capitol*, 9 Feb. 1936.

11. Charles E. Ross, "Charles Curtis of Kansas," *Outlook*, 16 May 1928, 84.

12. "Heap Big Chief," *American Mercury*, Aug. 1929, 410.

13. White, *Calvin Coolidge*, 181.

14. Ibid., 186; and *Topeka State Journal,* 22 Apr. 1920.

15. White, *Calvin Coolidge,* 183–84; and Villard, "Charles Curtis," 400. In 1912, Curtis reported a large following among members of the G.A.R., organized into Curtis Clubs throughout the state; see Curtis to H. L. Miller, 1 June 1912, Curtis Papers, MD, KSHS.

16. Curtis, "Autobiography," Colvin copy, art. 22, p. 2; and Miner, *Corporation and the Indian,* 173, 183–84, 197.

17. Miner, *Corporation and the Indian,* 178; Curtis, "Autobiography," Colvin copy, art. 22 ,p. 2.

18. *Muskogee Phoenix,* 9 Aug. 1900 and 15 Oct. 1903.

19. *Topeka Daily Capitol,* 4 Jan. 1892.

20. Ross, "Charles Curtis," 18; and "Heap Big Chief," 410.

21. "Heap Big Chief," 410.

22. *National Tribune* (Washington, D.C.), 27 July 1920; and *Washington* (D.C.) *Inquirer,* 7 Dec. 1924, in Curtis Scrapbooks, vols. 1907–23, LD, KSHS.

23. "Lo, the Poor Senator," 14.

24. "Charles Curtis, Indian," Kaw Indian Agency Collection.

25. Villard, "Charles Curtis," 400.

26. Curtis to Edson Watson, 29 June 2908, RG 75, LROIA, Potawatomi Agency, box 1795–1930, FRC, Kansas City; Curtis to Commissioner of Indian Affairs, 21 Nov. 1898, RG 75, LROIA, Land, NA; *Muskogee Phoenix,* 10 May 1894, 26 Mar. 1896, 16 Sept. 1897; Acting Commissioner of Indian Affairs to Secretary of the Interior, 28 Aug. 1900, RG 48, Records of the Office of the Secretary of the Interior, Indian Territory Div., Special Files, box 73, NA; Curtis to Commissioner of Indian Affairs, 15 May 1901, RG 75, LROIA, Finance, NA; Curtis to Commissioner of Indian Affairs, 7 Aug. 1900, RG 75, Education, NA; *Arkansas City* (Kans.) *Daily Traveler,* 5 Sept. 1901; and "Oklahoma Oil May Bring Riches to Indian Senator from Kansas," clipping, n.d., Curtis Scrapbooks, vols. 1907–23, LD KSHS. For additional details about Curtis's congressional activities regarding Indian affairs see William E. Unrau, "Charles Curtis," in *Indian Lives: Essays on Nineteenth and Twentieth Century Native American Leaders,* ed. L. G. Moses and Raymond Wilson (Albuquerque: University of New Mexico Press, 1985), 125–27.

27. Curtis to Ethan Allen Hitchcock, 10 Sept. 1900, RG 200, Private Papers Collection, Ethan Allen Hitchcock Papers, NA; and *Muskogee Phoenix,* 15 Oct. 1903.

28. Curtis to W. A. Jones, 14 Sept. 1897, RG 75, LROIA, Miscellaneous, NA; Curtis to Jones, 13 Sept. 1902, R. W. Johnson to Commissioner of Indian Affairs, 2 Sept. 1902, and Curtis to Commissioner of Indian Affairs, 28 May and 24 June 1898, RG 75, LROIA, Land, NA; and "Guthrie State Capitol," clipping, n.d., Hitchcock Papers, NA.

29. *Vinita* (Indian Terr.) *Indian Chieftain,* 23 Dec. 1897, 3 and 31 May 1900; and Frederick Babcock, "Curtis's Oily Hands," *Nation* 127 (26 Sept. 1928): 288.

30. *Vinita Indian Chieftain,* 25 Aug. 1898.

31. Curtis to Ethan Allen Hitchcock, 11 Sept. 1904; and Hitchcock to President Theodore Roosevelt, 26 Sept. 1906, Hitchcock Papers, NA.

32. Terry P. Wilson, *The Underground Reservation: Osage Oil* (Lincoln: University of Nebraska Press, 1985), 106–7; and Miner, *Corporation and the Indian,* 182.

33. Miner, *Corporation and the Indian,* 192–93.

34. *Leavenworth Daily Times,* 15, 16, and 19 Sept. 1903.

35. Francis Paul Prucha, *The Great Father: The United States Government and the Indian,* 2 vols. (Lincoln: University of Nebraska Press, 1984), 2:901.

36. *Leavenworth Daily Times,* 19 Sept. 1903; and *El Reno* (Oklahoma Terr.) *Americana,* 29 Oct. 1903, clipping, Hitchcock Papers, NA; and Prucha, *Great Father,* 902.

37. *Congressional Record,* 58th Cong., 2d sess., 19 Apr. 1904, 38:5121–22.

38. *U.S. Stat.,* 30:495–519; *Vinita Indian Chieftain,* 3 Mar. 1898 and 1 Mar. 1900; and *Cherokee Advocate* (Tahlequah, Cherokee Nation), 8 Sept. 1900.

39. *U.S. Stat.,* 30:495–519.

40. *Daily Oklahoma* (Oklahoma Terr.) *State Capital,* 16 Apr. and 8 June 1898; and *Vinita Indian Chieftain,* 14 July 1898; see also Kenny L. Brown, ''A Progressive from Oklahoma: Senator Robert Latham Owen, Jr.,'' *Chronicles of Oklahoma* 62 (Fall 1984): 232–65.

41. Arrell Morgan Gibson, *Oklahoma: A History of Five Centuries* (Norman: University of Oklahoma Press, 1981), 198; and Prucha, *Great Father,* 2:748.

42. D. W. C. Duncan, ''How Allotment Impoverishes the Indians: Testimony before a Senate Committee Investigating Conditions in the Indian Territory, November, 1906,'' in *Great Documents in American Indian History,* ed. Wayne Moquin and Charles Van Doren (New York: Praeger Publishers, 1973), 288–89.

CHAPTER 10. EASY ALLOTMENT

1. Prucha, *Great Father* 2:900–901; and *Congressional Record,* 59th Cong., 1st sess., 18 Jan. 1906, 40:1262.

2. *Congressional Record,* 59th Cong., 1st sess., 18 Jan. 1906, 40:1262.

3. Ibid., 1263–64; *U.S. Stat.,* 34:182–83; Senate Document 482 (ser. 5269), 27–31; Wilson, *Underground Reservation,* 91; and Prucha, *Great Father,* 2:773, 871–72.

4. *Osage Enrollment,* 91–92.

5. RCIA, 1874, 526–27.

6. Ibid.

7. T. D. Isaacs to Jas. I. Davids, 1 Sept. 1886, RG 75, LROIA, Osage Agency, box 9, FRC, Fort Worth; RCIA, 1880, 76; and RCIA, 1881, 86.

8. William Nicholson to Cyrus Beede, 31 Mar. 1876, RG 75, LROIA, General Records Correspondence, box 1, FRC, Fort Worth; and RCIA, 1877, 95.

9. Unrau, *Kaw People,* 69.

10. Affidavit of Gen. W. E. Hardy, 7 Jan. 1911, Kaw Indian Agency Records, box 45, WHC, UO. Hardy repeatedly referred to himself as a general, claiming that he had been an officer under General U. S. Grant during the Civil War; see, e.g., his interview with the *Guthrie* (Okla.) *Daily Leader,* 14 Sept. 1903. But he contradicts this in his 1911 affidavit, in which he states: ''That in 1858 this affiant again went to the Kaw Tribe . . . and ever since to this day has made his home and lived with them.'' In a search of the Consolidated Military and Pension Files, RG 94, Records of the Adjutant General's Office, NA, I found no official record of Hardy's service in the Civil War.

11. Kappler, *Treaties,* 223; Barry, *Beginning of the West,* 419; Senate Executive Document 58 (ser. 1122), 4, 15; and affidavit of Hardy.

12. H. Price to L. H. Miles, 20 June 1881, RG 75, LROIA, General Records Correspondence, box 6, FRC, Fort Worth; and *Victoria Hardy* v. *Pelagia Pougel,* 25 Jan. 1864, District Court of Kansas, 3d Judicial District, Jefferson County, Kans.

13. Affidavit of Hardy.

14. Hardy to Secretary of the Interior, 4 Feb. 1881, H. Price to L. J. Miles, 20 June 1881, RG 75, LROIA, General Records Correspondence, box 6, FRC, Fort Worth.

15. H. Price to L. J. Miles, 5 Sept. 1881, ibid.

16. Little Louis Pappan, Benjamin Fronkier, Joseph James, Nopawiah, and Allegahwahu (their Xs) to L. J. Miles, 13 Sept. 1883, ibid., box 8.

17. J. S. Smith to William Nicholson, 15 Dec. 1876, ibid., Osage Agency, box 2, Uriah Spray to Cyrus Beede, 12 May 1877, ibid., General Records Correspondence, box 3.

18. Kaw Council Tabular Vote, 16 Nov. 1883, at Kaw Agency, I.T., ibid., General Records Correspondence, box 8.

19. W. E. Hardy to H. Price, 23 Jan. 1885, ibid., box 8-A; and *Muskogee* (Okla.) *Phoenix*, 20 Jan. 1898.

20. *Arkansas City* (Kans.) *Daily Traveler*, 27 Oct. 1902; affidavit of Hardy; and *Wichita* (Kans.) *Daily Beacon*, 19 June 1899.

21. RCIA, 1900, 337; and Kaw Miscellaneous Volume, 1882-94.

22. C. W. Holcomb to Cyrus Beede, 3 Nov. 1880, RG 75, LROIA, General Records Correspondence, box 5, FRC, Fort Worth. Three years later, Commissioner Price wrote to agent Miles: "As a general rule the class of white men who desire adoption into an Indian tribe are too lazy and worthless to work for their own living and seek admission into an Indian tribe simply for the purpose of taking advantage of the Indian. . . . You will therefore inform any of these white people who apply, that any action the Indians may take looking to their adoption will not be approved by this Office." But Price refused to exclude white men who had *married Indian women* for purposes of tribal membership; see Price to Miles, 3 Oct. 1884, ibid., box 8-A.

23. A. Bupshaw to C. A. Potter, RG 75, LROIA, Osage Agency, box 11, FRC, Fort Worth; and *Kaw City Star*, 18 Sept. 1903. Curtis and his three children were listed on the official 1897 annuity roll of the Kaw Tribe; see Kaw Annuity Roll, 1897, RG 75, Pawnee Agency Miscellaneous Files, FRC, Fort Worth.

24. Curtis to W. A. Jones, 14 Sept. 1897, RG 75, LROIA, Miscellaneous Correspondence, NA.

25. Ibid.

26. *U.S. Stat.*, 34:391; and Prucha, *Great Father*, 2:746-47.

27. Wilson, *Underground Reservation*, 37-38; Berlin B. Chapman, "Charles Curtis and the Kaw Reservation," *Kansas Historical Quarterly* 15 (Nov. 1947): 340; Frank F. Finney, "The Kaw Indians and their Indian Territory Agency," *Chronicles of Oklahoma* 35 (Winter 1957/58): 421; and *Kaw City Star*, 18 Sept. 1903.

28. Report of Talk by Commissioner Jones with Delegation of Kaw Indians, Washington, D.C., 24 Dec. 1900, RG 75, LROIA, Osage Agency, box 33, FRC, Fort Worth.

29. W. David Baird, "William A. Jones," in *Commissioners of Indian Affairs*, 213; Jones to U.S. Indian Agent, Osage Agency, 9 Jan. 1902, RG 75, LROIA, Osage Agency, box 33, FRC, Fort Worth; and Wilson, *Underground Reservation*, 75-76.

30. Baird, "William A. Jones," 212; and W. A. Jones to Charles Curtis, 8 Sept. 1902, William A. Jones Letters, Archives Division, State Historical Society of Wisconsin.

31. *Kaw City Star*, 18 Sept. 1903.

32. Wilson, *Underground Reservation*, 76.

33. Memorial of Washungah (his X) and Kaw National Council, 23 Nov. 1898, Curtis to Commissioner of Indian Affairs, 5 Dec. 1898, RG 75, LROIA, Finance, NA.

34. *Muskogee Phoenix*, 6 Feb. 1898.

35. Resolution of Kaw National Council, 24 Aug. 1900, Curtis to Jones, 10 Sept. 1900, RG 75, LROIA, Finance, NA.

36. *Osage Journal*, 3 Jan. 1901; *Cherokee Advocate*, 5 Jan. 1901; and Commissioner Jones to Delegation of Kaw Indians, Washington, D.C., 24 Dec. 1900, RG 75, LROIA, Osage Agency, box 33, FRC, Fort Worth.

37. *Osage Journal*, 9 Jan. 1901; and Chapman, "Charles Curtis," 341.

38. Wahshungah (written by Forrest Chouteau) to Curtis, 15 Jan. 1902, Curtis to Commissioner of Indian Affairs, 27 Aug. 1901, RG 75, LROIA, Land, NA; and Curtis to Jones, 12 Nov. 1901, RG 75, LROIA, Special, NA.

39. Blackwell, Enid & Southwestern Railway, "Agreement across the Kaw Reservation," signed by O. A. Mitscher, 14 Jan. 1902, RG 75, LROIA, Osage Agency, box 36, FRC, Fort Worth; and Curtis to Commissioner of Indian Affairs, 21 Jan. 1902, RG 75, LROIA, Special, NA.

40. Curtis to Jones, 16 Dec. 1901, RG 75, LROIA, Authority, NA; and *U.S. Stat.*, 32:636.

41. Allotment Roll of Kaw Indians, 1 July 1902, RG 75, Pawnee Agency Miscellaneous Files, FRC, Fort Worth; and J. W. Clendening to Robert M. Sands, 20 Feb. 1920, Kaw Indians, Claims against the Government, IAD, OHS.

42. Prucha, *Great Father*, 2:775-76; and Hoxie, *Final Promise*, 154-56.

43. *Guthrie Daily Leader*, 14 Sept. 1903; *Wichita Daily Eagle*, 15 Sept. 1903; and *Kaw City Star*, 18 Sept. 1903.

44. *Kaw City Star*, 18 Sept. 1903.

45. *Coffeyville* (Kans.) *Daily Journal*, 8 Feb. 1902; *Arkansas City Daily Traveler*, 3 June 1902; and *Kaw City Star*, 30 Sept. 1904.

46. *Kaw City Star*, 28 Aug. 1903.

47. *Ponca City* (Indian Terr.) *Daily Courier*, 14 May 1902; *Kaw City Star*, 14 Nov. 1902, 1 May 1903, 29 Sept. 1905; J. W. Clendening to Robert M. Sands, Kaw Indians, Claims against the Government, IAD, OHS; and Edson Watson to Curtis, 7 May 1907, Kaw vol. 5, IAD, OHS.

48. *Kaw City Star*, 22 Jan. 1904; and Report of Edson Watson, Dec. 1905, Kaw vol. 1, memo., Office of Indian Affairs to Edson Watson, 6 Oct. 1906, Kaw vol. 5, IAD, OHS.

49. Curtis to J. W. Clendening, 22 Jan. 1923, Kaw Indian Agency Collection, box 45, WHC, UO.

50. Curtis to Ethan A. Hitchcock (marked personal), 10 July 1902, and O. A. Mitscher to Hitchcock, 23 June 1906, Hitchcock Papers; and *Kaw City Star*, 8 Apr. 1904.

51. O. A. Mitscher to Edson Watson, 21 June 1907, "Washungah Folder," Kaw Indian Agency Collection, box 45, WHC, UO.

52. Edson Watson to Curtis, 18 Feb. 1908, Kaw vol. 1, IAD, OHS.

CHAPTER 11. CONGRESSIONAL INCOMPETENT

1. W. A. Jones to Kaw Delegation, 24 Dec. 1900, RG 75, LROIA, Osage Agency, FRC, Fort Worth.

2. Chapman, "Charles Curtis," 348; Chapman's interview with Curtis took place in January 1932.

3. Roy Gittinger, *The Formation of the State of Oklahoma* (Norman: University of Oklahoma Press, 1939), 277; and *Congressional Record*, 58th Cong., 1st sess., 19 Apr. 1904, 38:521-22.

4. *Purcell* (Okla.) *Register,* 3 June 1903; see also *Osage Journal,* 4 June 1903.

5. Mitscher to Commissioner of Indian Affairs, RCIA, 1901, 328.

6. Mitscher to W. H. Robinson, 4 Apr. 1901, Minutes of Meeting of Kaw National Council, 13 Apr. 1901, and A. C. Tonner to Mitscher, 23 Apr. 1901, RG 75, LROIA, Osage Agency, box 34, FRC, Fort Worth.

7. W. A. Jones to Secretary of the Interior, 21 Dec. 1901, and Jones to Mitscher, 21 Jan. 1901, RG 75, LROIA, Land, boxes 513, 517, NA.

8. Ibid.

9. Blackwell, Enid & Southwestern Railway, "Agreement across Kaw Reservation," FRC, Fort Worth.

10. Allotment Roll of Kaw Indians; Unrau, *Kaw People,* 76; and *Kaw City Star,* 30 Jan. 1903.

11. *New York Times,* 16 June 1928; and *Kaw City Star,* 1 Dec. 1904.

12. Francis E. Leupp, *The Indian and His Problem* (New York: Charles Scribner's Sons, 1910), 344.

13. Michael D. Green, "Alexander McGillivray," in *American Indian Leaders: Studies in Diversity,* ed. R. David Edmunds (Lincoln: University of Nebraska Press, 1980), 41–63; Raymond Wilson, *Ohiyesa: Charles Eastman, Santee Sioux* (Urbana: University of Illinois Press, 1983), 12–13; and Brown, "Progressive from Oklahoma," 234–35.

14. *U.S. Stat.,* 32:686–90; *Kaw City Star,* 18 Sept. 1903; and Curtis to J. W. Clendening, 22 Jan. 1923, WHC, UO.

15. *U.S.* v. *Richert, U.S. Stat.,* 188:537–45; and Curtis to Edson Watson, 5 July 1906, Robert G. Valentine to Almond R. Miller, 5 and 16 Oct. 1909, C. P. Hanke to Almond R. Miller, 20 Dec. 1909, and Miller, "Statement of Incompetency, Charles Curtis," 9 Oct. 1909, WHC, UO.

16. Francis E. Leupp to Superintendent in Charge of Kaw School, 13 Sept. 1906, WHC, UO; *Congressional Record,* 67th Cong., 4th sess., 24 Feb. 1923, 64:4493, 5600; and 68th Cong., 2d sess., 27 Feb. 1925, 66:4833.

17. *Congressional Record,* 64th Cong., 1st sess., 22, 24, and 25 Mar. 1916, 53:4614–15, 4685, 4755, 4826; and Curtis, "Autobiography," Colvin copy, art. 20, pp. 7–8.

18. Ibid., art. 22, p. 9.

19. Lawrence C. Kelly, "Cato Sells," in *Commissioners of Indian Affairs,* 248–49; and RCIA, 1921, 25–26.

20. "Purchases, Accounts, Expenditures," Miscellaneous Kaw vol. 1917–32, IAD, OHS; and *New York Times* 12 Mar. 1930.

CHAPTER 12. A DIFFERENT PATH

1. Hoxie, *Final Promise,* x–xiii.

2. Morgan, *Indian Journals,* 94; see also Bieder, *Science Encounters the Indian,* 225–26.

3. *Congressional Record,* 59th Cong., 2d sess., 7 Feb. 1907, 41:2356–2414; and Prucha, *Great Father,* 2:783–84.

4. *Congressional Record,* 59th Cong., 2d sess., 7 Feb. 1907, 41:2357–58, 2411.

5. Hoxie, *Final Promise,* 242.

6. Ewy, "Charles Curtis," 31. Wesley M. Bagley views the meeting between Curtis, Brandegee, Lodge, and Harvey in the Blackstone Hotel as one of a series of interrelated causes leading to Harding's nomination; see "The 'Smoke Filled

Room' and the Nomination of Warren G. Harding," *Mississippi Valley Historical Review* 41 (Mar. 1955): 657–74.

7. Gann, *Dolly Gann's Book,* 66.

8. Ewy, "Charles Curtis," 32; Theodore M. Knappen, "The West at Washington: Turning the Spotlight on Statesmen from the Country's Better Half," *Sunset Magazine* 54 (Mar. 1925): 40; "The Kaw Indian Who Leads the Senate," *Literary Digest,* 3 Jan. 1925, 47; and "A Stoic in the Right Place," *Saturday Evening Post,* 26 Jan. 1924, 37.

9. Seitz, *From Kaw Teepee,* 173; *Topeka Daily Capitol,* 8 Aug. 1926; and Ewy, "Charles Curtis," 35.

10. Kelly, "Cato Sells," 255–56; Joseph C. Hart to Charles H. Burke, 23 Feb. 1923, Burke to Hart, 21 Sept. 1923, IAD, OHS; and *Wichita Eagle,* 27 Nov. 1927.

11. Ewy, "Charles Curtis," 37.

12. Ibid., 40; Gann, *Dolly Gann's Book,* 98; and Seitz, *From Kaw Teepee,* 208–9.

13. Ewy, "Charles Curtis," 40–41; *Wichita Eagle,* 5 Oct. 1927 and 18 Oct. 1928; Kelly, "Cato Sells," 260; and Lewis Merriam et al., *The Problem of Indian Administration* (Baltimore, Md.: Johns Hopkins Press, 1928), 199–201.

14. Sol Barzman, *Madmen and Geniuses: The Vice-Presidents of the United States* (Chicago: Follett, 1974), 214–16; Ewy, "Charles Curtis," 40; Viola, *Diplomats in Buckskins,* 191; and *Wichita Eagle,* 23 and 28 Sept. 1928.

15. *Wichita Eagle,* 21 and 28 Sept. 1928; Richard Norton Smith, *An Uncommon Man: The Triumph of Herbert Hoover* (New York: Simon & Schuster, 1984), 142.

16. *Congressional Record,* 70th Cong., 2d sess., 4 Mar. 1929, 70:5220–21.

17. "Heap Big Chief," 404–5.

18. Ibid., 411.

19. Ewy, "Charles Curtis," 43, 47, 54–56; and *New York Times,* 5 July 1930.

20. Francis W. Schruben, *Kansas in Turmoil, 1930–1936* (Columbia: University of Missouri Press, 1969), 28–29; and Gerald Carson, *The Roguish World of Doctor Brinkley* (New York: Rinehart, 1960), 121–77.

21. Schruben, *Kansas in Turmoil,* 81–82.

22. Ibid., 82; Carson, *Roguish World of Doctor Brinkley,* 134–35; and Walter Davenport, "Gland Time in Kansas," *Collier's,* 16 Jan. 1932, 12.

23. Davenport, "Gland Time in Kansas," 12.

24. Ewy, "Charles Curtis," 58.

25. Ibid., 54–55; and Schruben, *Kansas in Turmoil,* 86.

26. *New York Times,* 1 July 1928, 29 Mar. 1929, and 22 Nov. 1931. For a summary of President Hoover's commitment to the betterment of conditions among Indians see Prucha, *Great Father,* 2:921–31.

27. Ewy, "Charles Curtis," 56–58.

28. Ibid., 58; *Wichita Eagle,* 10, 11, and 12 Feb. 1936; and *Topeka Daily Capitol,* 12 Feb. 1936.

29. David M. Brugge, "Henry Chee Dodge: From the Long Walk to Self-Determination," and Valerie Shere Mathes, "Dr. Susan LaFlesche Picotte: The Reformed and the Reformer," in *Indian Lives,* 91–107, 61–89; William T. Hagan, "Quanah Parker, in *American Indian Leaders,* 175–91; Raymond Wilson, *Ohiyesa*; Terry P. Wilson, "Osage Oxonian: The Heritage of John Joseph Mathews," *Chronicles of Oklahoma* 59 (Fall 1981); 264–93; and Brown, "Progressive from Oklahoma," 232–65.

30. Miner, *Corporation and the Indian,* 212.

31. Unrau, *Kaw People,* 79–82; Hazel W. Hertzberg, *The Search for an American Indian Identity: Modern Pan-Indian Movements* (Syracuse, N.Y.: Syracuse University Press, 1971), 323–25.

32. *Wichita Eagle,* 9 Feb. 1936.

EPILOGUE. THE WHITE MAN'S LAW
AND THE CURTIS INDIAN ESTATE

1. Unrau, *Kaw People,* 75.

2. Kaw Allotment Boundaries (Beaver and Kaw Townships), *Map of Kay County, Oklahoma* (Newkirk, Okla.: Republican News Journal, 1905).

3. Ewy, "Charles Curtis," 15; Chapman, "Charles Curtis," 350–51.

4. Curtis, "Autobiography," Colvin copy, art. 5, pp. 8, 15, art. 7, p. 8, and art. 21, p. 1.

5. Ibid., art. 6, p. 6.

6. Ibid., art. 21, p. 2; Nyle H. Miller and Kenneth R. McLain to Honorable Robert B. Docking, Governor, and Members of the Legislature, 12 Jan. 1972, titled "Report on Topeka Homes of Charles Curtis," LD, KSHS.

7. Kaw Census, 1 Jan. 1940, compiled by Lem A. Towers, Pawnee Agency, Oklahoma, Pawnee Agency Miscellaneous Files, RG 75, FRC, Fort Worth; Unrau, *Kaw People,* 82.

8. Unrau, *Kaw People,* 83.

9. Ibid., 84–86.

10. Ibid., 88–92; Keckeisen, "Kansa 'Half-Breed' Lands," 123.

11. The bill was titled Private Law 90-318, 90th Cong., 2d sess., H.R. 8391, 8 Aug. 1968. For a discussion of the debate in Congress see Keckeisen, "Kansa 'Half-Breed' Lands," 125–29.

12. John Montgomery to James W. Denver, 30 June 1857, RG 75, LROIA, Kansas Agency, M 234, R 365, NA; Senate Executive Document 58 (ser. 1122), 22; and Warranty Deed, Louis and Julie Pappan to William Curtis, 19 May 1863 (copy), Miscellaneous Curtis Materials.

13. Keckeisen, "Kansa 'Half-Breed' Lands," 130.

14. Complaint 79-1668, United States District Court in and for the District of Kansas (11 Dec. 1979); and *Dennison v. Topeka Chambers Indus. Development,* 527 F.Supp. 611.

15. *Dennison v. Topeka Chambers.*

16. Ibid.

17. Ibid.

18. Ibid.

19. Ibid.

Bibliography

GOVERNMENT MANUSCRIPTS

National Archives, Washington, D.C.

RG 75, Letters Received by the Office of Indian Affairs
  Authority
  Central Superintendency (M 234)
  Documents Relating to the Negotiation of Ratified and Unratified Treaties (T 494)
  Education
  Finance
  Fort Leavenworth Agency (M 234)
  Kansas Agency (M 234)
  Land
  Miscellaneous
  St. Louis Superintendency (M 234)
RG 94, Records of the Adjutant General's Office Consolidated Military and Pension Files

Federal Records Center, Fort Worth, Texas

RG 75, Letters Received by the Office of Indian Affairs
  General Records Correspondence
  Miscellaneous Correspondence
  Osage Agency Files
  Pawnee Agency Miscellaneous Files

Federal Records Center, Kansas City, Missouri

RG 75, Letters Received by the Office of Indian Affairs
  Potawatomi Agency Files

MANUSCRIPTS AND SCRAPBOOKS

Charles Curtis, "Autobiography," William P. Colvin copy, typed copy in the possession of Tom Dennison, Ponca City, Oklahoma
Charles Curtis Family Articles, Library Division, Kansas State Historical Society, Topeka
Charles Curtis, "History of North Topeka," typed copy, Library Division, Kansas State Historical Society, Topeka
Charles Curtis Scrapbooks, Library Division, Kansas State Historical Society, Topeka
Chouteau Papers, Manuscript Division, Missouri Historical Society, St. Louis
Governor's Correspondence, Samuel J. Crawford, 1865–68, Subject File, Manuscript Division, Kansas State Historical Society, Topeka
Ethan Allen Hitchcock Papers, Private Papers Collection, National Archives (RG 200)
Edgar Watson Howe Papers, Manuscript Division, Kansas State Historical Society, Topeka
William A. Jones Letters, Archives Division, State Historical Society of Wisconsin, Madison
Kaw Files, Indian Archives Division, Oklahoma Historical Society, Oklahoma City
Kaw Indian Agency Collection, Western History Collection, University of Oklahoma Library, Norman
Isaac McCoy Papers (microfilm), Manuscript Division, Kansas State Historical Society, Topeka
Miscellaneous Material Relating to Charles Curtis and His Ancestors, Library Division, Kansas State Historical Society, Topeka
Michael Shine Papers, Nebraska Historical Society, Lincoln
George C. Sibley Papers, Manuscript Division, Missouri Historical Society, St. Louis

MAPS

Map of Kay County, Oklahoma. Newkirk, Okla.: Republican News Journal, 1905.

NEWSPAPERS

Arkansas City (Kans.) *Daily Traveler*
Cherokee Advocate, The (Tahlequah, Cherokee Nation)
Coffeyville (Kans.) *Daily Journal*
Commonwealth, The (Topeka, Kans.)
Council Grove (Kans.) *Press*
Daily Oklahoma State Capital, The (Oklahoma Terr.)
El Reno (Oklahoma Terr.) *American*
Emporia (Kans.) *News*
Guthrie (Oklahoma Terr.) *Daily Leader*
Kansas Press, The (Council Grove)
Kansas State Record (Topeka)

Kaw City (Indian Terr.) Star
Leavenworth (Kans.) Daily Times
Missouri Gazette and Louisiana Advertiser (St. Louis, Mo.)
Muskogee (Indian Terr.) Phoenix
National Intelligencer (Washington, D.C.)
National Tribune, The (Washington, D.C.)
New York Times
New York Tribune
North Topeka (Kans.) Times
Osage Journal, The (Pawhuska, Indian Terr.)
Ponca City (Indian Terr.) Daily Courier
Purcell (Oklahoma Terr.) Register
Topeka (Kans.) Daily Capitol
Topeka (Kans.) Mail and Breeze
Topeka (Kans.) State Journal
Topeka (Kans.) Tribune
Vinita (Indian Terr.) Indian Chieftain
Washington (D.C.) Inquirer, The
Western Spirit, The (Paola, Kans.)
Wichita (Kans.) Daily Beacon
Wichita (Kans.) Daily Eagle

PRINTED GOVERNMENT DOCUMENTS

American State Papers: Indian Affairs. Vol. 2.
Commissioner of Indian Affairs. Annual Reports.
Congressional Record. Washington, D.C., 1873–.
Indian Affairs: Laws and Treaties. Compiled by Charles J. Kappler. 5 vols. Washington, D.C.: Government Printing Office, 1904.
Private Laws of Kansas Territory, 1860.
United States, Congress. House. Committee on Indian Affairs. Osage Enrollment: Hearings before a Subcommittee of the House Committee on Indian Affairs on H.R. 17819 and H. 21199. 61st Cong., 2d sess., 1910.
United States, Congress. Senate. Joint Resolution for the Enrollment of Certain Persons as Members of the Osage Tribe of Indians, and for Other Purposes. 60th Cong., 1st sess., 29 Apr. 1908. Senate Document 482. Serial 5269.
United States, Department of Commerce, Bureau of the Census. Indian Population in the United States and Alaska, 1910. Washington, D.C.: Government Printing Office, 1910.

COURT CASES

John Brown and Jane Brown v. Adel [Clement] Belmarde. 3 Kan. 35.
William Curtis v. Orren A. Curtis, Guardian of Elizabeth Curtis and Charles Curtis, Minors, O. O. Kelsa, Louis and Julie Pappan. District Court of Shawnee County, Kansas. 21 May 1871.
Dennison and Dennison v. Topeka Chambers Industrial Development. 527 U.S. 611; 724 F. 2d 869.

George W. Ewing v. *John McManamy.* Kansas Territorial District Court. 1st Judicial District, Jefferson County. 10 Dec. 1858.
Victoria Hardy v. *Pelagia Pougel.* District Court of Kansas. 3d Judicial District, Jefferson County. 25 Jan. 1864.
Jacob Smith et al. v. *James H. Brown et al.* 8 Kan. 610–11.
U.S. v. *Richert.* 188 U.S. 537.

BOOKS

Alger, Horatio, Jr. *Risen from the Ranks; Or, Harry Walton's Success.* Philadelphia: John C. Winston, 1874.
Athearn, Robert G. *In Search of Canaan: Black Migration to Kansas, 1879–80.* Lawrence: Regents Press of Kansas, 1978.
Bader, Robert Smith. *Prohibition in Kansas: A History.* Lawrence: University Press of Kansas, 1986.
Barry, Louise. *The Beginning of the West: Annals of the Kansas Gateway to the American West, 1540–1854.* Topeka: Kansas State Historical Society, 1972.
Barzman, Sol. *Madmen and Geniuses: The Vice-Presidents of the United States.* Chicago: Follett, 1974.
Bieder, Robert E. *Science Encounters the Indian, 1820–1880.* Norman: University of Oklahoma Press, 1986.
Boynton, C. B., and T. B. Mason. *A Journey through Kansas, with Sketches of Nebraska: Describing the Country, Climate, Soil, Minerals, Manufacturing and Other Resources.* Cincinnati, Ohio: Moore, Wilstach, Keys, 1855.
Caldwell, Charles, M.D. *Thoughts on the Original Unity of Race.* New York: E. Bliss, 1930.
Carson, Gerald. *The Roguish World of Doctor Brinkley.* New York: Rinehart, 1960.
Castel, Albert. *A Frontier State at War: Kansas, 1861–1865.* Ithaca, N.Y.: Cornell University Press, 1958.
Caughey, John Walton. *McGillivray of the Creeks.* Norman: University of Oklahoma Press, 1938.
Clark, John G., ed. *The Frontier Challenge: Responses to the Trans-Mississippi West.* Lawrence: University Press of Kansas, 1971.
Clifton, James A. *The Prairie People: Continuity and Change in Potawatomi Indian Culture, 1665–1965.* Lawrence: Regents Press of Kansas, 1977.
[Cooper, Thomas]. *Strictures Addressed to James Madison on the Celebrated Report of William H. Crawford, Recommending the Intermarriage of Americans with the Indian Tribes, Ascribed to Judge Cooper, and Originally Published by John Binns, in the Democratic Press.* Philadelphia: Jesper Harding, 1824.
Crawford, Samuel J. *Kansas in the Sixties.* Chicago: A. C. McClurg, 1911.
Cutler, W. G. *History of the State of Kansas.* Chicago: A. T. Andreas, 1883.
Dictionary of American Biography. 1958 ed., suppl. 2, s.v. "Curtis, Charles," by James C. Malin.
Din, Gilbert C., and Abraham P. Nasatir. *The Imperial Osages: Spanish-Indian Diplomacy in the Mississippi Valley.* Norman: University of Oklahoma Press, 1983.
Dippie, Brian W. *The Vanishing American: White Attitudes and U.S. Indian Policy.* Middletown, Conn.: Wesleyan University Press, 1982.
Edmunds, R. David, ed. *American Indian Leaders: Studies in Diversity.* Lincoln: University of Nebraska Press, 1980.

Flint, Timothy. *Recollections of the Last Ten Years*. Introduction by James D. Norris. New York: Da Capo, 1968.

Foley, William E., and C. David Rice. *The First Chouteaus: River Barons of Early St. Louis*. Urbana: University of Illinois Press, 1983.

Gann, Dolly. *Dolly Gann's Book*. Garden City, N.Y.: Doubleday, Doran, 1933.

Gates, Paul Wallace. *Fifty Million Acres: Conflicts over Kansas Land Policy, 1854–1890*. Ithaca, N.Y.: Cornell University Press, 1954.

Gibson, Arrell Morgan. *Oklahoma: A History of Five Centuries*. Norman: University of Oklahoma Press, 1981.

Gihon, John H. *Geary and Kansas*. 1857. Reprint. Freeport, N.Y.: Books for Libraries, 1971.

Giraud, Marcel. *The Métis in the Canadian West*. Translated by George Woodcock. 2 vols. Lincoln: University of Nebraska Press, 1986. Originally published as *Le Métis Canadian*. Paris: Institut d'Ethnologie, Muséum National d'Histoire Naturelle, 1945.

Gittinger, Roy. *The Formation of the State of Oklahoma*. Norman: University of Oklahoma Press, 1939.

Gregg, Kate L., and John Francis McDermott. *Prairie and Mountain Sketches by Matthew C. Field*. Norman: University of Oklahoma Press, 1957.

Hertzberg, Hazel W. *The Search for an American Indian Identity: Modern Pan-Indian Movements*. Syracuse, N.Y.: Syracuse University Press, 1971.

Hoxie, Frederick E. *A Final Promise: The Campaign to Assimilate the Indians, 1880–1920*. Lincoln: University of Nebraska Press, 1984.

Irving, Washington. *Astoria: Or, Anecdotes of an Enterprise beyond the Mountains*. Rev. ed. New York: G. P. Putnam, 1859.

Johnson, James Hugo. *Race Relations in Virginia and Miscegenation in the South, 1776–1880*. Amherst: University of Massachusetts Press, 1970.

La Forte, Robert Sherman. *Leaders of Reform: Progressive Republicans in Kansas, 1900–1916*. Lawrence: University Press of Kansas, 1974.

Leupp, Francis E. *The Indian and His Problem*. New York: Charles Scribner's Sons, 1910.

McDermott, John Francis, ed. *Tixier's Travels on the Osage Prairies*. Norman: University of Oklahoma Press, 1940.

McReynolds, Edwin C. *Missouri: A History of the Crossroads State*. Norman: University of Oklahoma Press, 1962.

Mardock, Robert W. *The Reformers and the American Indian*. Columbia: University of Missouri Press, 1971.

Masterson, V. V. *The Katy Railroad and the Last Frontier*. Norman: University of Oklahoma Press, 1952.

Mathews, John Joseph. *The Osages: Children of the Middle Waters*. Norman: University of Oklahoma Press, 1961.

Merriam, Lewis, et al. *The Problem of Indian Administration*. Baltimore, Md.: Johns Hopkins Press, 1928.

Miner, H. Craig. *The Corporation and the Indian: Tribal Sovereignty and Industrial Civilization in Indian Territory, 1865–1907*. Columbia: University of Missouri Press, 1976.

——— and William E. Unrau. *The End of Indian Kansas: A Study of Cultural Revolution, 1854–1871*. Lawrence: Regents Press of Kansas, 1978.

Moquin, Wayne, and Charles Van Doren, eds. *Great Documents in American Indian History*. New York: Praeger Publishers, 1973.

Morgan, Lewis Henry, ed. *The Indian Journals, 1859–1862*. Ann Arbor: University of Michigan Press, 1957.

Moses, L. G., and Raymond Wilson, eds. *Indian Lives: Essays on Nineteenth and Twentieth Century Native American Leaders.* Albuquerque: University of New Mexico Press, 1985

Nasatir, Abraham P., ed. *Before Lewis and Clark: Documents Illustrating the History of Missouri, 1785–1804.* Vol. 2. St. Louis, Mo.: St. Louis Historical Documents Foundation, 1952.

Nash, Gary B. *Red, White and Black: The People of Early America.* Englewood Cliffs, N.J.: Prentice-Hall, 1974.

Nott, J. D., M.D., and George R. Glidden. *Types of Mankind: Or, Ethnological Researches, Based upon the Ancient Monuments, Paintings, Sculptures, and Crania of Races, and upon the Natural Geographical, Philological, and Biblical History.* 7th ed. Philadelphia: Lippincott, Grambo, 1855.

Oglesby, Richard Edward. *Manuel Lisa and the Opening of the Missouri Fur Trade.* Norman: University of Oklahoma Press, 1963.

Pearce, Roy Harvey. *The Savages of America: A Study of the Indian and the Idea of Civilization.* Baltimore, Md.: Johns Hopkins University Press, 1967.

Philips, Paul Chrisler. *The Fur Trade.* 2 vols. Norman: University of Oklahoma Press, 1961.

Phillips, William. *The Conquest of Kansas, by Missouri and Her Allies.* Boston, Mass.: Phillips, Sampson, 1856.

Plummer, Mark A. *Frontier Governor: Samuel J. Crawford of Kansas.* Lawrence: University Press of Kansas, 1971.

Prucha, Francis Paul. *American Indian Policy in Crisis: Christian Reformers and the Indian, 1865–1900.* Norman: University of Oklahoma Press, 1976.

———. *American Indian Policy in the Formative Years: The Indian Trade and Intercourse Acts, 1790–1834.* Cambridge: Harvard University Press, 1963.

———. *The Great Father: The United States Government and the Indian.* 2 vols. Lincoln: University of Nebraska Press, 1984.

———. *The Indian in American Society.* Berkeley: University of California Press, 1985.

———. *Indian Policy in the United States: Historical Essays.* Lincoln: University of Nebraska Press, 1981.

Richmond, Robert W. *Kansas: A Land of Contrasts.* St. Louis, Mo.: Forum, 1974.

Ross, Alexander. *The Fur Hunters of the Far West.* Edited by Kenneth A. Spaulding. Norman: University of Oklahoma Press, 1956.

———. *The Red River Settlement: Its Rise, Progress, and Present State, with Some Accounts of the Native Races and Its General History to the Present Day.* London: Smith, Elder, 1856.

Scheick, William J. *The Half-Blood: A Cultural Symbol in Nineteenth Century Fiction.* Lexington: University of Kentucky Press, 1979.

Schruben, Francis W. *Kansas in Turmoil, 1930–1936.* Columbia: University of Missouri Press, 1969.

Schultz, George A. *An Indian Canaan: Isaac McCoy and the Vision of an Indian State.* Norman: University of Oklahoma Press, 1972.

Seitz, Don C. *From Kaw Teepee to Capitol: The Life Story of Charles Curtis, Indian, Who Has Risen to High Estate.* New York: Frederick A. Stokes, 1928.

Sheehan, Bernard W. *Seeds of Extinction: Jeffersonian Philanthropy and the American Indian.* New York: W. W. Norton, 1974.

Smith, Henry Nash. *Virgin Land: The American West as Symbol and Myth.* New York: Vintage Books, 1957.

Smith, Richard Norton. *An Uncommon Man: The Triumph of Herbert Hoover.* New York: Simon & Schuster, 1984.

Starr, Stephen Z. *Jennison's Jayhawkers: A Civil War Cavalry Regiment and Its Commander.* Baton Rouge: Louisiana State University Press, 1973.

Turner, Katherine C. *Red Man Calling on the Great White Father.* Norman: University of Oklahoma Press, 1951.

United States Biographical Dictionary, Kansas Volume. Chicago: S. Lewis, 1879.

Unrau, William E. *The Kansa Indians: A History of the Wind People, 1673–1873.* Norman: University of Oklahoma Press, 1971.

―――. *The Kaw People.* Phoenix, Ariz.: Indian Tribal Series, 1975.

――― and H. Craig Miner. *Tribal Dispossession and the Ottawa Indian University Fraud.* Norman: University of Oklahoma Press, 1985.

Unruh, John D. *The Plains Across: The Overland Emigrants and the Trans-Mississippi West, 1840–1860.* Paperback ed. Urbana: University of Illinois Press, 1982.

Van Kirk, Sylvia. *Many Tender Ties: Women in Fur Trade Society, 1670–1870.* Norman: University of Oklahoma Press, 1980.

Viola, Herman J. *Diplomats in Buckskins: A History of Indian Delegations in Washington City.* Washington, D.C.: Smithsonian Institution Press, 1981.

―――. *Thomas L. McKenny: Architect of America's Early Indian Policy.* Chicago: Swallow, 1974.

Walker, Francis A. *The Indian Question.* Boston, Mass.: James R. Osgood, 1874.

Washington-Merry-Go-Round. New York: Blue Ribbon, 1931.

White, William Allen. *The Autobiography of William Allen White.* New York: Macmillan, 1946.

―――. *Calvin Coolidge: The Man Who Is President.* New York: Macmillan, 1925.

William W. Cone's Historical Sketch of Shawnee County, Kansas. Topeka: Kansas Farmer Printing Office, 1877.

Wilson, Raymond. *Ohiyesa: Charles Eastman, Santee Sioux.* Urbana: University of Illinois Press, 1983.

Wilson, Terry P. *The Underground Reservation: Osage Oil.* Lincoln: University of Nebraska Press, 1985.

ARTICLES

Babcock, Frederick. "Curtis's Oily Hands." *Nation,* 26 Sept. 1928, 288–89.

Bagley, Wesley M. "The 'Smoked Filled Room' and the Nomination of Warren G. Harding." *Mississippi Valley Historical Review* 41 (Mar. 1955): 657–74.

Baird, W. David. "William A. Jones." In *The Commissioners of Indian Affairs, 1824–1977,* edited by Robert M. Kvasnicka and Herman J. Viola, 211–20. Lincoln: University of Nebraska Press, 1979.

Barrows, William. "The Half-Breed Indians of North America." *Andover Review* 12 (July 1899): 15–36.

Barry, Louise. "The Kansa Indians and the Census of 1843." *Kansas Historical Quarterly* 39 (Winter 1973): 478–90.

Beaulieu, David L. "Curly Hair and Big Feet: Physical Anthropology and the Implementation of Land Allotment on the White Earth Chippewa Reservation." *American Indian Quarterly* 7 (Fall 1984): 281–311.

Bieder, Robert E. "Scientific Attitudes toward Indian Mixed-Bloods in Early Nineteenth Century America." *Journal of Ethnic Studies* 8 (Summer 1980): 17–30.

Boas, Franz. "The Half-Blood Indians: An Anthropometric Study." *Popular Science Monthly* 45 (Oct. 1894): 761–70.

Brooks, George R., ed. "George C. Sibley's Journal of a Trip to the Salines in 1811." *Missouri Historical Society Bulletin* 21 (Apr. 1965): 167–207.

Brown, Kenny L. "A Progressive from Oklahoma: Senator Robert Latham Owen, Jr." *Chronicles of Oklahoma* 62 (Fall 1984): 232–65.

Brugge, David M. "Henry Chee Dodge: From the Long Walk to Self-Determination." In *Indian Lives: Essays on Nineteenth and Twentieth Century Native American Leaders*, edited by L. G. Moses and Raymond Wilson, 61–89. Albuquerque: University of New Mexico Press, 1985.

Calloway, Colin G. "Neither White nor Red: White Renegades on the American Indian Frontier." *Western Historical Quarterly* 14 (Jan. 1986): 43–66.

Carruth, William H. "The New England Emigrant Aid Company as an Investment Society." *Kansas Historical Collections* 6 (1897–1900): 90–96.

Chapman, Berlin B. "Charles Curtis and the Kaw Reservation." *Kansas Historical Quarterly* 15 (Nov. 1947): 337–51.

Cole, Fannie E. "Pioneer Life in Kansas." *Kansas Historical Collections* 12 (1911/12): 353–58.

Davenport, Walter. "Gland Time in Kansas." *Collier's*, 16 Jan. 1932, 12–13, 50–51.

Ewers, John C. "'Chiefs of the Missouri and Mississippi' and Peale's Silhouettes of 1806." *Smithsonian Journal of History* 1 (Spring 1966): 1–26.

Ewy, Marvin. "Charles Curtis of Kansas: Vice President of the United States, 1929–1933." *Emporia State Research Studies* 10 (Dec. 1961): 1–58.

"Extracts from the Diary of Major Sibley." *Chronicles of Oklahoma* 5 (June 1927): 196–218.

Finney, Frank F. "The Kaw Indians and Their Indian Territory Agency." *Chronicles of Oklahoma* 35 (Winter 1957/58): 416–24.

"Governor Reeder's Administration." *Transactions of the Kansas State Historical Society* 5 (1891–96): 163–234.

Green, Michael D. "Alexander McGillivray." In *American Indian Leaders: Studies in Diversity*, edited by R. David Edmunds, 41–63. Lincoln: University of Nebraska Press, 1980.

Hagan, William T. "Full Blood, Mixed Blood, Generic, and Ersatz: The Problem of Indian Identity." *Arizona and the West* 27 (Winter 1985): 309–26.

———. "Quanah Parker." In *American Indian Leaders: Studies in Diversity*, edited by R. David Edmunds, 175–91. Lincoln: University of Nebraska Press, 1980.

———. "Squaw-Men on the Kiowa, Comanche, and Apache Reservation: Advance Agents of Civilization or Disturbers of the Peace?" In *The Frontier Challenge: Responses to the Trans-Mississippi West*, edited by John G. Clark, 171–202. Lawrence: University Press of Kansas, 1971.

"Heap Big Chief." *American Mercury*, Aug. 1929, 409–12.

Hoffhaus, Charles E. "Fort de Cavagnial: Imperial France in Kansas, 1744–1764." *Kansas Historical Quarterly* 30 (Winter 1964): 425–54.

Holman, Margaret. "The History of North Topeka." *Bulletin of the Shawnee County Historical Society* 24 (Dec. 1955): 1–32.

Horsman, Reginald. "Scientific Racism and the American Indian." *American Quarterly* 27 (May 1975): 152–68.

Jenness, Theodora R. "The Indian Territory." *Atlantic Monthly* 43 (Apr. 1879): 444–52.

"Kaw Indian Who Leads the Senate, The." *Literary Digest,* 3 Jan. 1925, 47.

Kelly, Lawrence C. "Cato Sells." In *The Commissioners of Indian Affairs, 1824–1977,* edited by Robert M. Kvasnicka and Herman J. Viola, 243–50. Lincoln: University of Nebraska Press, 1979.

Kiel, Eric. "Curtis's Indian Blood." *Nation,* 1 Aug. 1928, 109–10.

King, Edward. "The Great South: The New Route to the Gulf." *Scribner's Monthly* 6 (July 1873): 257–88.

Knappen, Theodore M. "The West at Washington: Turning the Spotlight on Statesmen from the Country's Better Half." *Sunset Magazine* 54 (Mar. 1925): 40.

"Lo, the Poor Senator." *Saturday Evening Post,* 9 Feb. 1907, 15–17.

McCluggage, Robert W. "The Senate and Indian Land Titles, 1800–1825." *Western Historical Quarterly* 1 (Oct. 1970): 415–25.

"Mackinac Register of Baptisms and Interments, 1695–1821." *Collections of the State Historical Society of Wisconsin* 19 (1910): 1–162.

Martin, George M. "Some of the Lost Towns of Kansas." *Collections of the Kansas State Historical Society* 22 (1911–12): 426–71.

Mathes, Valerie Shere. "Dr. Susan LaFlesche Picotte: The Reformed and the Reformer." In *Indian Lives: Essays on Nineteenth and Twentieth Century Native American Leaders,* edited by L. G. Moses and Raymond Wilson, 91–107. Albuquerque: University of New Mexico Press, 1985.

May, Thomas J. "The Future of the American Indian." *Popular Science Monthly* 45 (May 1888): 104–8.

Nott, J. C. "The Mulatto: A Hybrid—Probable Extermination of the Two Races if Whites and Blacks are Allowed to Intermarry." *American Journal of Medical Science* 6 (1843) 254–61.

Peterson, Jacqueline. "Ethnogenesis: The Settlement and Growth of a 'New People' in the Great Lakes Region, 1702–1815." *American Indian Culture and Research Journal* 6 (1982): 54–55.

Root, George A. "Ferries in Kansas: Part II: Kansas River." *Kansas Historical Quarterly* 4 (Nov. 1933): 363–66.

Ross, Charles E. "Charles Curtis of Kansas." *Outlook,* 16 May 1928, 83–86.

Rothensteiner, the Rev. John. "Early Missionary Efforts among the Indians in the Diocese of St. Louis." *St. Louis Catholic Historical Review* 2 (Apr.–July 1920): 57–96.

Schroeder, William A. "Spread of Settlement in Howard County, Missouri, 1810–1859." *Missouri Historical Review* 43 (Oct. 1968): 1–37.

Socolofsky, Homer E. "Wyandot Floats." *Kansas Historical Quarterly* 36 (Autumn 1970): 241–304.

"Stoic in the Right Place, A" *Saturday Evening Post,* 26 Jan. 1924, 37.

Swagerty, William R. "Marriage and Settlement Patterns of Rocky Mountain Trappers and Traders." *Western Historical Quarterly* 11 (Apr. 1980): 159–80.

Thompson, Gregory C. "John D. C. Atkins." In *The Commissioners of Indian Affairs, 1824–1977,* edited by Robert M. Kvasnicka and Herman J. Viola, 181–91. Lincoln: University of Nebraska Press, 1979.

Unrau, William E. "Charles Curtis." In *Indian Lives: Essays on Nineteenth and Twentieth Century Native American Leaders,* edited by L. G. Moses and Raymond Wilson, 113–37. Albuquerque: University of New Mexico Press, 1985.

———. "The Depopulation of the Dhegiha-Siouan Kansas Prior to Removal." *New Mexico Historical Review* 48 (Oct. 1973): 313–28.

———. "George C. Sibley's Pleas for the 'Garden of Missouri' in 1824." *Missouri Historical Society Bulletin* 17 (Oct. 1970): 3–13.

———. "The Mixed-Blood Connection: Charles Curtis and Kaw Detribalization." In *Kansas and the West: Bicentennial Essays in Honor of Nyle H. Miller,* edited by Forrest R. Blackburn, 151–61. Topeka: Kansas State Historical Society, 1976.

Villard, Oscar Garrison. "Charles Curtis." *Nation,* 7 Apr. 1928, 400–402.

Waltmann, Henry G. "Ely Samuel Parker." In *The Commissioners of Indian Affairs, 1824–1977,* edited by Robert M. Kvasnicka and Herman J. Viola, 123–31. Lincoln: University of Nebraska Press, 1979.

Wilhelm, Paul, duke of Wuerttenberg. *First Journey to North America in the Years 1822 to 1824.* Translated by William G. Beck. *South Dakota Historical Collections* 19 (1938): 7–466.

Wilson, Terry P. "Osage Oxonian: The Heritage of John Joseph Mathews." *Chronicles of Oklahoma* 59 (Fall 1981): 264–93.

THESES

Keckeisen, Robert Joseph. "The Kansa 'Half-Breed' Lands: Contravention and Transformation of United States Indian Policy in Kansas." Master's thesis, Wichita State University, 1982.

KANSAS STATE AGENCY REPORTS

Miller, Nyle H., and Kenneth R. McLain. "Report" to Hon. Robert B. Docking, Governor, and Members of the Legislature, 12 Jan. 1972. LD, KSHS.

Index